The Retirement Survival Guide

STERLING
New York

An Imprint of Sterling Publishing Co., Inc.
1166 Avenue of the Americas
New York, NY 10036

ISBN 978-1-4549-2733-4

Distributed in Canada by Sterling Publishing Co., Inc.
c/o Canadian Manda Group, 664 Annette Street
Toronto, Ontario, Canada M6S 2C8
Distributed in the United Kingdom by GMC Distribution Services
Castle Place, 166 High Street, Lewes, East Sussex, England BN7 1XU
Distributed in Australia by NewSouth Books
45 Beach Street, Coogee, NSW 2034, Australia

For information about custom editions, special sales, and premium and corporate purchases, please contact Sterling Special Sales at 800-805-5489 or specialsales@sterlingpublishing.com.

Manufactured in Canada

2 4 6 8 10 9 7 5 3 1

sterlingpublishing.com

The Retirement Survival Guide

How to Make Smart Financial Decisions
in Good Times and Bad

Julie Jason

STERLING
New York

To Howard G. Berg,
the wind beneath my wings.

Contents

Introduction   vii

Part I: Understanding the Basics

Chapter 1   Achieving a Secure Retirement   3

Chapter 2   Your Personal Cash Flow   13

Chapter 3   Sources of Retirement Income   23

Chapter 4   Income from Social Security   33

Chapter 5   Will Your Money Last as Long as You Do?   47

Chapter 6   Can You Improve Your Situation?   59

Chapter 7   Enter the Financial Adviser   73

Part II: Security for Sale:
              Evaluating Retirement-Income Products

Chapter 8   Guaranteed Lifelong Income   93

Chapter 9   Creating Your Own Personal Pension   103

Chapter 10   The Promise of Gain with No Pain: 121
              Equity-Indexed or Fixed Annuities

Chapter 11   It's Not Too Late to Catch Up:
              The Guaranteed Minimum Income Benefit   137

Chapter 12   Guaranteed Withdrawals So You Don't Run
              Out of Money: The Guaranteed Minimum
              Withdrawal Benefit, or GMWB   159

Chapter 13   Certificates of Deposit:
              Not All CDs Are Created Equal   175

Chapter 14   Cashing Out of Your Home   187

Part III: Investing in Your Future:
             Retirement-Income Planning and the Markets

Chapter 15   Tax-Deferred Account Decisions   203

Chapter 16   Making the Stock Market Work for You   217

Part IV: Pulling It All Together:
             Uncle Sam, Your Adviser, and You

Chapter 17   Taxes in Retirement   237

Chapter 18   Taking Money Out of IRAs and
             Other Tax-Deferred Accounts   249

Chapter 19   Sales Tactics, Scams, and Bad Advice:
             A "Perfect Storm" of Disaster for Retirees   259

Chapter 20   Do You Need a Retirement-Income Adviser?   273

Chapter 21   The Finish Line   285

Part V: More Retirement Resources

Appendix A: Prospective Adviser Notepad   297

Appendix B: Client Reference Notepad   298

Appendix C: Quick-Test Factors for Different Retirement Periods
             and Rates of Return   299

Appendix D: Retirement Income Management: A Case Study   300

Appendix E: Bibliography   321

Acknowledgments   322

About the Author   325

Index   326

Introduction

This book is about achieving retirement security—reaching a level of comfort in knowing that you will not outlive your money, whether economic times are good or bad. As an investment counsel (a type of money manager) to high net worth families, I make my living helping individuals of all ages do just that. I also interact with students and readers of my financial column, who pose questions about every aspect of retirement planning. Often they are seeking to untangle thorny financial predicaments—many of which I explore in the pages that follow.

All of these individuals are just like you, with similar needs, goals, and concerns. Some are well versed in the financial markets; others have little interest in the subject. Some have been investing all their lives; others are novices.

What they all share is the desire for some certainty in a time of transition—as they turn from today to the many tomorrows of retirement. Retirees face numerous unknowns, not the least of which is whether they can afford to retire and maintain their independence for the rest of their lives. But they need not face their retirement-income challenges alone, particularly in times of financial turmoil.

Let me reassure you on a couple of points.

Though the task at hand may seem overwhelming, it does not need to be. Together, in this book, we will address how you can create retirement income safely and carefully, regardless of your age, your financial circumstances, the economic times in which you live, and whether or not you have a financial adviser.

I promise you this: if you have never invested, never read an investment book, or never worked with a financial adviser, you will not be left behind. No matter who you are or what steps you have or have not taken up to this point, there is always something you can do to improve your situation.

How to Use
This Book
I've organized the material we will review together into four parts. Some chapters you will want to study closely and others you will want to skim, as I explain shortly. Because of the tools I've provided, such as self-assessments, tables, checklists, and questions to ask, I suggest keeping a pen and pad handy to note which sections of the book you want to revisit later. These tools will help you apply the concepts we discuss to your own personal affairs. You will also find sets of rules to follow in situations that people ordinarily face in their search for reliable lifelong income.

Part I   If you think about it, you'll realize that the essence of creating lifelong retirement income is being able to master cash flow—the money that comes into and goes out of a household. Because you can't retire on credit, your income must cover your expenses. In Part I, "Understanding the Basics," we'll review how to set up your own cash-management system so you can be secure in knowing your needs will be met.

By completing the exercises in Part I, you'll get a sense of how you're doing now, which will give you a chance to consider how to do even better. To help you, I'll share a way of managing spending that works well for people who don't like to budget. And, of course, we'll examine sources of income, including pensions and Social Security.

Then we'll talk about tools that help quantify some of the uncertainty every investor faces when trying to predict the future, such as Monte Carlo modeling programs that reflect some of the current professional thinking on how to solve the retirement-income puzzle. We'll also look at examples and case studies that illustrate how an adviser might work with a client to create a realistic retirement-income plan. (The case studies throughout this book present real people, their names and circumstances changed to preserve anonymity.)

If you are approaching retirement or are already retired, you will almost undoubtedly hear from financial advisers who want your business. At this time of life, it is important to distinguish among advisers in order to find one who is best suited for creating retirement income. Whether you are an old pro at investing or a newcomer, Chapter 7 will give you a fresh look at how advisers differ—and what they can do for you. We return to the topic of advisers in Part IV, after you have a sense of the different services you will likely be offered.

Part II   If you read magazines or watch television, you have probably noticed advertisements for financial products and services for retirees. Reverse mortgages and products that offer to pay income you cannot outlive are attractive because of their promises and guarantees. Part II, "Security for Sale: Evaluating Retirement-Income Products," is all about these retirement-income solutions.

Because these products are quite attractive at first blush, you may be tempted to proceed with a purchase after a quick sales presentation. It's important that you resist that urge until you have had a chance to contrast and compare the alternatives, so that you can choose the best for your situation. That's what Part II of the book will help you do. To guide you,

I've provided a five-point rating system to compare these financial products more easily, as well as questions to ask when you speak to a salesperson about them.

I suggest you read through Part II quickly to get an idea of the types of concepts and products you can expect to come across in your search for retirement income. Later, if your adviser recommends one of these products, review the relevant chapter carefully before buying anything. Keep in mind that you may have to talk to more than one adviser before making a decision about which (if any) retirement-income products are right for you.

In Part III, "Investing in Your Future: Retirement-Income Planning and the Markets," we'll discuss stocks, bonds, and other investments and what you can expect from them in good markets and bad. Because defined-contribution retirement accounts such as 401(k)s are an increasingly meaningful part of many people's assets, we'll talk about how to manage a 401(k), as well as Individual Retirement Accounts (IRAs) and other tax-deferred savings accounts, both before and after retirement. We'll also look at how much risk you should take on at different points in your life, how to deal with changing market environments, and how your financial goals may evolve as you progress from pre-retirement to retirement.

Part IV—"Pulling It All Together: Uncle Sam, Your Adviser, and You"— examines how to protect your retirement assets. First and foremost, no one needs to overpay taxes, especially after retiring. In Chapters 17 and 18, we'll discuss how taxes affect retirees and talk about ways to manage withdrawals from IRAs and 401(k)s.

Chapter 19 is my personal favorite. I am a believer in developing a sense of healthy skepticism, and this chapter will help you do that. It is intended for people of all ages. Millennials will benefit from understanding how to deal with sales pressures, as will retirees. People who have elderly parents will be able to sense when to get more involved. If you are married or have a partner who is not as interested as you are in making investment decisions, I recommend that the two of you read this chapter together.

By raising your awareness of persuasion techniques, you will be able to spot and avoid potential mistakes. This awareness will help you safeguard your assets. To make it easier to apply these principles to real life, I've created a set of "Don't-Be-Fooled Rules" that you can use when making financial decisions.

Most people need to work with an adviser after they retire, and it should be pretty clear that having a good adviser can make all the difference in the world—if not to you personally, then to the spouse or partner you may leave behind. In Chapter 20, I discuss how to go about the process of picking the right adviser—one who suits your particular needs. For your convenience, I've included a "Prospective Adviser Notepad" (Appendix A) to use when you interview candidates. Let me emphasize a key point here: Even if you decide you don't need an adviser, you should be aware that your spouse might outlive you—and may have difficulty managing the family finances on his* or her own without you. (* By the way, I use the male pronoun as shorthand throughout the book to denote both genders.)

Finally, in Chapter 21 ("The Finish Line") you'll find a step-by-step path to creating your own retirement-income plan. This chapter offers a retirement-readiness test you can take to determine whether you are ready to retire; a retirement risk self-assessment to use after you are retired; and a series of next steps to help you get started in reviewing your situation and devising a personal retirement strategy. Together these techniques and insights will help you on your journey to becoming a successful retiree—one who is secure in knowing how to make sound retirement-income decisions.

Looking Ahead

As you can tell from this introduction, there is quite a lot of material to cover, and much of it is new, reflecting the fact that the retirement-income field is still evolving. In thinking about how best to provide you with clear, practical, and thorough information, I've reached out to my clients, friends, readers, and students of diverse backgrounds, interests, and needs. Their insights and outlooks are woven throughout this manuscript.

The message of the book also reflects my experience as a lawyer on Wall Street at the beginning of my career (when I wrote prospectuses) and my involvement in matters legal (as a securities industry arbitrator and mediator).

When you are finished, you will be more aware of the options before you, how to improve your current situation, and how to avoid taking action that may not be in your best interest.

I hope you find this book helpful as you make retirement-investment decisions. If you do, please send me a note—I would love to hear from you (e-mail me at readers@juliejason.com). I wish you a healthy, happy, and financially secure retirement.

PART I

Understanding
the Basics

CHAPTER 1

Achieving a Secure Retirement

At some point in your life, you will stop working and begin enjoying a well-deserved retirement that may last thirty years or even longer. When you retire, you will stop receiving your paycheck. From that point on, you will have to rely on other sources of income—your "retirement income"— to support yourself. Some of these retirement-income sources will continue for as long as you live. They include Social Security, your company pension (if you have one), or a lifelong annuity— an insurance product that delivers a series of regular payments—that you purchased for yourself or that your employer purchased on your behalf.

Depending on your spending, you may need to create additional sources of income or continue to work longer. I'll show you how to use the financial assets you own at retirement—your bank account, your 401(k) plan, perhaps your home—for precisely that purpose: to create retirement income that will last a lifetime.

How Much Retirement Income Will You Need to Maintain Your Lifestyle?

Creating retirement income is all about making sure you can be financially secure for as long as you live. Will you be able to sustain—perhaps even to enhance—your lifestyle once you stop working? Will you be able to afford the activities and comforts you envisioned for yourself in retirement?

And what about the basics, such as medical expenses and utility bills? Additionally, ask yourself how long a retirement period you will need to fund: Ten years? Thirty years?

Will you need anything beyond your Social Security benefits and pension to cover your expenses after you retire? If you outspend those income sources and have to draw down your retirement savings to cover the gap, how can you be sure you won't outlive your nest egg? What if your assets are tied up in your house or your 401(k) account? Will you be able to arrange an alternative source of income?

Hint: To preserve your pre-retirement lifestyle, you will want to replace at least 80 percent of your paycheck. Each year after that, you will want to issue yourself a small "pay increase." In other words, you will want your retirement income to keep pace with inflation.

If you step back a moment to take in the big picture, you can see that all these questions deal with money flows and cash management. Essentially, creating retirement income comes down to this: how much money needs to flow in to your household to cover the money that flows out? And where will that money come from?

As you will see in the next few chapters, managing inflow and outflow is a central theme in retirement-income planning. No two situations are alike, making this a highly personal exercise. It's based not simply on paying bills but also on fulfilling—or, if need be, deferring—certain lifestyle expectations.

Everybody's financial situation at retirement differs. If your sole source of retirement income is Social Security, your Social Security check will define your retirement lifestyle. If you also have a pension, retirement savings, a 401(k), a house, and other assets, you will have more flexibility and a more complex financial picture.

What's Your Number?

Some experts suggest that you'll need a nest egg of a certain size before you can retire. The idea is that if you have the right amount of savings, you'll be able to withdraw what you need for the rest of your life.

These experts vigorously debate the correct withdrawal rate to use—and for good reason. As you can imagine, *withdrawal rates will depend on the financial markets, how money is invested, and the margin of safety one wants to assume.* To elaborate just briefly, consider your predicament if you retired at the beginning of a downturn in the stock market after investing heavily in stocks. Your experience will be quite different from that of someone who did the same but retired at the beginning of a market upturn.

Can You Do Better?

No matter what your age, your financial circumstances, or your current status in life (retired or working), you can look for ways to improve your financial situation. You always have options. For example:

You can get a handle on how you would like to live in retirement and decide which "indulgences" you want to enjoy.

You can delay using your retirement savings by working longer (or going back to work if you have already retired).

You can increase the value of your savings by maximizing compounding. ("Compounding"—earning interest on interest—is the math behind

Retirement Security: An Age-Old Problem

Facing life's uncertainties, the ancient Greeks turned to olive oil for security; it was nutritive and could be stored for a long time. In medieval Europe, the feudal lord took responsibility for the financial security of his serfs. Organized charities took hold during the Middle Ages, when individuals began contributing money to care for the needy. Today, achieving economic security increasingly falls to the individual, who must address this challenge through careful planning and saving.

the millionaire next door, allowing wealth to build by leveraging small investments made wisely over long periods of time. This is particularly important for millennials, who typically have long investment horizons. More on this phenomenon later.)

You can transfer the risk of outliving your money ("longevity risk") to an institution (an insurance company).

We'll explore your various options and discuss how to recognize and sidestep the pitfalls that can put your retirement savings in peril. Bear in mind this simple but powerful truth: it's never too late to change your financial future.

How Can You Be Certain
You'll Have Enough?
We'd all like to maintain our lifestyles as long as we live, without burdening our children, our grandchildren, our friends, or society at large. Assets, income sources, and lifestyle expectations differ, of course, but otherwise everyone is in the same boat: no one can predict the future. Rich or poor, we are all subject to events we don't control: the uncertainty of the markets, pensions, taxes, health, rising costs, and above all the impossibility of quantifying in advance

how long you will need retirement income. Indeed, unknowns of this sort have beset humankind throughout history. *Though many of these risks are part of life, the secret to a successful retirement is to address the challenges they present.*

Why You Need a Retirement Plan

If you knew for certain how long you would live, and if you were sure that your existing sources of income would cover all your expenses during that span, you wouldn't need a retirement-income plan. Because you can't predict with certainty either one of those eventualities, however, a secure retirement demands careful planning.

Even if you don't consider yourself a planner, together, in this book, we'll start the process. Importantly, you may find that you can take some simple steps to improve your situation, while avoiding some all-too-common missteps. Take your time. Get your spouse or partner involved.

When you're finished with your review, you may find that you are all set for a carefree retirement—or you may find that you still have some work to do. Though no plan can be ironclad for the duration of your retirement—too many variables can enter the equation—you can predict certain things with reasonable certainty, such as your expected pension and Social Security income. By the same token, you can make allowances for other things you cannot predict: changes in your health, for example, fluctuating health-care costs, growing family obligations, or the eventual need to care for aging parents or finance children's (or grandchildren's) education.

Turning Challenges into Successes

As you work out a plan that makes sense for you, you're likely to encounter certain commonplace obstacles. Here are a few typical snags.

Lack of Experience

Most people retire only once, so it's understandable that they have no experience making the transition from paycheck to retirement income. Everyone learns from experience. (Translation: we all learn from our mistakes.) Naturally you don't want to make mistakes with your retirement savings, yet many retirees lack any meaningful investment experience. They have never invested in anything beyond their retirement plan at work. Making 401(k) decisions in the sheltered work environment is nothing like making investments in the open financial marketplace, where retirees must learn to make investment decisions on their own.

A Closer Look:
Do You Need a Financial Adviser?

There is no hard-and-fast rule as to whether you need an adviser as you approach or enter retirement. I can tell you that many of you can and do go it alone. *To be a successful do-it-yourselfer, you need three qualifications: first, you have to be a successful investor in your own right; second, you need to know how to create retirement income; and third, your spouse has to share these skills.*

If you don't fit this profile—whether you need to amass retirement savings from scratch or have more money than you think you will ever need—some type of "financial adviser" will be an important ally for the rest of your life.

Note that I enclosed the term "financial adviser" in quotes just now. There are hundreds of thousands of advisers, and unless you're familiar with the financial-services industry you may not be able to differentiate among them readily. As you make financial decisions that affect your retirement security, however, you'll need to develop that skill. We'll talk about how to distinguish among financial advisers in Chapter 7; in Chapter 20 you'll find a quick self-assessment test to help you determine the type of adviser best for you.

WARNING!

When presented with a product that promises guaranteed income for life, people often don't ask how the guarantee works, who is behind it, what happens if the company making the guarantee goes out of business, how the product is regulated, or what costs, risks, liquidity restrictions, taxes, and the like are associated with the product. They buy the product with their retirement nest eggs based on a gut feeling about the adviser, without reading the financial documents that describe exactly what they are signing up for. Consequences may be as severe as the loss of irreplaceable retirement savings. So always be a skeptic. Never buy anything without a full understanding of whether the product can deliver on its promises and why the salesperson would recommend the product for you.

How many retirees are truly knowledgeable about how to invest retirement assets or create retirement income? Faced with so many uncertainties—and with new options cropping up in the financial marketplace every day—many of you will consider enlisting the advice of a financial adviser, if you haven't already. That's a step in the right direction—as long as you know what to expect, and how to manage the relationship.

Hint: You may not need a financial adviser if you are a serious do-it-yourself investor who uses discount brokers to execute stock, bond, and mutual-fund transactions. (Discount brokers, including online trading sites, typically charge lower fees because there is no commissioned salesperson between you and the execution of the trade.)

A do-it-yourselfer is first and foremost a researcher. His bookshelves overflow with investment books and retirement books. He is analytical and does his homework. He reads prospectuses and annual reports. He reads investment publications from Value Line and Morningstar, publishers of independent research reports and analyses; subscribes to charting software such as TeleChart (published by Worden Brothers); and is likely a member of the American Association of Individual Investors (AAII), an independent membership association of individuals who want to learn to invest.

You and Your Spouse:

Retirement Is a Joint Venture

During the working years, couples usually divvy up financial responsibilities, with one spouse often taking the lead. It's not uncommon to see one spouse make the important financial decisions for the family and deal with the financial adviser, the lawyer, and the accountant, while the other spouse is in charge of the household checkbook.

In such instances, the spouse taking the lead may not realize that retirement is—and needs to be treated as—a partnership, with the goal of creating satisfactory retirement income not only for the couple during their lifetime together, but also for the survivor.

Retirement-planning decisions affect both spouses, so both need to be aware of the decision points and their consequences. Take pension elections, for example. Before you retire, you are usually given the option of choosing between a higher pension that ends when you die ("sole" or "single life") or a lower pension that continues to pay your spouse after your death ("joint and survivor"). If you elect the single-life option, you will receive a higher payout during your own life, but your spouse will receive nothing after your death. If you elect a 50 percent survivor option, your spouse will receive 50 percent of your payment after your death for as long as your spouse lives.

As you can see, the financial decisions you make today can have a tremendous (and often irrevocable) impact on your spouse—and his or her quality of life—in the future. (Note: from this point forward, I'll use the male pronoun to denote genders.) So remember: retirement is a joint venture for you and your spouse. Neither one of you should proceed down this path alone.

Retirement

without Regret

If you ask retirees to name their biggest financial regret, they almost invariably say that it is having saved inadequately for retirement. The issue is not one of having a lot of money or the things that money can buy. Retirement planning is not about living an extrava-

A Closer Look:
For Better or for Worse

In my roles as a money manager and a columnist, I've met with and counseled all sorts of couples. But certain common strategies, explained below, seem to work best when planning for two.

Working Together   Here's one example of a couple with the right approach. Sam is the breadwinner, and his wife, Sheila, is a stay-at-home mother. Sam is aware that women tend to outlive men and is concerned about how Sheila will fare if he dies before she does. In our first planning session, the three of us considered the lifestyle they envisioned in retirement—and whether it was feasible, given their resources. Both Sheila and Sam remained involved as their retirement plan evolved over time. We met quarterly to review their progress. Periodically, Sheila and I met for lunch so she could feel free to ask any questions that came to mind. Through this process, Sam and Sheila reached a mutual understanding of how they wanted to live in retirement and how they would fund it. They also discussed how income flows would change if Sam died before Sheila.

What Doesn't Work   In contrast, consider the case of Jim, divorced with two adult children, who married Mary, also divorced with two adult children. Unknown to Mary, Jim shared the details of his financial situation with his children, including how much money he and Mary have and how much they spend. Jim's children called a family meeting and urged Jim and Mary to move to a smaller home and to make other cutbacks in their spending habits. Mary was distressed that Jim's children were involving themselves in Jim and Mary's lifestyle decisions. Jim felt he was being a good father and was unaware of the effect his relationship with his children was having on Mary. This situation was fraught with danger—both to the couple's financial plans and to their relationship.

As you can see, communication between spouses is essential in working together toward a solid financial future.

gant lifestyle. Rather, it's about making choices now, when you still have time to influence your future. Let's start with the first step to a simplified retirement-income plan—understanding cash flow, the subject of the next chapter.

CHAPTER 2

Your Personal Cash Flow

Do this exercise with me.

Imagine that you will retire this Monday. From that day forward, your paycheck will stop and you will have to pay your bills with nothing but your savings. How long will your retirement last?

Let's consider a few likely scenarios.

Say you normally spend $5,000 a month and that you have $60,000 in the bank. Because you will be able to pay for twelve months of living expenses, your "retirement" will last precisely one year before you must return to work.

Now re-examine the situation, but this time factor in taking that vacation you've been dreaming about, which eats up $10,000—two months' savings. Your remaining savings will last only ten months.

Of necessity, you reconsider.

You decide you'd like to stretch out your retirement as long as possible. How? You can't go back in time and save more, of course, but you can control your spending in the present—and into the future. Rather than spending $5,000 a month, you decide you can live on $2,500 a month by sharing living quarters with friends or family. Good move: it buys you an additional year of retirement.

This exercise is an example of a point-in-time retirement-survival plan. In real life, we would factor in the earnings on your savings, which would increase the value of the account over the period in question—but those earnings would also be reduced by income taxes. We would also factor in pensions and Social Security, as well as inflation (to account for the loss of purchasing power as time passes). In addition, we would consider your lifestyle and probable longevity, and make projections based on reasonable assumptions for these variables. All of these are important pieces of the puzzle, and we'll explore them together in this book.

You Can't
Retire on Plastic
Despite the easy availability of credit cards, you can't retire on plastic. Unfortunately, debt is a problem that plagues many retirees: according to the Federal Reserve, almost seven out of ten households headed by retirees age 65 to 74 hold some kind of debt, including mortgages, loans, and credit-card balances (the median debt is $44,000). About four out of ten households headed by retirees age 75 and older have some kind of debt, with the median debt being $20,000.

Boomers and Budgeting
I'm convinced that people approaching retirement have a fear of budgeting. People who were born after World War II—the boomers—have been using credit cards and home-equity loans to buy consumer goods and pay for other "wants" as opposed to "needs," something previous generations simply did not do.

Boomers grew up with childhood memories of air-raid drills and fallout shelters. As teens and young adults, some blossomed into flower children, pacifists, and nonconformists, with not a thought about money or the future. Freedom, nonconformity, spirit, and individuality were the ideals. Scrimping, saving, and budgeting were matters addressed by the previous generation that grew up during the Great Depression—boomers' parents and grandparents.

Yet here we are.

If you're a boomer, I won't ask you to renounce your spending habits. Instead, I'll show you a technique to prioritize and time your expenditures. But first let me share some insights about how to look at expenses.

Start with
Your Expenses
What you need to know first is how much you spend on "musts" and how much you spend on "wants." Musts are the basics you need to survive and function, such as rent (or mortgage), utilities, medical expenses, food, transportation, and taxes. Let's call these "Essential Expenses." *The most financially secure retirees are able to pay for Essential Expenses with monthly income from Social Security and pensions or pension substitutes, such as immediate annuities.*

All other expenses are "wants." These expenses are not essential to survival, and may include entertainment, vacations, gifts, and the like. Let's call them "Lifestyle Expenses" (some people call them "discretionary expenses").

In contrast to Essential Expenses, which you must pay in full and on time, your Lifestyle spending is entirely up to you. That gives most people the power to control their financial destinies.

Hint: Categorizing your expenses is relatively straightforward: you must pay your rent or mortgage, or you won't have a place to live—hence that's an Essential Expense. By contrast, whereas you have the option of buying a second TV, you don't need one to survive—therefore that's a Lifestyle Expense.

What's the Difference? Vacations, gifts, club memberships, and tickets to entertainment or sporting events all belong in the Lifestyle category, as do magazines, new clothes, an extra pair of sneakers, fancy hors d'oeuvres for your dinner party, flowers for your kitchen table, pottery classes, extra plants for your garden—you get the picture. These are pure indulgences, by which I mean you could easily live without them if you

A Closer Look:
Know Where You Stand

After they retired, Sandy and Ira deposited their Social Security and pension checks in their joint checking account to pay their monthly bills, but there was never enough money in the account to cover all of their living expenses. Month after month, they had to sell off investments to free up money to pay bills, which was unsettling.

Both looked for ways to save. Ira started giving up the things he enjoyed, such as playing golf with his friends. In conversations with Sandy, he frequently brought up how much things cost. Sandy began to worry; did they have enough money to last a lifetime?

The problem was this: Sandy and Ira lacked the information they needed to assess their situation. First they needed to understand where their money was going by looking at their expenses and categorizing them. Then they needed to look at their income to see where there was a mismatch.

After studying their cash flow, Sandy and Ira discovered why they felt they never had enough money. They were spending $1,500 a month on Essential Expenses (such as housing and utilities) and $500 to $700 a month on Lifestyle Expenses (such as movies and trips), whereas their income (Social Security and pension) came to only $1,500 a month.

That was useful information. They could relax about basic needs and focus on managing their Lifestyle spending. If their investments were sufficient to support withdrawals of $500 to $700 a month, they could maintain their current lifestyle. If not, they would have to limit their spending.

had to—or at least for a while, until the money was in your bank account to pay for these items.

How Not
to Spend Your Future Now let me give you the timing tool, which I call the "Lifestyle Balance Register."

To track your expenditures, get a check register from a bank. This is a booklet the bank gives you to monitor your check writing. (See Table 2-1 for an example.)

Give yourself a beginning balance—the dollar amount you can afford to spend on Lifestyle Expenses for the month. This is your Lifestyle Balance. Like the balance in a checking account, use it as a starting point each month. Spend the balance as you wish on Lifestyle items such as gifts or entertainment, or save it for bigger items such as vacations. As with a checking account, be careful not to overdraw this balance.

Carry the register with you at all times. Enter every amount you spend on lifestyle items, no matter how small. As you make purchases—whether you pay by check, cash, credit card, or debit card—subtract each expense from your updated Lifestyle Balance.

In the example below, I've purchased two items and deducted them from my Lifestyle Balance of $500. Keep in mind that this register covers only my Lifestyle Expenses. In this example, I did not need to use the register to record Essential Expenses, because those were already covered by my pension and Social Security.

Date	Check #	Payee	Amount	Lifestyle Balance
January		Beginning Balance:		$500
Jan 5	Cash	Movie Tickets	$24	$476
Jan 7	Cash	Magazines	$12	$464

Table 2-1: Check register showing a $500 beginning Lifestyle Balance

WARNING!

Some people may think they can overspend their Lifestyle Balance and then make up the deficit by spending that much less the next month. That's spending money you don't have, which is what people do when they live on credit. Spend every last penny of your monthly Lifestyle Balance any way you want, but don't spend a penny of next month's deposit until next month arrives. Stick to the present. Don't spend the future.

As a new month begins, give yourself another lifestyle deposit of $500, adding that to any money remaining in your Lifestyle Balance from the previous month, and start spending as you wish. The only rule is that you cannot over-draw this account.

Budgeting is hard on just about everyone, but timing expenditures is manageable. Whereas a budgeting system is about saying "No," this timing system is all about asking "When?" If you want to spend money that would overdraw the Lifestyle Balance, all you have to do is wait until the balance increases on the first of the next month with the deposit of your next $500.

Where Does
the Money Go?
I have yet to meet anyone whose idea of a good time is poring over bills, checks, and credit-card receipts. So let me share some tips on how to get the information you need with the least amount of effort.

For a rough estimate of your expenses, compare your take-home pay with what you have left at the end of the month. For example, if you take home $1,000 a month and you have $100 left at the end of the month, you are spending $900 a month.

That's a good start. If you have more time to devote to this exercise, you can learn even more. Gather up the last three months of bills, bank statements, and credit-card and debit-card receipts, and make a list of cash expenditures. Set aside a weekend afternoon and, if you are married, get your spouse involved. Go through the records for the most recent month first. Review your checks and any other withdrawals from your bank account, which will also show debit-card activity. Then review your credit-card bills. Scrutinize each expenditure.

A Closer Look:

The Lifestyle Balance Register

Here's an example of how timing expenditures works. Harry and Joan receive pension and Social Security income of $5,000 a month (which covers their Essential Expenses) and withdraw $2,000 a month from their savings for Lifestyle Expenses. They normally spend $7,000 a month but are distressed because they often exceed that amount. On reviewing their spending, we uncovered the problem: spontaneous credit-card purchases of lifestyle "wants," such as gifts for their grandchildren. We decided to give the Lifestyle Balance Register a try. Harry and Joan started the month with a "Lifestyle Deposit" of $1,000 each. They agreed to record each expenditure (whether by plastic, check, or cash) and to deduct that amount from their Lifestyle Balance on a running basis. If they wanted to make a purchase when the balance had fallen too low, they were forced to wait until the next deposit.

Did the regimen work? You be the judge. By tracking their expenditures and timing their lifestyle spending, Harry and Joan stopped worrying about money. They knew that they could buy what they wanted so long as they made purchases only as their Lifestyle Balance permitted.

Now let's put the concepts and tools we've been discussing into practice, by taking a closer look at your own expenses.

Have your spouse do the same for his or her expenditures. Record each one in a ledger like the one shown in Table 2-2. Repeat the process for the two previous months.

You won't capture all your expenses this way (you'll be missing one-time expenses, such as a major purchase made earlier in the year), but you should arrive at a fairly sound estimate. For greater accuracy, review the last twelve months of your financial records, keeping an eye peeled for

Expense	Amount	Paid By	Date	Type
Home Insurance	$115	Check	June	Essential
Mortgage	500	Check	June	Essential
Electricity	120	Check	June	Essential
Phone	130	Check	June	Essential
Groceries	400	Credit Card	June	Essential
Entertainment	500	Credit Card	June	Lifestyle
Restaurants	150	Credit Card	June	Lifestyle
Newspapers	20	Cash	June	Lifestyle
Commuting	60	Cash	June	Essential
Gas	190	Cash	June	Essential
Car Repairs	200	Check	June	Essential
Magazines	20	Credit Card	June	Lifestyle
Medical	40	Check	June	Essential
Total Expenses	$2,445			

Table 2-2: Sample record of expenses

semiannual or annual expenditures such as real-estate taxes, life-insurance payments, car repairs, and the like.

The result will be an estimate of your monthly expenses. The next step is to categorize those expenses, as we discussed earlier, with the goal of identifying decision points. In Table 2-2, you can see that $690 was spent on Lifestyle Expenses and the rest ($1,755) was spent on Essential Expenses.

The purpose of this exercise is to enable you to plan. Whereas many of the elements that determine retirement security are beyond your control, how much you spend is very much within it.

How Much
Can You Safely Spend?   Now that you understand how much you
currently spend, you must figure out whether you can continue spending
at that rate for the rest of your life. And any time we address the future,
we have to consider ways of projecting what will happen.

So first let's talk about what we know—always the best place to start.

Inflation
Based on personal experience, we know that costs will rise over time.
For example, I bought my first car—a yellow Karmann Ghia—for about
$2,000 in 1967. With inflation having averaged 4.7 percent annually
over the forty-some years since then, that car (were it still being made)
would cost about $14,500 in 2017 dollars.

We can't avoid inflation, so we need to factor it into the puzzle. To calculate future costs, use 3 percent—the average annual inflation rate since
1926 (as published by Ibbotson Associates, a subsidiary of the invest-
ment-research firm Morningstar). To be more conservative, use a higher
number such as 4 percent. To be more conservative still, use 6 percent—
the inflation rate for the twenty years ending in 1992.

Let me show you how that works. You can project that if your Essential Expenses are $1,000 today, in twelve years they will be roughly
$1,500 (assuming a 3 percent inflation rate) or $2,000 (assuming a 6
percent inflation rate). The rate you choose to plan with depends on how
risk-averse you are, but in order to be certain of covering your Essential
Expenses as you grow older, you must plan for a retirement income that
will cover this rising cost of living. Because medical costs may rise faster
than other expenses, it might be safer to use a higher inflation rate.

Longevity
Demographic studies tell us that boomers (people born in the years 1946
to 1964) will live much longer than any previous generation. According
to the National Center for Health Statistics, the median life expectancy
for a man who reaches the age of 65 is 18 years (age 83). (The "median"

simply means that an equal number of people will either outlive or fail to reach this age.) For a woman who attains that milestone (age 65), the median life expectancy is 20.5 years (age 85.5).

Hint: For a couple age 65, there is a 50 percent chance that one of them will live to age 93—and a 25 percent chance that one will live to age 97.

When projecting for your own personal situation, it's best to be optimistic. Unless medical concerns dictate otherwise, budget for a long life—thirty to forty years—in retirement.

Why Your Expenses Matter

As we discussed earlier, you can simplify retirement planning into a basic cash-flow equation between your income and your expenses. We've examined your spending habits before anything else for two reasons:

First, by understanding your expenses in retirement, you can better determine how much income you really need to generate right now. With that information in hand, you can then determine whether you have realistic expectations of continuing your current lifestyle—or whether some adjustments will need to be made.

Second, to a large degree, your expenses are within your control. Reduce your spending and you won't need to generate as much income; add to your expenses in retirement and you'll need to generate more.

Now let's turn to the other part of the cash-flow equation: sources of retirement income.

CHAPTER 3

Sources of Retirement Income

Having discussed how to manage the outflow part of cash-flow management in Chapter 2, we're now ready to look at the inflow part of the equation. Your inflow may include various sources of income, such as Social Security, a pension, or income you create from savings or assets.

How Much

Will You Need? After you retire, you won't be contributing to your 401(k)* plan at work. You won't be commuting to work or buying work clothes, lunches, and the like. It's possible that you will actually need less—perhaps only 80 percent—of your pre-retirement income. (*Throughout this book, when I refer to 401(k)s, I'm not excluding other types of employer retirement plans, such as 403(b) plans.)

On the other hand, you may plan to travel in retirement, make gifts to grandchildren, or take up an expensive hobby. In that case, you may need more—perhaps 120 percent of your pre-retirement income. The same holds true if you run into medical or dental problems.

Now let's look more closely at various types and sources of retirement income. First we will consider assets or activities that create income in retirement. Next we will talk about income that is coming to you based on decisions you made while you were still working.

Action Required

Three sources of retirement income require some action on your part:

1. Income created from personal assets
2   Income from a business you own
3. Income from work during retirement

Let's explore each income source in some detail, beginning with personal assets.

Personal Assets Personal assets—including your savings, investments, IRAs, 401(k) plan, investment real estate, and anything else you own at retirement—can all be redeployed to create retirement income. (In Parts II and III, you'll learn how to use the equity in your home to create retirement income and how to use savings, investments, or your 401(k) to create a flow of monthly checks for life.)

Even if you are an experienced investor, prudently creating income from assets is the single most difficult task ahead of you. The reason? Until 2006,

A Closer Look:

Replacement Ratios: Before Inflation

Depending on how you want to live in retirement, your desired ratio of post-retirement income to pre-retirement income (your "replacement ratio") will be lower than, higher than, or equal to your pre-retirement earnings. Although it's hard to generalize about individual situations, here's a rule of thumb to consider: if you want to live more modestly than you did before retirement, your replacement ratio will be lower than 100 percent. If you want to live larger, your replacement ratio will be higher than 100 percent. If you want the same lifestyle, your replacement ratio will equal 100 percent.

Here is an example, using $100,000 of pre-retirement income.

- 100 percent replacement ratio = $100,000
- 70 percent replacement ratio = $70,000
- 120 percent replacement ratio = $120,000

when the first boomers began turning 60, advisers generally focused their efforts on wealth accumulation, which is all about growth, not income.

Wealth creation is an essential skill to have if you are young and want to build a retirement portfolio for the future. As you get closer to retirement, however, you also need to know how to turn accumulated wealth into an income stream that can support you for the rest of your life.

That skill is not easily learned, even for the financial adviser. It calls for a shift in mind-set—from creating growth to creating income plus growth.

Let's take a look at some specific assets you're likely to have available.

Your home A home can be an asset that you can sell, as many retirees do, when they scale down and move to a smaller residence. Of course, you'll need sufficient equity in your home to make this work. (Equity is the value of the home after deducting mortgages and other debts, such as equity lines of credit.)

You also may have the option of staying in the home and benefiting from a reverse mortgage, as we'll discuss in Chapter 14.

Everything else you own besides your home can create retirement income for you. Some assets create income through earnings (dividends or interest), which you can withdraw to pay bills. Other assets must be sold to free up money.

In either case, you must understand the tax ramifications of your actions. As a result, it's helpful to consider assets as taxable, tax-deferred, or tax-free:

- Taxable assets include your bank account, investments, credit-union accounts, or collectibles (such as art or antiques). In a taxable account, earnings (dividends and interest) are subject to income taxes at ordinary income tax rates, somewhat like your paycheck. (Note that some dividends, called "qualified dividends," may be taxed at a lower tax rate than your paycheck.) The tax is payable whether or not you withdraw the earnings.

   As mentioned, gains on sales (profits you make when you sell an asset) are generally taxed at capital-gains tax rates. Once you make a sale, the gain is taxable whether or not you withdraw the proceeds from your account.

- Tax-deferred assets include your traditional IRA (Individual Retirement Account); employer retirement plans such as your 401(k), 403(b), or SEP (Simplified Employee Pension); and any other financial products that are tax-deferred, such as variable annuities (see Chapter 11). Tax-deferred accounts are free of income-tax liability during the time you leave the money in the account. *When you take money out of the account, the amounts you withdraw generally are taxed as ordinary income.* There are nuances that you need to review with your tax adviser; for example, if you made nondeductible contributions, those withdrawals are not taxable.

- Tax-free assets include Roth IRAs and tax-free municipal bonds. "Tax-free" means earnings are free from income tax, provided certain conditions are met. You don't have to pay taxes on the earnings or gains in a Roth IRA, or on withdrawals from a Roth IRA after five years. (See Chapter 17 for more information.) The Internal Revenue Service (IRS) does not tax the interest you earn on municipal bonds. However, you will be taxed on gains if you sell a municipal bond for more than you paid for it. There is no tax on withdrawals of earnings.

See Table 3-1 for a comparison of how different types of assets are taxed.

Asset	Taxable	Tax-Deferred	Tax Free
Earnings	Taxed at Ordinary Income-Tax Rates	Not Taxed	Not Taxed
Gains	Taxed at Capital-Gains Tax Rates	Not Taxed	Taxed at Capital-Gains Tax Rates
Withdrawals	Not Applicable	Taxed at Ordinary Income-Tax Rates	Not Applicable

Table 3-1: Comparison of taxable, tax-deferred, and tax-free assets

WARNING!

Understand how your withdrawals are taxed. If you withdraw $200 from your IRA to pay for a car repair, you're actually paying $267 for that bill ($200 for the repair and $67 to the "tax man," assuming you pay taxes at a rate of 25 percent).

Sequencing If you have all three of the types of assets listed in Table 3-1, you will need a sequencing plan. In other words, which assets will you turn to first when you need to generate cash flow for retirement?

Financial advisers debate the question of sequencing among themselves. Some believe it is wiser to hold on to tax-deferred assets as long as possible to take advantage of the tax-free growth they offer during the holding period. Others disagree, pointing out that when you withdraw your money, the withdrawal triggers an income tax, so you may as well pay the tax sooner rather than later.

There is no general rule that applies to everyone. Just be aware of this issue when you talk to your tax and financial advisers before you make any withdrawals. My personal preference is to let tax-deferred assets grow as long as possible, assuming other assets are available for emergencies and Essential Expenses.

Income from

a Business If you start or own a business after you retire, you can create retirement income for yourself. The business needs to generate income without too much day-to-day effort, unless you plan to "un-retire" and manage the business yourself full-time. Commercial real estate is an example of a cash-flow business that can be operated by an absentee owner.

One individual I know ran an auto-parts store until he retired. Now he receives monthly income from a small commercial building in a warehouse district that he bought more than thirty years ago. He rents the space to a few small local retail stores. The building takes virtually no time or effort to keep up, and his leases provide a substantial retirement income.

Income

from Work   If you retire with no business and no personal assets, you may be one of the rising number of retirees who must go back to work full- or part-time after leaving a regular job. Around 30.8 percent of people age 65 to 69 work, the Bureau of Labor Statistics reported in 2015, as do 17.8 percent of those age 70 to 74.

As boomers age, those numbers are expected to climb. According to a 2013 MetLife study (the most recent one available), one of every two boomers expects to work past traditional retirement age. One in five believes he will never be able to afford to retire.

Some retirees put their knowledge to work by becoming consultants. Others find themselves in different jobs altogether. Though the following story may be distressing, you will not suffer the same fate if you take the time to prepare for retirement. A few years ago, a former plant manager contacted me after his financial adviser had persuaded him to retire early. He soon found that he couldn't make ends meet. Failing to get reinstated in his old job, he drove a school bus for a time, then was forced to sell his house in the Northeast and move in with his daughter, who lived in the Midwest. If you assess your situation realistically before retirement—the crucial step this man omitted—you will be able to choose to work in retirement rather than being forced to do so.

No Action

Required Up to now, we've been talking about assets that you need to turn into income after you retire. But you may have other sources of retirement income coming to you that call for no action on your part after you retire, such as company pensions and Social Security retirement benefits. This income is yours thanks to credits you earned while you were working. After you make initial elections to start payments, you have no control over how much you will receive—but no action is required on your part to keep the checks coming.

What Can You Expect

from Social Security? The first recipient of a monthly Social Security retirement check was Ida May Fuller of Ludlow, Vermont. She died in January 1975 at the age of 100, having received almost $23,000 in benefits. Her first check was for $22.54.

Today, ninety percent of the U.S. population age 65 or older receives Social Security retirement benefits, either as retired workers who have paid into the system or as the spouses or survivors of such workers.

Social Security was designed to replace a portion of the wages that a retired worker or a disabled worker had earned while he was still in the

A Closer Look:

By the Numbers

How important are Social Security benefits to those 65 and over? Very. Social Security provides a lifetime retirement benefit that is adjusted annually for inflation. According to 2016 statistics from the Social Security Administration (SSA):

• For two out of three beneficiaries, Social Security retirement benefits are their major source (50 to 100 percent) of income.

• One out of five married couples and two out of five unmarried individuals rely on Social Security for 90 percent or more of their retirement income.

• According to the most recently available SSA statistics (2003), Social Security represents the sole source of income for one out of five beneficiaries.

workforce. It was also intended to aid the survivors of deceased workers. It was never meant to cover all of an individual's retirement needs.

Let's see just how much of your pre-retirement income will be replaced through Social Security.

How Much Do Social Security Beneficiaries Receive?

Though averages don't tell the full story, consider this: according to the Social Security Administration (SSA), the estimated average monthly Social Security retirement benefit paid in 2017 was $1,360 ($16,320 for the year). The maximum benefit for a worker retiring at full retirement age in 2017 was $2,687 per month ($32,244 for the year).

Women and men are treated the same in terms of their benefits. That is, individuals with identical earnings histories receive the same benefits whether they are male or female.

A Progressive Formula Social Security has a "progressive benefit formula," which provides lower-wage earners with a larger share of their pre-retirement earnings than higher-wage earners.

Social Security benefits replace at most about one-third of the income of maximum-earning individuals (wages above $108,570 in 2013; see Figure 3-1) who apply for Social Security at full retirement age.

For medium-earning individuals (career average earnings of $45,128), Social Security benefits replace 40 percent of income.

And for lower earners (career average earnings of $20,308), Social Security replaces about 54 percent of their income.

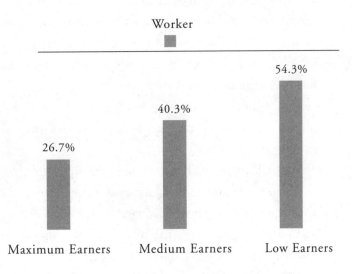

Figure 3-1: A closer look at social security replacement ratios

For example, let's compare two people, both single. Anne earned $20,000 before she retired and Mary earned $120,000. Anne will receive just over 54 percent of her pre-retirement income from Social Security, while Mary will receive less than 30 percent. This progressive formula was designed to protect those who are less likely to have savings or a pension.

WARNING!

One out of two American workers is not covered by a private pension. One out of three American workers has saved nothing for retirement. If you're one of the millions of Americans counting on Social Security to replace your pre-retirement income, you need to understand replacement ratios—and how they may affect the amount of your retirement benefit. Try to determine in advance how big a role your Social Security benefits can realistically be expected to play in that plan.

So. . . Can You Afford to Retire?

After you stop working, you will need to provide food, shelter, and clothing for yourself. That's a fact. If you do no planning and have no personal assets to turn into retirement income, you may have to learn to live on less. For example, one of my readers, a widower, knows the location of every thrift shop within twenty miles of his home. He grows his own vegetables. And by helping out friends and neighbors when he sees the opportunity (it helps to be handy), he gets invited to homemade dinners at least once a week. He has lots of friends and is very active and happy.

You will define your lifestyle in retirement by the personal resources you have when you retire. If those resources don't make you happy, you'll have choices: you can work longer, start a business, or reduce your wants and needs. If you are accustomed to borrowing money to pay for living expenses, though, you'll have to break that habit.

Now that we've discussed possible sources of income, let's explore Social Security in greater detail.

CHAPTER 4

Income from Social Security

Just about everyone you know will receive Social Security retirement benefits after they retire. As discussed in Chapter 3, lower earners will benefit proportionately the most because their benefits are based on higher replacement ratios. By contrast, higher earners will need to rely on their own personal savings and pensions to supplement their Social Security benefits and maintain their standards of living in retirement.

Because Social Security is such a critical retirement-income topic, let's examine a few of its details. Even if you already receive Social Security, some of the information below will be of interest to you—notably the taxation of Social Security retirement benefits, the reduction of benefits if you go back to work, and benefits for surviving spouses.

First let's discuss some general concepts, such as how one qualifies for benefits and how payments are calculated. Then we'll go into specifics that may affect your individual situation, as well as details about Supplemental Security Income (SSI), a government program designed to help those with incomes and resources below the poverty level.

Before we begin, I'd like to thank the subject matter experts at the Social Security Administration for help with this chapter.

Who Is
Eligible? Normally, you have to be a U.S. citizen (living here or abroad) or a lawfully admitted noncitizen (living in the United States) to receive butions for forty calendar quarters (see "Credits," below).

According to 2016 data, about ninety percent of people over 65 are receiving benefits, and 94 percent of working Americans (171 million people) pay into the Social Security system through payroll deductions to FICA or SECA. The 6 percent of the working population that does not contribute to FICA or SECA (because most of them work for state or local governments) is not covered by Social Security.

How Much
Will You Receive? The size of your monthly Social Security check depends on your earnings history and your age. That is, the Social Security Administration (SSA) determines your retirement benefit based on earnings (wages and self-employment income covered by Social Security) over your working career, and on whether you retire before or after your full retire-ment age.

Credits To qualify for Social Security retirement benefits, a covered worker must have worked in Social Security–covered employment (or self-employment) and paid FICA or SECA long enough to earn forty credits over the course of his* lifetime. A credit—the basic unit for determining whether a worker is insured under the Social Security program—is often referred to as a QC, or quarter of coverage. (*"His" denotes both genders.)

Before 1978, quarters counted were actual calendar quarters in which wages of $50 or more were paid. After 1978, wage reporting switched from quarters to years. One quarter of coverage was credited for each $250 of an individual's wages for the year, up to a maximum of four quarters for the year. That dollar amount has increased over time; as of 2017, you need 1,300 in earnings to earn one quarter of coverage.

Your Monthly Check The SSA will determine your retirement benefits based on your highest thirty-five years of earnings, selected from all of your years of contributions. The actual earnings are first indexed (adjusted to account for changes in average wages since your earnings were received). A formula is then applied to arrive at the amount you will receive at your full retirement age.

Hint: The SSA has a benefit estimator at http://www.socialsecurity.gov/estimator/. Using your current benefit record, you can see how your benefits would change based on different future earnings, or different future dates when you stop working.

When to Apply Your sixty-second birthday is a turning point. It's the earliest date at which you can start receiving Social Security retirement benefits as a worker. (Some people, such as survivors and disabled workers, can apply earlier. See the discussion of survivor and disability benefits later in this chapter for more details.) However, the age at which you apply for your benefits affects how much you receive. As a result, you will want to give this decision careful consideration.

WARNING!

You can elect to receive Social Security retirement benefits as early as age 62. If you do, however, your monthly checks will be permanently reduced. To collect your full benefit, you must wait to apply until your full retirement age (see Table 4-1).

Applying Early If you apply before your full retirement age, you will receive a smaller, permanently reduced benefit, based on when you decide to apply.

For example, if you choose to receive benefits in 2017 at the age of 62, your benefit will be approximately three-fourths (a reduction of about 25.8 percent) of the amount you would receive if you wait just a few years until your full retirement age. The closer you get to full retirement age before accepting benefits, the more of your benefit you can receive. In fact, every month you wait makes a difference.

Let's look at an example. Mary earns $40,000 a year. She turns 62 in September of 2017 and wants to consider retiring immediately. How much will she receive in Social Security benefits if she retires at 62?

To answer this question, I logged onto the Quick Calculator at http://www.socialsecurity.gov/planners/benefitcalculators.htm and inserted Mary's date of birth and current salary. The calculator tells me that Mary will receive $910 a month in Social Security benefits if she retires now.

But if Mary waits until her full retirement age (66 and two months in this case, given that she was born in 1955), she will receive $1,284 a month in Social Security benefits in today's dollars.

To determine your full retirement age, see Table 4-1, opposite.

In Sickness and in Health If before full retirement age you become seriously disabled and cannot work, consider filing for disability benefits before applying for retirement benefits. Why? Because your disability benefit will be higher than the reduced retirement benefit you would receive before full retirement age. Once you reach full retirement age, your disability benefits will convert to retirement benefits.

For an example, let's return to Mary. At age 62, if she is disabled, she will receive a monthly disability benefit of $1,220—significantly higher than the $910 retirement benefit for which she otherwise would have qualified at that age. However, Mary must meet stringent disability requirements.

Year Of Birth	Full Retirement Age (FRA)
1937 and Prior	65
1938	65 and 2 Months
1939	65 and 4 Months
1940	65 and 6 Months
1941	65 and 8 Months
1942	65 and 10 Months
1943–54	66
1955	66 and 2 Months
1956	66 and 4 Months
1957	66 and 6 Months
1958	66 and 8 Months
1959	66 and 10 Months
1960 and Later	67

Table 4-1: Social Security full retirement ages (FRA)

Breaking Even Still not convinced you should wait until your full retirement age to apply for your benefits? Try using one of the break-even age calculators you can find online, or create your own using a spreadsheet.

Using one such online tool, I entered Mary's monthly benefit at age 62 ($910) and her benefit at age 66 and two months ($1,284). The calculator estimated her break-even age as 76 years. That's the age at which her cumulative payments from age 62 equal the cumulative payments she would have received if she had retired at age 66 and two months. If Mary outlives her break-even age, the cumulative payments she received after retiring at age 62 will be less than if she had waited until age 66 and two months to begin her Social Security benefits.

Applying Later   If you apply for Social Security retirement benefits after your full retirement age, you will receive a higher benefit. The higher amount is due to something called the "delayed-retirement credit," which increases your Social Security retirement benefit and is calculated based on your year of birth.

For example, if you were born in 1943 or later, your delayed-retirement credit is 8 percent. This means that for each year you delay retiring after your full retirement date, 8 percent (two-thirds of 1 percent monthly) is added to your annual benefit amount.

To qualify for delayed-retirement credits, all you have to do is wait to apply—if you can. Your retirement benefit will increase automatically.

It may be possible to increase your Social Security retirement benefit even further by working and making additional FICA or SECA contributions. As discussed on page 35, the highest thirty-five years of earnings are used in the computation. If your continued earnings are higher than the prior earnings used to figure your Social Security benefit, the SSA will automatically increase your benefit to reflect the new earnings.

Spousal
Benefits   Social Security provides a benefit for spouses (both current and former) as well as for widows and widowers. Let's ex-plore a few of the rules and how they may affect you.

If Your Spouse Did Not Work   If your spouse is not eligible for
Social Security on his own employment record, he can nonetheless receive a spousal benefit of up to one-half of your benefit when your spouse retires. (He may file as early as age 62 but will incur some reduction in the benefit amount he receives.) The spousal benefit will turn into a survivor benefit at your death (see opposite page), increasing the surviving spouse's payment to up to 100 percent of your benefit if he is at full retirement age or above when you die. A survivor who has not remarried may draw benefits as early as age 60, or age 50 if disabled. Remarriage after age 60 does

not affect eligibility for survivor benefits, which continue for the survivor's life unless the new spouse has a higher benefit.

For example, Harry is married to Susan, who has never been employed. Assuming Harry retires at age 66 and Susan has reached her full retirement age (66 years old in this case) at the time, she will receive a payment equal to one-half of Harry's $1,161 monthly payment ($580) for as long as Harry lives, even though she has no earnings record of her own. If Harry dies, Susan will receive 100 percent of Harry's $1,161 monthly as a survivor benefit for as long as she lives. (Note that this example does not reflect increases for inflation, which you would receive in real life. If inflation adjustments had boosted Harry's benefit to $1,300 by the time he died, Susan would receive 100 percent of that increased benefit, or $1,300 a month. She would also receive any additional inflation adjustments applicable to Harry's benefit in the decades following his death.)

Note that your spouse cannot apply for spousal benefits before you, as the covered worker, apply for your own Social Security retirement benefit. He can file only after you do. However, the most a never-employed spouse can receive is 50 percent of the retired worker's benefit at full retirement age.

If Your Spouse Is Covered Your spouse may qualify for his own Social Security retirement benefit based on his own record as well as a spousal benefit (up to ½) based on your work record. SSA will pay the higher benefit of the two. When a married individual files for either his own retirement benefit or his spouse's benefit, he is "deemed" to file for the other benefit as well. (Under prior law, the spouse at full retirement age could apply for spousal benefits and postpone applying for his own retirement benefits in order to take advantage of delayed-retirement credits. That is no longer the case for individuals who turn 62 on or after 1/2/2016.)

There is an exception, however: you can no longer postpone your own benefit as before, unless you 1) act before January 2020 and 2) will have reached full retirement age before then. If you turned 62 *prior* to January 2, 2016, you may file for either your own or your spouse's benefit or your retirement benefit without being "deemed" to file for the other. You may also restrict your application to apply only for spouse's benefits and delay filing for your own retirement in order to earn delayed retirement credits.

Survivor Benefits   If you are widowed (regardless of the age of your spouse at death), you can apply for Social Security survivor benefits when you are age 60, or age 50 if you are disabled. "Disabled" for this purpose means you cannot work because you have a severe medical condition that is expected to last at least one year or result in death. The disabling condition must occur before age sixty and within seven years of the later of two dates: either the spouse's death or the last month of entitlement to a mother's or father's benefit.

The survivor benefit will depend on the age of the survivor at the time he applies.

The benefit will equal the deceased spouse's benefit if the survivor is at or over full retirement age. If the survivor is under full retirement age, the payment is reduced by a formula that is tied to age: the younger the survivor, the smaller the payment. The survivor can switch to his own retirement benefit when he reaches full retirement age.

Generally, to qualify for the survivor benefit, you must have been married for at least nine months just before the covered worker died. However, there are exceptions. There is no nine-month minimum under the following circumstances: if you are the biological parent of the worker's biological child; if you legally adopted the worker's child while you were married to him and before the child turned 18; if the worker's death was accidental (on or off the job); or if the worker died in the line of duty while he was a member of a uniformed service serving on active duty. (For additional exceptions, see sections 401 and 404 of the Social Security Handbook at http://www.ssa.gov/OP_Home/handbook/handbook.html.)

Social Security
and Divorce   If you get divorced after your Social Security benefits begin, your spousal benefits do not terminate because of the divorce, provided you were married for at least ten years. They continue throughout

your lifetime as if you were still married. (Your spousal benefits do end, however, if you remarry.)

Divorce before Retirement If you are divorced, you may still be eligible for benefits based on your former spouse's earnings. If you were married to a covered worker for more than ten years and subsequently divorced, essentially you are treated as a spouse for purposes of Social Security benefits. As long as you are age 62 or older and have not remarried, you can apply to receive up to one-half of the covered worker's Social Security retirement benefit for his life—and 100 percent of his benefit after his death. (If your ex predeceases you, be sure to check if you qualify for survivor benefits, even if you are younger than 62. Survivor benefits may be payable even if you have not applied for retirement benefits.)

A Closer Look:
The "Benefits" of Divorce

If you are divorced, you can receive benefits on your former spouse's Social Security record, provided he is at least 62 years old and you:

- Were married to your ex-spouse for at least ten years
- Are at least 62 years old
- Are unmarried (although your former spouse can be remarried)
- Are not entitled to a higher Social Security benefit on your own record

In addition, your former spouse must be entitled to receive his own retirement or disability benefit. If he is eligible for a benefit but has not yet applied for it, you can still receive a benefit if you meet the eligibility requirements above and have been divorced from your former spouse for at least two years.

In most cases, the benefits paid to a divorced spouse or a surviving divorced spouse will not affect the benefit amount paid to other family members who receive benefits on the same record.

If you are claiming spousal benefits based on a previous marriage that ended in divorce at least two years ago, you do not have to wait until your former spouse begins to take his retirement benefits to claim yours. In fact, if you remarry but that remarriage ends by death, divorce, or annulment, the earlier benefits may be reinstated.

Working While Retired

We've talked about how you can increase your Social Security retirement benefits by continuing to work and waiting to apply for Social Security until after your full retirement age. Now let's discuss going back to work after you start to receive your Social Security retirement benefits. How will this affect the amount you receive from Social Security?

It all depends on your age.

If you are working at or after your full retirement age, your Social Security retirement benefits will not be reduced.

If, on the other hand, you started receiving your benefits before your full retirement date and you are working, your Social Security checks will be reduced until you reach full retirement age. So that there are no surprises, be sure you understand how this works.

The law provides for a two-tiered earnings test: one for beneficiaries below their full retirement age, and a different one for beneficiaries who are in the calendar year when they will reach full retirement age. The earnings test was established as the limit below which a person meets the definition of being "retired." Both tiers are explained below.

Before Year of Retirement Age

Here's how the earnings test works for retirees below full retirement age: the SSA deducts $1 for every $2 you earn above a limit for the year ($16,920 in 2017). "Earnings" can be W-2 wages if you have a job, Form 1099 compensation if you work as an independent contractor, or your net income if you are self-employed. So if you are below full retirement age, regardless of how old you are, apply this earnings test to see if your Social Security retirement benefits will be reduced.

Let's look at an example. Henry is 62 years old and receives $700 monthly from the SSA. He notifies the SSA in advance that he expects to make $20,000 in 2017, exceeding the annual limit by $3,080 ($20,000 minus $16,920). The SSA withholds Henry's $700 monthly Social Security benefits from January through March to make up for the $1,540 that he owes the SSA ($1 for every $2 of his earnings above $16,920), and he starts receiving his regular $700 benefit again in April. However, since the withheld benefits total $2,100—$560 more than Henry owes—he also receives a check for the remaining $560 in January of 2018.

To notify the SSA of your expected annual income, call its main number at 800-772-1213.

During Year

of Full Retirement Age If you work in the year in which you attain full retirement age, things are different. In that year, your benefits will be reduced $1 for every $3 you earn over a different limit ($44,880 in 2017) until you reach full retirement age. In other words, if you expect to earn $48,000 between January and the date on which you reach full retirement age, the SSA will withhold your benefits starting in January until it has collected the $1,040 you owe ($48,000 minus $44,800 is $3,120). Once you reach your full retirement age, you receive your normal Social Security benefit payments, no matter how much you earn. Starting with the month in which you reach normal retirement age, there is no limit on earnings.

Taxation of

Benefits Let's consider a few common questions relating to the taxation of Social Security retirement benefits. (For more detail on tax issues, see Chapter 17.)

Two out of five beneficiaries currently pay taxes on their benefits. Income taxes are triggered only when other income pushes these individuals over a base amount.

If you do have other income, you'll have to figure out whether your Social Security retirement benefits will be subject to income taxes. To do that, add up your total taxable income, plus your tax-free income, plus one-half of your Social Security retirement benefits. If that sum is more than $25,000 for a single filer, or $32,000 for a married couple filing jointly, or zero for a married couple filing singly, your Social Security retirement benefit will be subject to income taxes.

The best way to figure out whether your Social Security retirement-income benefit will be taxable is to use the Social Security Benefits Worksheet in the Internal Revenue Service (IRS) publication "Instructions for Form 1040," which you can get online at www.irs.gov or by calling 800-829-3676.

How to Apply for

Benefits You can apply for retirement benefits online at www.ssa.gov or you can visit your local Social Security office to apply in person. Call 800-772-1213 for more information. The SSA advises that you should apply three months before the date you want your benefits to begin.

Required Information You will need to provide documentation to begin the application process, but it is important not to delay if you do not have all the documents. The SSA can help you obtain information that you may not be able to furnish, such as a former spouse's Social Security number.

Here is a list of information you will need to bring with you, but again, don't wait if you are missing something. Delays in applying can cause delays in benefits.

- Your Social Security number
- Your birth certificate
- Your W-2 forms or self-employment tax return for the previous year
- Your military discharge papers if you served
- Your spouse's birth certificate and Social Security number if he is applying for benefits

- Children's birth certificates and Social Security numbers if you are applying for children's benefits
- Proof of U.S. citizenship or lawful-alien status if you (or a spouse or child applying for benefits) were not born in the United States
- The name of your bank, your account number, and the routing number so your benefits can be deposited directly into your account

Supplemental Security Income Program

Income Program The Supplemental Security Income program, or SSI, provides another source of income for people who are aged, blind or otherwise disabled, and who have very limited income and resources. SSI is a public assistance program that is administered by the Social Security Administration. Unlike Social Security retirement benefits, SSI benefits are financed from general tax revenues, not the Social Security Trust Funds.

To qualify for SSI, your monthly income must be under a certain monthly limit that changes annually. In 2017, the monthly limit for individuals whose income derived exclusively from wages and other "earned income" was $1,555 ($2,285 for couples). Keep in mind that states also provide SSI-type benefits, so depending on where you live you may qualify for assistance even if you exceed SSI income limits. To find whether you are eligible for SSI, complete the screening tool at https://ssabest.benefits.gov.

Your Social Security benefit (which is "unearned income") will be counted against the monthly income limit for SSI eligibility. But if your Social Security benefit is low, SSI will pay you the extra amount needed to bring your monthly income up to the SSI maximum amount. Based on the most recent data available (2016), 56 percent of SSI recipients age 65 and older also received Social Security retirement benefits. SSI benefits are not subject to income taxes.

Someone eligible for SSI may also be eligible for food stamps and other assistance. When you apply for SSI, if everyone else in your home signs up for (or already receives) SSI, Social Security will help you fill out the food-stamp application and will forward it to the servicing food-stamp agency. To qualify for food stamps, individuals must meet strict income and asset requirements. Generally, to receive food stamps, an individual over age 60 cannot have more than $3,250 in assets. To see if you are eligible, run the food-stamp tool at http://www.snap-step1.usda.gov/fns.

CHAPTER 5

Will Your Money Last as Long as You Do?

Every retiree wants to know that he will be financially secure for the rest of his life. As discussed in earlier chapters, part of the equation includes income from Social Security, pensions, and other lifelong sources of income such as immediate annuities. These sources will be sufficient for you to live on if you spend less than you receive—in other words, if your outflow does not exceed your inflow. As long as your inflow increases year after year to keep up with rising costs (inflation), you will have enough money to live on for the rest of your life.

However, if your sources of lifelong income do not cover your expenses, you have to take an extra step. You have to create retirement income from your assets—your savings accounts, 401(k)s, IRAs, investment accounts, business holdings, real estate, and any other assets that you can use for this purpose. (Let's use the term "savings" as a catch-all for these assets.)

Hint: The term "income" refers to earnings (interest and dividends). By contrast, we use the term "retirement income" broadly to denote any money you withdraw from your investment accounts. That includes both earnings and principal.

Your Optimal Withdrawal Rate

To answer the question posed by this chapter—will your money last as long as you do?—you must first answer another, closely related question: how much can you reasonably expect to withdraw from your savings over your lifetime?

People have different points of view on how much one can safely withdraw from savings over a lifetime without running out of money. Forty two percent of pre-retirees surveyed by a major financial institution in 2017 believed four to five percent was the correct figure. But an almost equal number (38 percent), thought seven percent or more was a safe withdrawal rate. Fifteen percent thought a safe withdrawal rate was 10 to 12 percent. The remainder had no opinion.

The financial institution's answer was this: no more than four to five percent of your initial retirement assets, adjusted each year for inflation.

When academics study this question, they look to historical data for inflation and market data for different types of investments to determine the optimal rate for individuals—which is usually around 3–4 percent. While that's an interesting exercise, it misses one important real-life element: everyone's situation is different. How people spend money is different. How long their retirements will last is different. Some will want to leave an inheritance. Some won't. Some are astute investors. Others have never made investment decisions. Some have financial advisers; others are do-it-yourselfers.

Creating your own withdrawal rate is a very personal exercise. One person's optimal withdrawal rate will differ from another's.

These questions will help you start thinking about your own:

- How much money will you need to withdraw yearly from your retirement savings?
- For how long? (This deals with longevity and is called your "payout period.")
- Do you want any money to go to your heirs (that is, is there a need to create "terminal value")?
- Do you want to leave a legacy to charity?
- Do you have tax deferred or taxable savings?
- How experienced are you as an investor?
- Have you experienced a down market? Importantly, were you a stock market investor during down market periods, such as October 19, 1987 (Black Friday, the day the stock market fell more than 20 percent), when the Internet Bubble burst (2000–2003), or during the Financial Crisis (October 2007–March 2009)?
- How comfortable are you with volatility?

These questions are relatively easy to answer. Here are the more difficult: how do you predict future markets, inflation rates, and taxes? And, there are a few more: What is your financial adviser's role now? Do you want that role to change as you approach retirement and after you retire?

The purpose of this chapter is to lay out mistakes to avoid. We'll do that by looking at advisers first. Then we'll look at high withdrawals in down market periods.

Optimistic

Advisors People will go with the adviser who presents the more optimistic outlook: they believe that adviser knows something his competitors do not. In a bid to seal the deal, that adviser may even provide references from happy clients who have withdrawn money from their savings for a number of years. That does not mean this adviser can deliver for you, however. (Your personal time-frame will be different, and even if the investments are identical, results will not be.) You will want to know more: 1) how did the adviser accomplish those results for his other clients? and 2) how does he propose to do the same for you?

Once you ask those two questions, listen carefully to the answers. Pay attention to the types of investments the adviser used to achieve his prior performance. If he promises to repeat the feat for you, consider whether those investments are likely to be as effective in today's financial climate as they were in yesterday's.

The strategies he used for his clients in the past may no longer make sense. In the late 1970s and early 1980s, for example, retirees were able to earn more than 10 percent annually on safe U.S. Treasury bills (T-bills), money-market mutual funds, or bank certificates of deposit (CDs). More recently, though, yields have been under one percent.

Hint: Double-digit interest on T-bills lasted from 1979 to 1982. Interest rates then declined over time and have not topped 6 percent since 1991. (Recently, interest on T-bills dropped to near zero.) Thus an adviser who earned more than 10 percent returns for his clients in the 1970s had better have a new plan for you today.

If you were retiring in a high-interest-rate environment such as the one that prevailed in 1979, you could easily have invested your savings in a money-market mutual fund and withdrawn 10 percent for a few years. However, that market period also had high inflation, which would have eroded your money's purchasing power. In fact, inflation averaged 13.3 percent in 1979, 12.5 percent in 1980, and 8.9 percent in 1981 before declining to 3.8 percent in 1982, translating to an average inflation rate of 9.6 percent from 1979 through 1982. So even though you would have achieved double-digit returns, inflation would have offset their results.

Had you retired in a double digit market, you could have purchased long-term U.S. government bonds (see "Terms of Retirement). Had you purchased $100,000 worth of government bonds with twenty-year matur-

A Closer Look:

Terms of Retirement

A money-market mutual fund is a fund that you can buy for the purpose of earning money from short-term, interest-bearing investments that mature within a year. A bank certificate of deposit is a deposit account at a bank that earns interest, usually for a set term at a predetermined rate. U.S. Treasury bills (called T-bills) are notes backed by the U.S. government; they mature within a year. U.S. government bonds are financial instruments issued by the U.S. government that promise to pay interest to the investor for the term of the bond.

ities in August of 1981, for example, you would have locked in interest payments of $14,520 a year (14.52 percent) for twenty years (from August 1981 through 2001).

So what's the lesson? Current market conditions will dictate a course of action; but don't build your retirement-income plan on the assumption that those conditions will prevail forever.

If you purchased the same U.S. government bonds discussed above during a period of low interest rates you would have had far different results. A twenty-year U.S. government bond purchased in January 2017 and maturing in January 2037 pays interest of 2.7 percent, or $2,700 per year until 2037 per $100,000 invested. (You can find current interest rates online at www.federal.gov/releases/h15. Bonds are sold in $1,000 face amounts.)

Your adviser's ability to deliver on his promises will hinge largely on how the financial markets perform after you retire. High returns are possible during good markets, not bad. If the adviser promises such returns during down markets, press him on how he intends to achieve them—and understand the extra risk he is taking to do so.

What if the adviser tells you, "Stocks return 10 percent per year, so we'll invest everything you've saved in stocks"?

From time to time, you may, in fact, run into this very recommendation—and for good reason. Historical data corroborate the 10 percent figure when savings are invested in a broadly diversified stock portfolio for long periods of time. According to Ibbotson, the average annual return for the broad stock market from 1926 to 2016 (which includes the Great Depression and the Financial Crisis) was about 10 percent. This number represents the market's "total return," which combines dividends (income distributions to stockholders, somewhat comparable to bank interest) with changes in market value (stock prices).

Although it is true that over long periods the broad stock market has averaged about 10 percent per year, it did not return 10 percent each and every year; things don't work out that way, because the market has its ups and downs. (The "broad stock market" refers to a diversified basket of stocks, such as the S&P 500 Index, which an individual investor can replicate with the purchase of a mutual fund that tracks the S&P 500 Index.)

So although there is historical support for buying and holding such an investment for twenty or thirty years with the expectation of growing your savings at 10 percent returns, it's another matter altogether to assume that you can withdraw 10 percent per year after you retire. Why the distinction? When you invest for growth over long periods of time, you can ride out down-market periods. If you want to withdraw 10 percent per year, on the other hand, you are assuming that the market will return 10 percent or more each and every year—simply not the case. (No one with a stock investment during the 2008 market crash should have any doubts about this point.)

Since 1926, we've had a number of severe down stock-market periods, as reflected by these annual returns: −43.3 percent (1931), −26.5 percent (1974), −22.1 percent (2002), −11.9 percent (2001), and of course 2008, when the market declined precipitously (−37 percent). But we've also experienced significant up markets: 47.7 percent (1935), 36.4 percent

(1945), 52.6 percent (1954), 37.4 percent (1995), and, more recently, 28.7 percent (2003), 26.5 percent (2009), and, 32.4 percent (2013), according to Ibbotson.

Hint: Variation in returns is called "volatility," which can be measured by "standard deviation." Standard deviation is a measure of the variations around an average or mean. The higher the standard deviation, the greater the risk.

Withdrawing in a Down Market

To understand how volatility and high withdrawal rates can affect retirees, let's see what would have happened if you had retired at a market peak. Let's go back to the year 2000 to capture two down market periods.

Assume you invested $100,000 in an S&P 500 Index fund at the beginning of 2000 and withdrew 10 percent ($10,000) a year from that point on. Your money would have lasted you about 9 years. The S&P 500 Index fund dropped in value in 2000, 2001, and 2002. When the market is declining and you're withdrawing more than your investment can deliver, capital is dissipated before the next uptrend.

What were the annual total returns of the S&P 500 Index fund during this period? The first three years caused the problem, with negative returns totaling 43 percent. In 2003, however, returns rebounded nicely with a 30 percent increase, followed by positive returns in 2004 through 2006, then followed by the Financial Crisis and a bull market that sprung from the bottom of March 2009.

Figure 5-1 (next page) shows the annual returns for a representative S&P 500 Index fund starting in 2000, through 2016.

Before we move on, let's examine an alternative investment possibility—one that adds bonds to the mix. The likely investment vehicle here is a balanced index, which represents about 60 percent of its assets in the S&P 500 Index and 40 percent in a broad index of bonds.

You would have fared much better by investing $100,000 in a balanced fund at the beginning of 2000 and withdrawing 10 percent ($10,000) a

Annual Change in Value, S&P 500 Fund

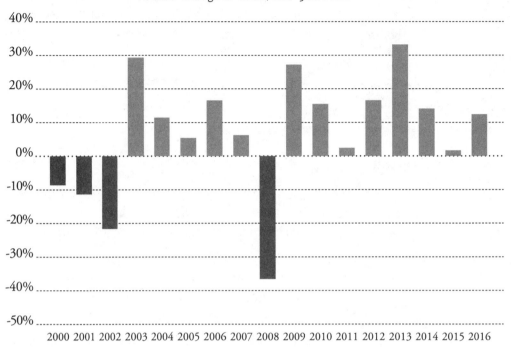

Figure 5-1: Representative S&P 500 Index Fund Returns, 2000–2016

year from that point on. You would have run out of money in about 10 years. Figure 5–2 (next page) shows the annual returns for a representative balanced fund from 2000 to 2016.

Finally, let's consider one more possibility: an investment in ninety-day U.S. Treasury bills, the safest investment of all.

T-bills never declined in value during this period. Yet if you had invested $100,000 in T-bills at the beginning of 2000 and withdrawn 10 percent of the original investment each year after that, your investment would have lasted 12 years. That's because withdrawals exceeded the returns generated by T-bill yields.

As you can see from this discussion, you cannot go into retirement with the idea that you can support yourself by withdrawing 10 percent from your original investment each and every year.

Annual Change in Value, Balanced Index

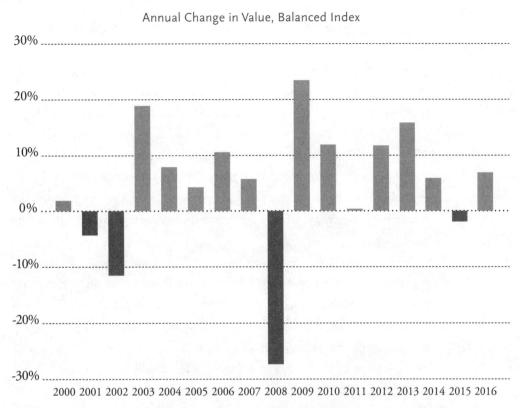

Figure 5-2: Representative Balanced Index Returns, 2000–2016

Hint: When considering safe withdrawal rates, you must always be acutely aware that your assets may decline in value before they rise—even if the investment you are considering has historically averaged a high rate of return.

Predicting the Future Until now we've been talking about history. Now let's see what we can do about predicting the future. I want to take you from the certainty of today—how much you have in assets and what you control (your spending decisions)—into the unknown of tomorrow.

The future involves projections. Some projections take today's economic environment and assume that tomorrow's will be the same. That is very dangerous indeed, especially if you are dealing with long time periods, such as retirement. As in space flights, one slight miscalculation can land you on the moon instead of Mars.

Although the severe declines of the 2008 financial markets are fresher in our minds, there are some equally important lessons to be drawn from the turn-of-the-century Internet bubble. If you were an investor during the late 1990s, for example, you may recall that people were projecting astronomical returns based on the belief that we had crossed some sort of threshold into a new era where the old rules no longer applied.

By March 2000, some stocks had achieved returns as high as 3,000 to 9,000 percent. Technological advances and the Internet seemed to justify the belief that the stock market could go nowhere but up. Even normally cautious people started feeling left out if they weren't at least doubling their money.

Some retirees and pre-retirees believed they could not lose their retirement savings. When the tech bubble burst shortly thereafter, they were devastated. Indeed, many of the companies that fueled the stock-market boom turned out to be far from profitable. After the bubble burst, many of those stocks fell as much as 99 percent from their peaks. Some companies went out of business and their stocks fell to zero.

Moral of the story: when it comes to rates of return on investments and inflation—the two elements you must factor in when projecting future returns—today is not tomorrow. "Tomorrow" may be a period of thirty years or more. For these reasons, the financial-services industry is developing more complex and comprehensive ways to estimate what your financial future may hold.

Monte Carlo Projections
and Financial Modeling
Although it's impossible to predict the exact percentage of your original investment that you personally can safely withdraw each year, you can assign a probability of achieving the desired outcome by modeling different withdrawal rates.

You can also factor in various investment-return and inflation assumptions with the help of retirement-income modeling tools known as "Monte Carlo simulators" (after the well-known gambling mecca in Monaco).

By running through hundreds of possible permutations of a given set of conditions at random, a Monte Carlo simulation can calculate the probability of achieving your desired results—such as whether you are saving, investing, and spending in such a way that your money will last as long as you do. And by tweaking the variables, such as how long you live or how much you save, you can see whether you can improve your chances of success—and come up with a better plan to address your unique situation.

A number of such programs are available through advisers. You can find some free programs online for your personal use, such as the "Retirement Income Calculator" at www.troweprice.com or the similar service offered at the Vanguard Retirement Plans website.

A Closer Look

Simulations are artificial models that attempt to predict real-world outcomes. As such, they are still somewhat controversial. A model is only as good as its underlying assumptions, and those assumptions vary. As a result, different simulators can produce different results.

What's Safe for You?

A safe withdrawal rate for one person will not be safe for another in different circumstances. For example, in order to leave a meaningful inheritance for your children or a charity, you may need to save more or work longer than someone who has no legacy interests. You may be married and want to be sure your spouse has enough to live on should something happen to you, whereas someone who is not married won't have to plan for a surviving spouse.

If your savings are lower than you would like, you will need to devote a lot of thought to your investments and your withdrawal strategy.

(Investment techniques are addressed in Part III.) If you are working with an adviser, make sure you are both in sync on this very basic planning point.

If you are uncertain about whether you have enough money for retirement, check out the "Quick Test" formula in Chapter 21. Identify potential areas of improvement, as I discuss in Chapter 6. You may find that working just a few more years will make a huge difference in your retirement security. Or you may find that changing your investment mix will help.

Now that we've discussed some important foundational concepts, let's focus on your particular situation.

Can You
Improve Your Situation?

Is there something you are doing (or failing to
do) that you could change today in order to
brighten your outlook for tomorrow? While you
are still working and even after you retire, the
simple answer is yes—and it goes by the name
"compounding."

Compounding:

Why Time is Money

The math behind compounding makes millionaires of average people who save a little bit over a long time.

Here's how it works: you make an investment. The investment makes money (in the form of interest or dividends) for you, which is added to the initial investment. That new total makes more money, and so on. Over time, the "interest on interest" multiplies many times over.

This concept can be illustrated with a simple question: would you rather have a penny that doubles daily for thirty days or $1 million?

Believe it or not, you're better off taking the doubling penny. A single penny earning 100 percent daily interest would grow to $10.7 million within thirty days. You'll never see a 100 percent daily return in real life, of course, but you get the idea: compounding is such a powerful tool that you should capitalize on it right away.

The longer you have, the better. Time is of the essence.

You're Never Too Young—

or Too Old—to Start

Consider a 30-year-old who can achieve a growth rate of 8 percent over a long time period with a diversified stock portfolio. His modest investment of $100 a month ($42,000 over thirty-five years) will be worth more than $200,000 by age 65. (Be mindful that we're ignoring taxes here, as you would be doing if you were investing that money in a Roth IRA or a Roth 401(k).)

But here's the bigger picture. As shown in Table 6-1, that original investment of $100 a month will be worth almost $500,000 at age 75, about $1 million at age 85, and more than $2.2 million at age 95 (assuming an 8 percent annual return).

You may be wondering: what 30-year-old is willing to wait until age 95 for the big payoff? The answer: one who thinks in terms of different age targets. If you're planning for the long term, set milestones: invest a portion of your savings for age 95, another for 85, 75, and 65. Think of these as "target decades," which we'll discuss later in the chapter.

$100 per Month from Age 30 to 65 ($42,000 Total)

Rate Of Return:	6%	8%	10%
Total Invested Over 35 Years	$42,000	$42,000	$42,000
Value at Age 65	138,000	215,600	342,600
Value at Age 75	247,200	465,500	888,600
Value at Age 85	442,700	1,605,000	2,304,800
Value at Age 95	792,800	2,169,900	5,978,000

Table 6-1

You may likewise be curious (considering the stock-market plunge of 2008) whether the 30-year-old in my example can actually earn an 8 percent lifetime return. No one knows what the future will hold, of course, which explains why conscientious investment advisers are quick to caution you that "past performance does not guarantee future results." That admonition ever in mind, the historical record reveals that past markets have delivered an 8 percent return—or higher, for patient investors who consistently invest month after month, regardless of the direction the market is moving. Indeed, for every 35-year period from 1928 through 2016—including those that contained the Great Depression and the Financial Crisis—the strategy of investing monthly in a diversified, large-company portfolio* has averaged 9 to 14 percent per year over time. (* I'll use an S&P 500 Index Fund to represent such an investment.)

As you can see, even a small investment can reap great rewards—provided it is given time to do so. But you needn't be 30 years old to take advantage of compounding. There is no reason a 50-year-old can't carve out a portion of his savings for the sole purpose of maximizing compounding.

A 50-year-old can turn that same $42,000 investment ($233.33 a month for fifteen years, until age 65) at an 8 percent return into about $170,000 by age 75. By age 85, he would have almost $370,000 to show for his efforts, and by 95 he would have just under $800,000. As in the previous example, this investment can be free of income taxes if done within a Roth IRA.

$42,000 Invested Over 15 Years ($233.33 per Month for 15 Years)

Rate of Return	6%	8%	10%
Total Invested over 15 Years	$42,000	$42,000	$42,000
Value after 15 Years	67,300	79,300	93,700
Value after 25 Years	120,500	171,100	243,000
Value after 35 Years	215,700	369,500	630,400
Value after 45 Years	386,400	797,800	1,635,200

Table 6-2

Unlike the hypothetical 30-year-old profiled above, who can legitimately feel confident about achieving an 8 percent return by investing in an S&P 500 Index Fund over the 35-year investment horizon before him, a 50-year-old facing an investment term of only 15 years will need to temper his expectations. Why? Because a hypothetical monthly investment in an S&P 500 Index Fund would have failed to achieve 8 percent in 17 of the 75 fifteen-year holding periods from 1928 through 2016. The worst periods—1960 to 1974 and 1994 to 2008—averaged only 1.54 to 1.70 percent per year.

On the bright side, by contrast, more than 42 of these 75 fifteen-year periods average annual returns in excess of 10 percent. And 32 of those 42 fifteen-year periods averaged more than 13 percent per year. Indeed, during the best 15-year period, from 1941 through 1955, monthly investments returned more than 19 percent per year. The 15 years ending 2016 resulted in an average annual return of 9.11 percent.

Avoiding Lost Opportunities
Now let's look at the power of compounding in reverse—"negative compounding," if you will.

Think of it this way: not only is every dollar you spend today lost to you in retirement, but there's an even higher price to pay. If you are 50 years old, every dollar you spend today deprives you of almost $7 at age 75 (figured at 8 percent), since you're failing to take advantage of compounding. So that extra pair of shoes you buy for $90 today actually costs you more than $600 of retirement money. (Use Table 6-3 to calculate lost opportunity. At age 50, the "lost opportunity factor" for age 75 is $6.85: $90 x $6.85 = $616.50.)

How $1 Spent at Various Ages Translates into Lost Opportunity
(Based on an 8 Percent Return on Investment)

Age at Time $1 is Spent	Loss by Age 65	Loss by Age 75	Loss by Age 85	Loss by Age 95
Your Age Now: 30	$14.79	$31.93	$68.93	$148.82
40	6.85	14.79	31.93	68.93
50	3.17	6.85	14.79	31.93
60	1.47	3.17	6.85	14.79

Table 6-3

Viewed this way, that same $90 pair of shoes costs a 30-year-old almost $2,900 in lost opportunity at age 75, and more than $13,000 at age 95.

Hint: Will inflation erode the value of your savings? Yes. To stay ahead, your investments need to earn more than inflation eats away. From 1926 through 2016, inflation has averaged about 3 percent per year.

Assuming 3 percent inflation, an individual will need more than $2 at age 75 to pay for something that cost $1 at age 50. However, if your return on your investment is higher than the inflation rate, you come out ahead. For example, assuming a return of 8 percent after taxes, a $1 investment at age 50 would be worth $6.85 at age 75—which, as you can see in Figure 6-1 (overleaf), far outpaces the effect of inflation.

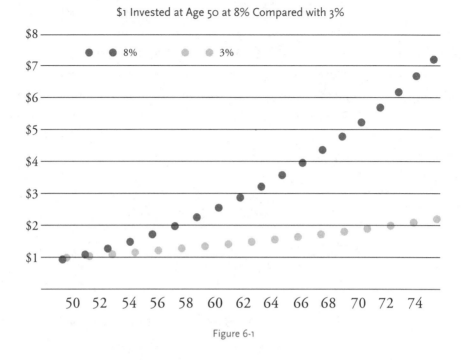

Figure 6-1

From Spendthrift to Saver So how can you use compounding and the other strategies we've discussed so far to improve your current situation? Let me share with you the seemingly impossible situation of an individual whose lifestyle obligations had spiraled out of control. His "inability" to save abounds with instructive lessons for us all—and, happily, his seemingly hopeless situation turns out to be salvageable.

Nick is a father of two young children, ages 5 and 7, and two college-age children from a previous marriage. He finds it impossible to save for his own retirement.

Even though he is 50, Nick thinks he will never be able to retire. Indeed, he resists talking or even thinking about the topic. As with many other people his age, Nick moved from a good job to a better job at several points in his career. In so doing, however, he sacrificed his chance to become vested in a pension plan somewhere along the way.

By the time he sought advice, Nick had accumulated $100,000 in a rollover IRA, thanks to his participation in the 401(k) plan at each of his previous jobs. He also recently bought a home but has not yet built up much equity in it.

All of Nick's take-home pay is being eaten up by his daily living expenses, which include tuition for his older children. Not a dime—he thinks—is left over for retirement savings.

WARNING!

If you're banking on working after age 65, consider this: many people who want to keep working cannot, due to illness, disability, or lack of available jobs. To hedge your bets, be sure you make saving for retirement a priority.

Room for Improvement?

Nick's primary challenge is that he has nothing remaining at the end of the month to invest for retirement.

How can Nick turn things around? First, he needs to split his spending into Essential Expenses and Lifestyle Expenses (as discussed in Chapter 2). But here he runs into a problem: Nick doesn't see anything as discretionary. His children's educational expenses are essential, he argues, as are their babysitters, classes, clothing, and everything else pertaining to their upbringing.

Nor can Nick imagine himself relinquishing his charitable contributions—he's an active member of his church, after all—and family vacations are essential for preserving his peace of mind and keeping his blended family intact. In fact, he's unwilling to classify even one expenditure as nonessential. So we've arrived at an impasse.

Today's Indulgences
or Tomorrow's Needs? Nick is like everyone else who hasn't prepared for retirement but knows he should. Facing—and fearing—the unknown, he is immobilized. That's understandable. He focuses his energies on his day-to-day routine, as most people do.

In the meantime, Nick is paying for today's lifestyle wants with tomorrow's essential needs (see Chapter 2). Every $1 Nick spends on indulgences today at age 50 leaves him with $3 less for absolute necessities at age 65; almost $7 less at age 75; approximately $15 less at age 85; and almost $32 less at age 95 (assuming a hypothetical 8 percent return on his investments).

Some cold, hard numbers may persuade Nick to change his ways, and soon, while there is still time for him to take advantage of compounding. He needs to face his fear and channel that energy to take charge of his future. It doesn't take much to make a difference. However, the longer Nick waits, the more he loses.

Small Sacrifices
for Big Returns
If Nick confronts the problem, he will quickly ascertain that even a few changes will help him get on track. By maximizing his 401(k) at work and recapturing a few hundred dollars a month that is currently spent on "wants," Nick can achieve significant progress.

For the next set of examples, I do some planned investing to cover different periods of retirement. I'm using an 8 percent annual return, not as a projection, but just to see what the possibilities might be over long periods of time. Real returns will be a reflection of how these accounts are invested.

I'm assuming that Nick will work another fifteen years before he retires, which opens up the possibility of delaying some indulgences and diverting that money into retirement savings. I'm also going to assume that he doesn't touch his savings until the time frame I identify below, which I've split into three periods. And, for the sake of isolating my point, I don't address taxes right now. We'll talk about how to factor in taxes in Chapter 17.

Targeting
Retirement Decades
When you're trying to save money you don't have, you need to use tools that maximize your results. To help Nick do that, let's divide his retirement into three "target decades." Then we'll figure out how he can optimize compounding in each one.

- Target decade #1 (age 65 through 74)

- Target decade #2 (age 75 through 84)
- Target decade #3 (age 85 and older, and legacy)

This exercise is meant to show Nick that small steps taken now can reap great rewards in the future. Ideally, he'll be able to pay for each decade of expenses this way, although he may have to make some changes when he evaluates what he needs. For now, it's important that he—and you—have a big-picture understanding of possibilities in order to identify how to improve your own situation.

Target Decade #1

(Age 65 through 74) If Nick (age 50) achieves an 8 percent annual return on his $100,000 IRA, he will have roughly $317,000 by the time he is 65. Ideally, that will pay for that decade's (age 65 through 74) expenses.

Target Decade #2

(Age 75 through 84) If Nick (age 50) contributes an ever-so-modest $150 a month—that's less than $5 per day—to his 401(k) at work from now until he retires at age 65 ($1,800 a year for fifteen years, for a total of $27,000), his company will contribute an additional $75 a month (that's $900 a year for fifteen years, for a total of $13,500) as a 50 percent match. (A 50 percent match is not unusual.)

By the time Nick is 75, those modest savings would be worth almost $160,000 to him, assuming an 8 percent annual return over that time period. He would have withdrawn about $24,000 from age 70.5 through 75 to cover required minimum distributions (RMDs), or $18,000 after paying taxes on those RMDs, assuming a 25 percent effective tax rate. (For more on RMDs, see Chapter 18.) Plus, he would still have $135,000 left in his 401(k). So Nick is ahead by $$130,000 at age 75 even after taxes—all achieved at the price of $5 a day.

Of course, Nick should contribute more—at least enough to maximize his company's match, and ideally as much as it takes to cover Decade #2's projected expenses.

WARNING!

You lose big-time if you don't contribute enough to your 401(k) or other retirement plan at work. How much should you contribute? At the very least, enough to maximize your match; if your plan matches up to 6 percent of your salary, then you should contribute at least 6 percent.

Target Decade #3 (Age 85 and Older, and Legacy)

Assume, starting today (at age 50), that Nick can limit his Lifestyle Expenses (see Chapter 2) by $5 a day ($150 a month) until he retires in fifteen years. If he invests that extra money between now and the time he retires at age 65, then keeps it invested for another twenty years, until he turns 85, he will have an additional $246,000, assuming an 8 percent annual return. Of course, the more he can spare now, the more he will benefit in the future.

To summarize, if Nick thinks in terms of target decades, he can see the huge benefits he can reap from saving a little money now in order to take advantage of compounding. That can give him the motivation he needs to save and invest for the future.

Table 6-4 summarizes his results (figured at 8 percent) at ages 65, 75, and 85.

The Results of Implementing Nick's Savings Plan at Age 50

		Value	Nick Invested
IRA	at 65	$317,000	$100,000
401(k)	at 75	157,800	27,000
Savings	at 85	237,550	27,000

Table 6-4

After considering this information, Nick says he understands the program, but he wants to wait until two of his children graduate from college five years from now. This is a common reaction. It's hard to change habits. Nick needs to understand the consequences.

By waiting five years (until age 55) to start saving, Nick will substantially impair his results (compare Table 6-4 to Table 6-5). That half-decade's delay costs Nick plenty: his 401(k) will have $73,650 less in it at age 75, and his savings will be $110,800 lower at age 85.

The Results of Implementing Nick's Savings Plan at Age 55

		Value	Nick Invested
IRA	at 65	$317,000	$100,000
401(k)	at 75	84,150	18,000
Savings	at 85	126,750	18,000

Table 6-5

The bottom line: the longer you allow the earnings on your investments to be reinvested, the more money you will have after you retire. Give yourself a little money and a lot of time, and you can attain retirement security.

A Closer Look

If you want to calculate the benefits of monthly savings, use the future-value table in Table 6-6, which assumes an 8 percent annual return. Here's an example:

Say you are 45 years old. If you save $1 a month until you are 65, you will have $593, assuming an 8 percent per year return, even though you set aside only $240 during that time.

At that same age (45), if you save $50 a month ($12,000 over twenty years), you will have $29,650 by age 65 (50 * $593). If you leave that money invested at the same rate, you will have $64,000 by age 75 (50 * $1,280), $138,200 by age 85 (50 * $2,764), and $298,400 by age 95 (50 * $5,968).

As I discussed earlier, your purchasing power will be lower in the future because of inflation—all the more reason to save a little bit over long periods of time, and to invest those savings wisely.

Monthly Investment of $1 at 8% from Age Shown to Age 65,
Then Held until Ages 75, 85, and 95

Age Investment Begins	Amount Invested by Age 65	Value at Age 65, When Investing Stops	Value at Age 75	Value at Age 85	Value at Age 95
45	$240	$573	$1,240	$2,670	$5,760
50	180	340	734	1,580	3,420
55	120	181	391	739	1,825
60	60	73	159	342	739

Table 6-6

Building a Reserve for the Future

The target-decade exercise gives Nick a different perspective on money. He now sees that his attitude about spending can result in lost opportunity. Focusing on target decade #2, Nick realizes that if he can turn his $5 a day 401(k) contribution into a total of $157,800 by age 75, he can double his results by contributing $10 a day. Given the benefit of time, there is an exponential benefit to contributing to an employer-matched retirement plan such as a 401(k).

The Effect of Contributing $300 a Month for 15 Years (Age 50–65) to a 401(K)
with a 50% Match at an 8% Return, Compared with Higher Contributions

	$150 a Month	$300 a Month	$600 a Month
401(K) Value at Age 75 (a)	$135,300	$270,700	$541,400
Rmds Reduced by 25% For Taxes (b)	22,500	44,900	89,700
Total after Taxes at Age 75 (a+b)	157,800	315,500	631,100
Total Contributed over 15 Years	27,000	54,000	108,000
Ahead by	130,800	261,500	523,100

Table 6-7

With this knowledge, Nick sees that if he changes his mindset from "I don't have anything left over at the end of the month to save for retirement" to "What can I cut out today so that I start compounding right away?", he can make small changes in his spending habits today to provide for tomorrow. He will focus his efforts on optimizing compounding for target decades #2 and #3. His goal will be to save enough for each target decade to cover that decade's expenses. Even after factoring in the effect of taxes, Nick will be far ahead of where he is today.

Can You Improve Your Situation?

I hope that Nick's eleventh-hour awakening inspires you to take a closer look at your own circumstances. What small but significant changes can you make today to improve your chances of retiring when you want to? To find out, you'll need to do the following:

1. Review your current expenses.
2. Identify Essential Expenses and Lifestyle Expenses (Chapter 2).
3. Catalogue your assets.
4. Project your Social Security and pension income.
5. Complete the "Retire Monday" exercise described in Chapter 2.
6. Evaluate whether you, like Nick, should be saving more now. If so, identify Lifestyle Expenses that you can hold off on for a while, then redeploy those funds into retirement savings. Think of how each dollar you save today translates into a larger nest egg at different target decades of your retirement (see Table 6-6).
7. Check out your 401(k) or other retirement plan at work. Are you taking full advantage of your company's matching contributions? Are you putting in the maximum permitted by the plan? If you are age 50 or older, ask your plan administrator about "catch-up" contributions to your 401(k). No employer is required to make catch-up provisions part of its plan, but if your plan includes this feature, take advantage of it if you can. It could enable you to sock away an extra $6,000 or more each year above and beyond what younger employees are permitted to contribute. (The catch-up contribution for 2017 is $6,000.)

If you believe you can't afford to contribute more to your 401(k) but you get a tax refund every year, you are missing out on retirement savings big-time—especially if your plan offers a matching feature. You can even adjust how much is withheld from your paycheck so that your future tax refund pays for your 401(k) contribution without lowering the net amount of your paycheck. (More on this appears in Chapter 15.)

8. Make sure you are making good investment decisions so that your return beats inflation. (For more on investing, see Chapters 15 and 16). In situations where you have little motivation to save, you'll find it helpful to focus on target decade #3; doing so gives you the longest investment horizon and will make the most of compounding. If you are retired and unable to save, use the concept of target decades to set aside certain assets for the future. This will help you visualize and maximize your opportunities.

Nick's situation shows us that there is always room for improvement, and that small changes can make a huge difference.

For additional ideas on how you can improve your personal circumstances, see the case study on retirement-income management in Appendix D.

So, now that you've saved all this money—or have a plan to do so—how do you turn the surplus into retirement income that will last a lifetime? That will be the topic of Part II of the book. Before we jump to those retirement-income solutions, though, let's discuss the financial adviser's role in presenting them to you.

CHAPTER 7

Enter the
Financial Adviser

Most solutions to your retirement-income needs will be presented to you by an associate or employee of a regulated financial firm, such as a broker-dealer or a registered investment adviser. I'l call that person a "financial adviser." I use that term advisedly, as it does cause confusion on the part of even experienced investors, according to the US Securities and Exchange Commission (SEC).

Let me explain, quoting the Investment Adviser Association:

"Under the current regulatory regime, retail customers seeking non-discretionary investment advice may choose a broker-dealer or an investment adviser, and may not know which type of financial professional they have hired. This is especially true if they are referred to a specific person who has provided such advice to a friend, relative, or co-worker. Furthermore, even if the retail customer knows that he or she has hired a broker-dealer or an investment adviser, he or she is not likely to understand that there are different standards of care applicable to each." (Investment Adviser Association's July 3, 2013 comment letter to SEC in response Rel. No. IA 3558).

Quoting further: "A bright line separated traditional brokerage services from traditional investment advisory services. During the last two decades, however, broker-dealers have moved toward offering more traditional investment advisory activities and marketing themselves as 'advisors,' resulting in a blurring of this line."

Let me give you some insight into how to tell one adviser from another so that you can manage the relationship with your adviser accordingly.

Regulation
Is the Secret
Here is a simple truth: sometimes—many times, in fact— investors play by a different set of rules than their advisers do, causing confusion and leading to unmet expectations. If you want to know what to expect from a financial professional, you need a glimpse inside his "rule book"—that is, you need to find out how he is regulated and paid.

Think about it for a moment: if your financial adviser is legally allowed to sell you insurance products and nothing else, what type of product do you think he will recommend? Although certain insurance products do indeed fulfill retirement-income needs (see Part II), it is wise to know if your adviser is limited in the products and services he can offer you.

It would also be good to know if your adviser is permitted to receive an undisclosed fee. And you'll want to find out who is responsible for monitoring your investments over time—is that the adviser's job or yours? Many times, people assume the adviser is responsible for more—everything having to do with investments, from assessing your situation to making recommendations for specific buys and sells, structuring an income-producing portfolio, managing cash needs, offering tax advice, monitoring your investments, and so on. Your adviser may or may not provide these services, depending on how he defines his job, how he is regulated, and how he is paid.

With these points in mind, let's go over the playing field. We'll talk about types of advisers, the standards of care they must live by, and how they are paid.

The Four Categories
of Advisers Among professionals addressing investment and retirement-income needs, you will likely encounter four general types of "financial advisers." Regulation focuses on the type of service or product the adviser offers. An individual can be licensed to sell more than one service or product.

1. "Registered representatives" (historically known as "stock brokers" or just "brokers") are licensed to sell securities such as stocks, bonds, and mutual funds. (As we'll discuss in a moment, registered representatives must hold either a Series 6 or a Series 7 license. See "A Closer Look: Licensed to Sell," page 83.) Some registered representatives sell retirement-income products, such as "variable annuities," requiring them to be licensed as insurance agents as well.

2. "Insurance agents," also called insurance producers, are licensed to sell life-insurance products. These include retirement-income products such as immediate annuities, which we'll discuss in the next chapter. Some states license "insurance advisers" whom you can pay to review and recommend insurance contracts.

3. "Registered investment advisers" sell investment advice. Registered investment advisers are regulated under federal and state securities laws. Certain states require employees who provide investment advice to be licensed as "investment adviser representatives" or "agents."

4. "Financial planners"—a self-selected term—sell financial-planning services. Financial planners (including Certified Financial Planners™ or "fee-only planners") are not regulated or licensed, unless they also sell securities, insurance, or advice under one of the three categories above.

Hint: Don't be unduly impressed by titles—wealth manager, financial consultant, account executive, financial adviser, vice president of investments, senior specialist. Although such labels may hint at special status or expertise, they are in fact mere titles of convenience, conferred more often for marketing purposes (or to indicate sales ability) than for anything else. These titles and many others can be (and are) used by registered representatives, insurance agents, investment advisers, and financial planners alike.

Now let's examine each of our four categories through a slightly more focused lens. As you read ahead, think of the types of services you want from your financial professional as you move into retirement. (At the end of this chapter, we'll talk about how to apply this information to your own particular situation. Once you've had a chance to review the various retirement-income solutions in Part II, we'll discuss how to search for—and find—an appropriate adviser, should you need one.)

Registered Representatives In all likelihood, your financial adviser sells securities, such as stocks, bonds, or mutual funds. Whether he works out of a brokerage office, a financial planner's office, a bank lobby, or his own living room, anyone who sells you a security must be licensed as a registered representative of a brokerage firm ("broker-dealer"). There are about 640,000 registered representatives in the United States, and licensing is administered by the Financial Industry Regulatory Authority, or FINRA. FINRA is the private-sector regulator of the U.S. securities industry. The professional must pass criminal, personal, and financial background checks; be sponsored by a brokerage firm; pass at least one of several licensing examinations, some of which I summarize in Table 7-1; and meet continuing-education requirements.

You should be aware that you can check a registered representative's background through FINRA, which maintains qualification, employment, and disclosure histories of registered representatives on an automated system called the Central Registration Depository, or CRD, accessible at www.finra.org.

From your point of view, the two most important licenses are the Series 6, which is a limited license to sell mutual funds (and variable annuities, assuming the representative also has a life-insurance license), and the Series 7, a more comprehensive license to sell all types of securities (including variable annuities, again assuming he is also licensed to sell life insurance).

When a registered representative recommends that you buy a security such as a stock or bond, he is required to adhere to a "suitability" standard. That is, your registered representative must have a reasonable basis for believing the recommendation "makes sense for you" (I'm using layman's terms here)—having first assessed your risk tolerance, financial situation, and investment objectives. (Note that the suitability requirement is triggered by a recommendation and does not apply if you place an unsolicited order.)

Here is an example of what would not be suitable: say you are a widow, age 88, with no investment experience and a total of $100,000 in savings, which you cannot afford to lose. Your goal is to create retirement income of $250 a month. Your registered representative sells you $100,000 worth of a single stock in a company that was started a few years ago to conduct innovative cancer research. The representative feels the stock is bound to be a winner that will make you lots of money. You buy the stock, and in a few months your $100,000 is worth $40,000.

Suitability calls for making recommendations that are appropriate for you, given your experience, financial circumstances, and goals. The registered representative's recommendation in my example would not have fit this standard. You would have the right to seek recourse—by complaining to the brokerage firm employing the registered representative (the firm has a duty to supervise the broker), or by filing a claim (usually in an arbitration proceeding) against him and his firm for damages you suffered as a result of his violating his duty to you.

A more suitable recommendation might have been a few appropriately selected balanced mutual funds, recognizing your need for growth and income as opposed to aggressive growth, your need for safety, and your lack of investment experience.

ALERT!

The registered representative's suitability standard focuses on the recommendation at the point of purchase or sale. This standard of care does not require that your registered representative provide you with ongoing advice. Nor is there a requirement to disclose conflicts of interest in most cases. Keep that in mind as you read on.

Hint: A registered representative may be a "fiduciary" in certain circumstances. (A fiduciary must put your interests ahead of his own.) One example is if you authorize him in writing to make buy and sell decisions in your account without checking with you in advance. In this case you are granting him "discretion," so the account is called a "discretionary account."

Suitability is an important concept to understand. For more information on suitability, go to the SEC website at www.sec.gov and search for "suitability" under "Investor Information."

Insurance Agents

Your financial adviser may recommend retirement-income products that are not securities. Some are pure insurance products, such as immediate annuities, that can be sold only by licensed life-insurance agents who pass an examination and a background check and meet continuing-education requirements.

These agents are regulated by state insurance commissioners. If someone wanted to sell insurance to residents of Chicago, he would have to be licensed to sell insurance by the state of Illinois.

Like registered representatives, insurance agents can be expected to put together retirement-income plans that feature the particular products they are licensed to sell. Unlike registered representatives, however, not all insurance agents are subject to suitability standards.

Historically, state regulation of insurance sales focused on consumer protection, and in some states that standard still applies to transactions between insurance agents and their customers. The consumer-protection standard of care means that insurance agents are prohibited from engaging in unfair or deceptive acts or practices, such as misrepresenting the terms of the policy or the financial condition of the insurance company.

A number of states have adopted laws to strengthen the legal standard of care for insurance agents to include a "suitability" obligation. At this time, thirty-seven states plus D.C. have adopted the 2010 version of the National Association of Insurance Commissioners (NAIC) Suitability in Annuity Transactions Model Regulation, and other states will no doubt follow suit. Among its requirements, the suitability regulation mandates that insurance agents make reasonable efforts to assess your financial and tax status, investment objectives, and any other information that might be useful before making an investment recommendation to you. (To determine exactly how insurance agents are regulated in your state, contact your state insurance commissioner's office or check the NAIC website at www.naic.org.) However, no matter what rules and regulations come into play, as a prospective investor you must be sure to research thoroughly any product that you are offered and determine if it fits your objectives.

Before we leave the subject of insurance, you need to be aware that some retirement-income products have elements of both securities and insurance, such as the "living-benefit" products discussed in Chapters 11 and 12. Salespeople who sell these products must hold both securities and life-insurance licenses.

Registered
Investment Advisers Registered investment advisers provide investment advice and portfolio-management services. They are regulated by either the states in which they have clients or the SEC. Generally, if their clients' accounts equal or exceed $100 million, they are regulated by the SEC; if the value of their clients' accounts is less than $100 million, they are regulated by the individual states in which they have clients.

The registered investment adviser is a fiduciary under the law—the highest standard of care of all those we've considered. What does that mean to you?

First, the investment advice must be suitable—that's the standard that applies to the broker-dealer registered representative—but the investment adviser who agrees to manage your investments has a duty that extends beyond the recommendation to buy or sell a security; it is an ongoing responsibility during the client relationship. Second, the registered investment adviser is obligated to have a reasonable, independent basis for his investment advice. Third, he has a duty to be loyal to clients, which includes the duty to disclose conflicts of interest and how he is compensated. Exercising self-interest to the detriment of the client is not an option.

Federally regulated advisers are under the SEC's supervision and are subject to an onsite inspection of the adviser's practices and procedures. Registered investment advisers must enforce written codes of ethics that establish standards of conduct for their personnel and reflect their fiduciary obligations.

Registered investment advisers might call themselves investment managers, portfolio managers, money managers, or investment counsel. But only one of those titles—"investment counsel"—is a legally defined term. An investment counsel (such as my firm, Jackson, Grant Investment Advisers, Inc.) is an adviser whose principal activity is to provide continuous advice about the investment of funds according to the individual needs of each client (technically, "investment supervisory services"). It is illegal for other types of registered advisers to use that title. Another title—"portfolio manager"—is not a legally defined term, but it carries a specific meaning within the financial-services industry. Typically, a portfolio manager is responsible for directing the trading decisions of a pool of assets, such as a mutual fund or a pension fund.

"Money manager," a more general label, can include portfolio managers. It also can denote that the manager provides more personal service for individuals, as opposed to pools such as mutual funds.

Registered investment advisers make their services available to individuals directly in one-on-one relationships, or indirectly by offering their management expertise to a larger pool of clients through a mutual fund or a managed account that the adviser manages. Individual one-on-one service is usually limited to larger portfolios, because these advisers usually have minimum-account requirements (for example, my firm has a $5 million minimum). Typically, clients compensate the adviser based on a percentage of assets managed.

You can check information on SEC-registered investment advisers at www.adviserinfo.sec.gov.

Financial Planners

There is a lot of confusion about financial planners. The acting financial planner is not regulated as such. That opens the door for anyone to call himself a "financial planner."

This does not mean, however, that anyone can call himself a Certified Financial Planner™, or CFP®. That designation—it's not a license—is conferred by the Certified Financial Planner Board of Standards, Inc. There is an educational requirement (waived for lawyers and accountants) and an examination, as well as ethics and continuing-education requirements. (You may also come across accountants who have earned the designation of Personal Financial Specialist for Certified Public Accountants [CPA/PFS], which is offered by the American Institute of Certified Public Accountants.)

Licensing is required, however, if the financial planner (certified or not) offers to sell you a financial product or investment advice. A registered representative or an insurance agent can likewise call himself a financial planner without meeting any additional educational or licensing requirements. In that case, if you hire the financial planner to draw up a course of action for you, confirm whether the plan includes a product purchase that will trigger a commission for the planner.

Who's Who?

Any time you encounter someone who wants to give you financial advice or sell you a product, you'll want to find out how he is regulated—before you reveal any personal information or turn over any money. A good way to go about this is simply to ask the prospective adviser the following questions:

- Who regulates your business?
- Are you licensed? By whom and for what?

continued on page 84

Official Title

Requirements	Permitted Sales	Regulatory Body
Registered Representative		
Series 6 or Series 7 license; Background Check, Examinations, Continuing-Education Requirements	Securities, Including Stocks, Bonds, and Mutual Funds	FINRA and State Securities Regulators
Insurance Agent		
State Life-Insurance License; Background Check, Examinations, Continuing-Education Requirements	Life-Insurance Products, Including Some Retirement-Income Products such as Annuities	State Insurance Commissioners
Registered Investment Adviser		
Registration with the SEC or Individual States; Series 65 License Required in Some States; Background Check, Examinations, Continuing-Education Requirements	Investment Advice	SEC or State Securities Regulators
"Financial Planner"		
No License or Registration	None	None; but a Financial Planner is Subject to Regulation if He Acts as an Insurance Agent, Registered Representative, or Registered Investment Adviser
Certified Financial Planner™		
No License or Registration; Board of Standards Certified Financial Planner Requires CFP® Holders to Meet Educational, Examination, and Continuing-Education Requirements	None	None as Such, but a CFP® is Subject to Regulation if He Acts as an Insurance Agent, Registered Representative, or Registered Investment Adviser

Table 7-1: Whom are you dealing with?

A Closer Look:
Licensed to Sell

In evaluating advisers, you will want to know what they are licensed to sell. If your adviser sells financial products or services, he will need to have one or more of these licenses.

- Series 6: License to sell mutual funds and variable annuities; to sell the latter, however, the salesperson must also have a life-insurance license—see below.

- Series 7: License to sell securities, including stocks, bonds, mutual funds, and (if life-insurance-licensed) variable annuities.

- Series 65: License to provide investment-advisory services on behalf of a registered-investment advisory firm or to solicit business for the firm—technically, to act as an "investment-adviser representative" or "invest-ment-adviser agent" of the firm. This license may or may not be required in your state; to find out, see NASAA's Investment Adviser Guide at www.nasaa.org. (NASAA is the North American Securities Administrators Association.)

- Series 66: This license is comparable to the Series 65; however, only employees of broker-dealers can sit for the Series 66, and the employee must also pass the Series 7 exam in order for the Series 66 exam to be valid.

- Life Insurance: License to sell life-insurance products to residents of the state that issued the license. Anyone selling a "variable annuity" (see Part II) must have an insurance license as well as either a Series 7 or a Series 6 license.

Compare what you're told to the descriptions of the four categories we've discussed. To help you, I've created a chart (Table 7-1) showing the characteristics of each type of adviser.

By comparing your adviser's licenses to the chart, you can see which categories he falls into and what services he will be able to offer you (and what he *cannot* or may not be offering you, simply because he is not licensed to do so). This method is far more helpful than trying to rely on titles, which don't always tell you what to expect.

ALERT !

At this writing, the SEC is reviewing standards of care and coordinating with the US Department of Labor in connection with a fiduciary rule that the DOL implemented in 2017 for IRA and other retirement accounts. For more information, see www.dol.gov and search for "Conflict of Interest Final Rule."

Standards of Conduct As we've discussed, various types of advisers are held to different standards of conduct. Table 7-2 summarizes the differences.

Legal Violations As explained above, it's against the law for anyone to sell securities, insurance, or investment advice without being properly registered or licensed with their state or the SEC. (The notable exception is for investment advice that is dispensed "solely incidental to the practice of a profession," such as accounting or law.)

Violations of the laws regulating different types of advisers can trigger severe consequences. (See "Disciplinary and Other Actions" at finra.org.) For example, FINRA fined a brokerage firm $20 million for sales of two hundred thousand variable life-insurance policies to its customers in violation of federal and FINRA rules. If you have a problem with your adviser, knowing how he is regulated will tell you whom to contact for help. (Chapter 19 explains how to protect yourself from fraud and what to do if you experience a problem with your adviser.)

Official Title Standard of Care	Definition	Required Written Disclosures
Registered Representative Suitability if Making a Recommendation (Fiduciary if Acting with Discretion)	Must Have a Reasonable Basis for Believing that Each Recommendation to a Customer is Suitable Based on the Information that the Customer Provided (Transaction Based)	None, Unless Also Acting as a Fiduciary
Insurance Agent State Consumer-Protection Standards, Perhaps Suitability (Depending on State)	Varies by State	Usually None
Registered Investment Adviser ("RIA") Fiduciary Duty	Must Put your Interests Ahead of His Own	Qualifications; Compensation; Potential Conflicts of Interest
"Financial Planner" N/A	N/A	N/A

Table 7-2: What can you expect from your adviser?

Compensation

Investors are often confused about the way financial advisers get paid. In talking to the readers of my newspaper column, in fact, I've encountered many who believe the adviser works for free.

Here's an example of a situation one of my readers encountered:

"I asked the adviser if I had to pay a commission on an investment I was considering buying, and he said, 'No.'

"Then I asked if all my money would be invested, or if something would be deducted from my investment to pay him, and he said, 'All your money is invested. Nothing is deducted.'

"So then I asked him how he gets paid. He said, 'The people behind the product pay me—nothing comes from you. You get me for free.'"

Happy to hear that, my reader went ahead with the purchase without doing any further research.

Experienced investors know better. They know that most financial products are distributed through commissioned salespeople whose compensation—directly or indirectly—comes from you, the buyer, not from the manufacturer of the product.

How does that work? In my reader's situation, the salesperson's commission (6 percent of the purchase price, in this case) is advanced by the sponsor against ongoing fees deducted from the investment. Usually these types of products have higher ongoing fees and penalties associated with them.

If my reader wants to get out of the investment before she has held it for ten years—to pay for unexpected medical expenses, for example—she will have to pay a penalty (a "surrender charge") that can be as high as 15 percent (in this case) of the money she wants to withdraw. This form of pricing may surprise you if you don't read the prospectus and your adviser doesn't bring it to your attention. The penalty compensates the sponsor for having advanced the adviser his 6 percent commission.

So, who is really paying the adviser: you or the sponsor? Ultimately it's you, reinforcing my point that there's no such thing as "free" when a financial adviser is providing you with a service. He gets paid only when you buy or sell a financial product or sign up for a financial service.

Commissions

and Fees Fees and commissions vary from product to product. The registered representative (or insurance agent) receives some percentage of the commission or fee, usually ranging from 40 percent to 100 percent, depending on the firm he works for and his sales production.

Registered investment advisers are required by law to disclose their fees, which they do in writing. The adviser is required to give you a copy of part 2 of Form ADV (an abbreviation for "adviser"), which is also called the "brochure," along with a copy of the contract that you sign when you become a client. Make sure you read both carefully.

Here is a quick summary (I go into more detail in the chapters that follow):

- Stocks: When you buy or sell a stock, you normally pay a commission, which is printed on your confirmation of the transaction. In some cases, you'll see a "markup" or "markdown" instead of a commission on your confirmation. A markup is a broker-dealer's fee that is embedded in your purchase price when a broker-dealer sells a stock to you out of its own inventory. The markup inflates the price at which you purchase the stock; the markdown reduces your proceeds when you sell.

- Bonds: When you buy or sell a bond, you could pay a commission, or the bond price could reflect a markup/markdown instead of a commission. (See "Stocks," above.) Investors can find current bond prices online at www.finra.org. Click on "For Investors," then "Market Data" under the "Tools and Calculators" tab.

- Mutual funds: A mutual fund may have a commission (or "load") that is visible and paid up front, reducing your investment in the fund at the time you make the purchase. (A load share is usually referred to as an "A" share.) Or the commission may not be visible because it does not reduce your investment at the time of purchase. You can find this type of pricing in a Class "B" or "C" share. You don't get a free ride, however, because it can cost more to own a "B" or "C" share than an "A" share." (You will find this information in the fund's prospectus.)

- Insurance products: Insurance products are priced in a way that includes a payment to the agent; these payments are built into the structure of the product and are not visible to you.

- SMAs: Separately Managed Accounts (SMAs) are offered to customers of brokerage firms but managed by registered investment advisers who may or may not be affiliated with the brokerage firm. Instead of commissions or markups/markdowns, the brokerage firm charges a percentage of your account value. The rate can be lower for larger accounts (for example, 1 percent per year for a $1 million account) and higher for smaller accounts (2 or even 3 percent for a $250,000 account). "Wrap accounts," typically managed by a broker, usually charge the same way.

- Investment advisory services: Investment advisers typically charge a management fee based on the value of your account. The client's securities are frequently housed with an independent custodian, who charges transaction fees for securities purchases and sales at reduced (that is, institutional) rates.

Bank Employees
and Trust Companies
Before we leave the subject of financial advisers, we need to talk about banks. In 1933, the Glass-Steagall Act separated commercial banking from investment banking after the financial failures of the Great Depression. Banks could not actively engage in the brokerage business until after 1999, when Congress passed the Gramm-Leach-Bliley Act (GLBA).

The GLBA repealed most of the Glass-Steagall Act's separation of commercial and investment banking, permitting banks to engage in third-party brokerage arrangements without having to register as brokers. These third-party brokerage arrangements, called "networking," now allow banks to enter into contracts with broker-dealers to offer brokerage services—that is, to sell stocks, bonds, and financial products—to bank customers.

Though bank employees today are not permitted to sell securities at the teller window, they can refer a banking customer to a broker in the lobby. In exchange, the law allows the registered representative to pay the bank employee a small referral fee.

Trust companies and the trust departments of banks operate in a similar fashion. In addition to serving as trustees for trusts and as executors of wills, bank trust departments can offer investment advisory services. Because they are subject to federal and state banking regulations, they are not required to register as investment advisers with the SEC or the states. If they wish to sell you securities or annuities, they must register as broker-dealers or insurance agents. Most do not register, however, but rather set up a separate affiliate who registers with the appropriate agency. Or they utilize the license of an independent firm through a networking agreement. If you're working with someone in a bank, you should ask how he is licensed, if at all, and how he is compensated.

Your Job Is to
Ask Questions
As you can see from this chapter, the regulatory system that governs financial advisers creates standards of care that differ based on the type of service being offered. Titles are not determinative. A further complication is that an adviser can be regulated under multiple legal regimes; for example, a financial adviser working for a major brokerage firm can be regulated under the broker-dealer suitability rules if he handles broker-dealer accounts as well as the fiduciary standard if he handles investment adviser accounts.

An ever further complication is the DOL's fiduciary rule affecting IRAs and 401(k)s (partially effective June 9, 2017, with full effectiveness anticipated in 2018). The rule introduces an additional "best-interest" standard. In a comment letter filed with the DOL, the Financial Industry Regulatory Authority (FINRA), noted that the best interest standard on broker-dealers differs significantly from fiduciary standards applicable to investment advisers. Since the rule is being challenged at this writing, how the rule will impact IRA and retirement plan participants is yet to be determined.

Given this scenario, the most important take-away is this: advisers are not all the same. As a result, the burden is on the shoulders of you, the client, to inquire about what to expect in a working relationship with the adviser. That will help the relationship and it will help avoid misunderstandings. The next question is how this information can help you determine the type of adviser you would like on your side as you move into retirement.

Whom Should

You Hire? As you approach retirement, you will face some unique decisions. Whom you decide to hire as your financial adviser will hinge on many factors, including your experience, your goals, your financial circumstances, and what kind of financial advice and services you need.

People of more modest means looking for retirement-income solutions will likely be shown the types of products and services that we will discuss in the next part of the book. Most of these products are sold by registered representatives or insurance agents. You will have to take the initiative in understanding costs, fees, and why recommendations made are in your interest. (More details about this process—including specific questions to ask—appear in Part III.)

A smaller number of people with greater wealth will likely work with a registered investment adviser, either directly (if they meet the minimums) or indirectly through an SMA.

You'll get a much better sense of what kind of adviser you might need after you learn how several retirement-income products and services work, and how they are sold—the subject of the next few chapters. Be sure to read Chapters 19 and 20 before you buy any financial product or sign up for any service.

PART II

Security for Sale:
Evaluating Retirement
Income Products

Guaranteed Lifelong Income

Ever since demographic trends made it clear that large numbers of boomers would need retirement income, the financial-services industry has been searching for the perfect solution. The industry's stated goal is to address retirees' fear of outliving their money by offering products that promise "guaranteed income for life." Some firms offer to deliver one better—income for life plus "upside appreciation." (Translation: not only will the company behind the product take care of you, it will also help your money grow.)

Most of these products—which I discuss in Chapters 9 through 12—are marketed to consumers, rather than actively sought out by them. They appeal to the natural desire we all have for security. Because of that you may feel tempted to go along with the salesperson on faith alone before understanding how the product works.

Wishful thinking goes only so far. The reality is that these products are not the perfect solution for everyone.

In addition, they all have risks that you need to understand. "Risks?" you might ask. "Isn't a guarantee all about doing away with risk?"

Though it's true that guarantees are intended to eliminate risk, life doesn't work that way—and neither do these products. The company making the promise of lifelong income must be able to deliver it not only to you for your entire lifetime, but also to everyone else who buys the same promise. That means the company has to be very good at projecting longevity over the course of more than a quarter-century. That's an awesome task indeed.

Faced with this simple truth—that the conditions behind the promises must be understood—you should always be a detective. This part of the book will help you understand and evaluate the facts and risks behind sales presentations—and to determine which of the popular retirement-income solutions available might be right for you.

Who's Minding Your Money?

Let's start at the heart of the matter: the guarantees. After all, this is what makes products offering "retirement income for life" so appealing.

Financial-product guarantees, such as a promise of lifelong income, are contractual obligations. You are relying on the financial strength of the company issuing the product.

What exactly does that mean? Think about the types of guarantees you might make in your own life: if you have a child in college, you may have to guarantee that he will pay the rent on his first apartment.

If you're self-employed, you may have to sign a personal guarantee for a small-business line of credit. In either case, the obligation is not secured by collateral. If you are unable to make good on your guarantee, the party to which you extended the guarantee will find it worthless if you lack the funds to fulfill your obligations.

By contrast, suppose the loan were secured by collateral. If you were unable to repay your debt, the lender could sell the property you had used to secure the loan. A mortgage lender, for example, can foreclose on your house if you miss your mortgage payments, then sell your house to recover its investment.

Because retirement-income product guarantees are not secured by collateral, they are only as good as the company standing behind them. As a result, you have to assure yourself that the company from which you buy a guaranteed product will be able to meet its financial obligations to you throughout the term of that guarantee. If you are buying a lifelong guarantee, you will want to assure yourself that the issuing company will be around as long as you live.

But how do you do that? How, in other words, do you assess the financial strength of the company behind the guarantee?

You can get some comfort from rating agencies, such as Moody's Investors Service, a provider of independent credit ratings, research, and financial information (www.moodys.com; see sidebar); Fitch Ratings, a global rating agency (www.fitchratings.com); A. M. Best, a full-service, global credit-rating organization that subjects all insurers to the same rigorous criteria, providing a valuable benchmark for comparing insurers (www.ambest.com); and Standard & Poor's, a source of independent financial data (www.standardandpoors.com).

Although you can't choose a financial product based on ratings alone, common sense dictates that you should avoid lower-rated companies. The more cautious retiree might eliminate all companies other than those receiving the highest ratings.

A Closer Look:

Moody's Insurance Financial Strength Ratings

Here are Moody's official rating symbols for insurance financial strength.
(Note: if you're interested in buying bonds, these ratings are similar to Moody's bond ratings.)

Aaa Insurance companies rated Aaa offer exceptional financial security. While the credit profile of these companies is likely to change, such changes as can be visualized are most unlikely to impair their fundamentally strong position.

Aa Insurance companies rated Aa offer excellent financial security. Together with the Aaa group they constitute what are generally known as high-grade companies. They are rated lower than Aaa companies because long-term risks appear somewhat larger.

A Insurance companies rated A offer good financial security. However, elements may be present that suggest a susceptibility to impairment sometime in the future.

Baa Insurance companies rated Baa offer adequate financial security. However, certain protective elements may be lacking or may be characteristically unreliable over any great length of time.

Ba Insurance companies rated Ba offer questionable financial security. Often the ability of these companies to meet policy-holder obligations may be very moderate and thereby not well safeguarded in the future.

B Insurance companies rated B offer poor financial security. Assurance of punctual payment of policyholder obligations over any long period of time is small.

Caa Insurance companies rated Caa offer very poor financial security. They may be in default on their policyholder obligations or there may be present elements of danger with respect to punctual payment of policyholder obligations and claims.

Ca Insurance companies rated Ca offer extremely poor financial security. Such companies are often in default on their policyholder obligations or have other marked shortcomings.

C Insurance companies rated C are the lowest-rated class of insurance company and can be regarded as having extremely poor prospects of ever offering financial security.

Moody's appends numerical modifiers 1, 2 and 3 to each generic rating classification from Aa to Caa: the modifier 1 indicates that the security ranks in the higher end of its generic rating category; the modifier 2 indicates a midrange ranking; and the modifier 3 indicates that the issue ranks in the lower end of its generic rating category.

How do you interpret these ratings? A company rated Aaa would be a better choice than a company rated Aa1. If Moody's drops a rating from B3 to Caa1, it means that Moody's has reconsidered its rating in light of new financial information and has downgraded it.

What If the Insurance Company

Goes Broke? Although the life-insurance industry remains one of America's most highly regulated business sectors, you should be aware that an insurance company can go out of business. An insolvent company may not have funds to meet its obligations in full.

Even highly rated companies can find themselves in unexpected situations. Here are two things you need to know:

1. Insurance regulation lessens the likelihood of potential insolvencies; and

2. When insolvency does occur, state guaranty funds can come into play, as we'll discuss below.

Hint: For a partial list of insurance companies that have had financial difficulties or failed, go to the website of the National Organization of Life and Health Insurance Guaranty Associations (NOLHGA): www.nolhga.com. Check out the Frequently Asked Questions.

Insurance companies are regulated by the states and are required to calculate reserves—estimates of all future benefits the companies must pay on all types of policies, including annuities and life insurance. Companies need to have assets equal to their reserves, plus a cushion. This cushion is called a "surplus."

If a company's surplus falls below minimum levels, state regulators require the company to correct the problem by various means, including arranging for an infusion of additional capital, reducing operating expenses, or restricting the writing of new business. If that fails, insurance regulators seize the company and a state-appointed receiver takes over the company's operation. If assets fall below reserves, a form of insurance (state guaranty funds) provides some protection to the policyholder.

Each state has a life- and health-insurance guaranty association that provides continuing coverage to the policyholders of failed insurers. The associations pay for this coverage by assessing (charging) healthy insurance companies in their states to make up shortfalls in the policies of failed companies.

There are limits to coverage, just as there are limits on bank-deposit insurance through the Federal Deposit Insurance Corporation (FDIC). Most state insurance-guaranty associations cover up to $250,000 of the present value of the underlying obligation, and a number of state associations provide additional coverage (four cover up to $500,000, for example).

The present value of an "immediate annuity"—a product we'll discuss in the next chapter—is calculated by adding up the future income stream, then determining what it would cost to pay for that future stream today, using a present-value interest factor.

Let's take a few examples of how coverage would work. Say you have an immediate annuity with a present value of $200,000 and you reside in a state with $500,000 of coverage. You would be fully covered, which means that you would continue to receive your full annuity payments for the life of the annuity, either from your state guaranty association or, if the guaranty association had arranged the transfer of the failed insurer's business to a financially sound insurer, from your new insurer.

What happens if your present value is higher than the state's limits? Let's look at another example. Your annuity has a present value of $350,000 and the state guaranty association in your state covers up to $250,000. You will receive $250,000 in coverage from the guaranty fund. That leaves $100,000 ($350,000–$250,000 = $100,000) not covered. That difference is called the "excess of cap amount." You may be able to recover some or all of the excess of cap amount, as I explain below.

As a policyholder of the insurance company that issued the annuity, you are a creditor; as such, you take precedence over general creditors when the insurer's assets are distributed in a bankruptcy-like proceeding run by the insurance department of the state in which the insurer is domiciled. In such a proceeding, a recovery will be partially covered (based a ratio of the amount covered by the present value).

In this example ($250,000/$350,000), your excess of cap amount is $100,000. Assuming 71 percent recovery, you could receive a payment of $71,000 (for a grand total of $321,000). In the alternative, the receiver (the person overseeing the proceeding) may decide to continue paying the monthly annuity payments on the $100,000 excess of cap portion of the annuity in full until the insurer's money runs out. Or the receiver might opt to reduce scheduled periodic payments on the excess of cap amount in proportion to the company's projected balance-sheet deficit.

A Closer Look:
Deferred versus Payout Annuities

If your annuity is in the build-up stage (a "deferred annuity"), its "present value" will be determined by its net cash-surrender value. If you are already receiving periodic payments under your annuity (a "payout annuity"), the amount and duration of your payments will generally be used to determine its present value.

For deferred annuities, the receiver will likely limit the amount you would receive from the insurer (the "excess of cap amount") to 85 percent (that is, your pro rata share of the insolvent insurer's assets). But you may get additional amounts in the future if the receiver is successful in possible litigation recoveries, or if the insurer's assets realize more than is anticipated.

Hint: To research the coverage limits applicable in your state, visit www.nolhga.com, the website for the National Organization of Life and Health Insurance Guaranty Associations. The site's "Guaranty Association Laws" section offers contact information for your state's insurance guaranty association. Most state guaranty associations have their own websites; the NOLHGA site provides links to them as well.

In my experience, when people deal with more-complicated insurance products, they tend to rely on the salesperson to set expectations. Depending on verbal explanations boosts your risk of misunderstanding what to expect. It's human nature. It's tempting to stop asking questions whenever the word "guaranteed" is used in a presentation.

Whenever you are assessing a guaranteed financial product of any sort, ask questions. You want to know 1) what is guaranteed, 2) who is making the guarantee, 3) how the guarantee works, and 4) when the guarantee doesn't apply. Ultimately, you want to know what the guarantee is worth to you.

Evaluating Guaranteed
Products
In your search for guaranteed retirement income, you are likely to come across many of the financial products we'll discuss in Chapters 9 through 12, which focus on annuities and "living benefits." (In Chapters 13 and 14, I discuss two well-established products that retirees often seek out on their own: CDs and reverse mortgages.) To help you get a good understanding of these products without overwhelming you, I've developed a product-specific rating system. Watch for these assessments as you read the chapters that follow:

1. How Motivated Is Your Salesperson? (Not Especially or Eager to Sign You Up)
2. Complexity (Easy to Understand, Complicated, or For Ph.D.s)
3. Safety (Lets You Sleep at Night, Think Twice, or Watch Out)
4. Value (Good Value, Hard to Judge, or Poor Value)
5. Overall Recommendation (Consider, Proceed with Caution, or Avoid)

The first rating (How Motivated Is Your Salesperson?) helps you see yourself from the salesperson's point of view. With this insight, you will be more likely to recognize sales incentives that you will want to know about.

Be sure to note the Complexity and Safety ratings. Certain products seem to "sell themselves" because of their "guarantees," but they may be more complex, requiring more effort on your part to avoid misunderstanding.

When we zero in on costs, we'll be looking at three types: 1) your cost to buy the product, 2) your cost of ownership, and 3) what you need to pay if you want to sell or liquidate (get your money out of) the product.

I use the following shorthand when we talk about costs: cost to buy, cost to own, and cost to sell.

I also address how the salesperson is compensated if you buy the product. This is especially important because, at first blush, the purchase of some of these products appears to be free of fees or commissions—which might imply that the salesperson works for free. That's not the case, of course. As explained in Chapter 7, in many cases you pay the salesperson indirectly: the sponsor of the product pays the salesperson, but the sponsor typically recoups the money to pay the salesperson from your cost of ownership. Further, you want to know if the salesperson is getting paid more to sell you this product than he would to sell you another suitable product that might be less risky, less complicated, and less costly to own.

To further assist you, in each of the guaranteed-income chapters (9 through 12) I include answers to the following questions, which are intended to raise your awareness of potential benefits, expose possible pitfalls, and stimulate your thinking:

- Why is this product important to retirees?
- How does the product work?
- What does the product promise?
- When do you get your money?
- How is the product sold?
- How easy is the sale?
- What does the salesperson make if you buy the product?
- How easy is the product to understand?
- How risky is the product?
- How good is the guarantee?
- What is the cost to buy, the cost to own, and the cost to sell?
- What happens if you die while you own the product?
- What can go wrong?
- What should you read before buying this product?
- What questions should you ask before you buy?
- Who should consider buying the product? Who should not?

As you can see from this list, there is much to consider when buying a product to address your retirement-income needs. After all, you're looking for a lifelong solution. The last thing you want to do is rush the decision, especially if you intend to make a large purchase—and by "large" I mean any sum of money that is important to you.

So take your time as you weigh your options. No product or service, no matter how compelling it looks, sounds, or feels, should be purchased on the spot. Instead, slow down and make the effort to assess your options. Finally, never buy any product, especially one that you want to last a lifetime, until you understand it well enough to explain its pros—and, more important, its cons—to a friend.

CHAPTER

9

Creating Your Own Personal Pension

How would you like to have your boss continue to pay you after you retire? That's what it's like to receive a pension. If you have a pension, more power to you. If you don't, you can buy a product that will create one for you, called an "immediate annuity," which is the oldest product of its kind in the marketplace.

I think of the immediate annuity as a "personal pension." Like a pension, the immediate annuity can provide you with lifelong income. And, like a pension, this product carries certain risks, as we'll discuss shortly.

The Vanishing
Company Pension

People who work for companies that offer life-long pensions are the envy of many. What's so attractive about a company pension? First, you know that once you retire you will be getting a check for the same amount (or more, if your pension is indexed for inflation) every month for as long as you live. Second, if you die before your spouse, he may be entitled to receive all or a portion of your pension payments. Third, it's the company's responsibility, not yours, to invest wisely enough to fund that monthly payout to you and your fellow retirees. Fourth, your check doesn't decrease in value if the stock market declines. Fifth, you don't have to make any decisions after you start drawing the pension: all you have to do is have your pension deposited automatically into your bank account. What could be easier?

Hint: Keep in mind that most pensions are fixed monthly payments: they do not increase over your lifetime. As a result, the purchasing power of your pension check diminishes as you grow older. If you do have a company pension, be sure to monitor your spending carefully, or plan to cover rising living expenses from savings.

How risky is your pension? Your pension is a promised benefit from your company. Your company can fail to meet its pension obligations, as United Airlines did in May 2005. Should that happen, government protections come into play. The Pension Benefit Guaranty Corporation (PBGC) steps in to guarantee the pension responsibilities of bankrupt employers with insolvent pension plans (go to pbcg.gov to learn more). However, few people know that the benefits are capped based on the amount of your pension, the year in which the PBGC takes over your plan, and your age of retirement. For example, if your pension plan terminated in 2017 and you retired at age 65 in any year after 2017, the PBGC would pay you a maximum of $64,431 per annum, even if your pension was higher than that. If you had already retired when your plan terminated, however, your benefits would be based on your age at the time of termination, not the age at which you originally retired. For example, if you were 68 and already retired when your plan became insolvent in 2017, the maximum the PBGC would pay you is $86,338 per annum. In 2016, the PBGC paid about $5.6 billion to about 860,000 retirees in pensions that terminated.

If present trends continue, there will be fewer and fewer private pensions in the future. From the mid-1980s to 2007, the number of pension plans offered by employers fell from 112,000 to 30,000, further declining to about 22,500 by 2014. There is no reason to suspect this trend will end.

Ensuring You Won't Outlive

Your Money The problem a pension may solve is the risk of outliving your money ("longevity risk"). If you do not have a company pension, or if your pension is small compared with the cash flow you need to have coming in each month, you will want to make the following strategic decision before or soon after you retire.

Do you want to "self-insure" against longevity risk (meaning you take on the risk of outliving your money)? Or do you want to pay someone else to take on this risk? If you self-insure, you will need to be certain that you have enough money to live longer than you might expect. Who knows? Due to medical and lifestyle advances, you may live to 100 or longer.

To "insure" means to eliminate the probability of risk. How do you self-insure against the risk of outliving your money? You would need enough capital to last a lifetime even if you lived to be 120—and you would need to make sure you didn't lose it. You couldn't eliminate the risk altogether, however, because you would always have to contend with the possibility of loss of capital resulting from down markets or poor investment choices.

Your other option is to have someone else assume your longevity risk—someone who insures a large number of retirees against precisely this danger. The insurer can pool the risk that you will live a long life with that of other people facing the same scenario, some of whom will die sooner, thereby spreading the risk across many retirees. A pool is less risky to insure than a single person.

That's the concept behind the immediate annuity: you don't assume the risk of outliving your money; the insurance company does. You pass on the risk of a long life to the insurance company.

The Nuts and Bolts
of Immediate Annuities   Let's take a closer look at how the immediate annuity operates, and why certain retirees might benefit from buying an immediate annuity with part (but never all) of their savings.

Why Are Immediate
Annuities Important to Retirees?   Many retirees want a fixed income stream for life to replicate a pension that others receive from their employers after they retire. That's exactly what an immediate annuity offers. The immediate annuity is the closest financial-product solution for someone who wants the security of a company pension but doesn't have one.

How Does an Immediate
Annuity Work?   An immediate annuity (also called an "income annuity," a "fixed immediate annuity," or a "single premium immediate annuity") is an insurance product you buy, not an investment you make. The immediate annuity is a contract between you and the insurance company under which the insurance company promises to pay you a fixed dollar amount, typically every month, for a certain length of time as long as you live. Unlike a deferred annuity, which is meant to grow in preparation for your retirement, an immediate annuity is a contract that pays out a stream of income checks to you right away. There is no deferral period. Some immediate annuities offer inflation features that increase your monthly payout to offset rising costs.

The money used to pay for an immediate annuity (usually a lump sum) becomes the property of the insurance company when you buy the annuity. The insurance company pays you as agreed (for example, a life annuity pays income for life), but normally you cannot get your money back if you change your mind after a short cancellation period called a "free-look period." The owner (that's you) of the traditional life-only annuity has no claim to the money (called the "premium") used to buy the annuity—and neither will his estate after he dies. (Be aware, however, that you can buy an immediate annuity with survivorship benefits for heirs, as we will discuss.) The annuity is a contractual obligation between the owner of the annuity and the insurance company that issued the annuity. The contract spells out the terms of the annuity.

WARNING

Your decision to buy an immediate annuity is irrevocable (after the "free-look" period). If you change your mind after then, you cannot ask the insurance company to send your money back to you, unless your contract has a special feature that allows you to do so.

What Does an
Immediate Annuity Promise?   An immediate annuity promises that you will not outlive your money. Just like a pension, it does not promise that you will have enough to live on—that will depend on your spending habits. As with your pension, there is normally nothing to pass on to your heirs, unless you buy an immediate annuity with a "period-certain" or "refund" feature, as you will see shortly.

When Do You
Get Your Money?   Most immediate annuities are lifelong promises, meaning you receive a fixed amount each month for as long as you live. However, you can also buy an immediate annuity that pays out for a limited term, such as ten to fifty years; you get nothing if you live longer than the term specified. The term can also be combined with a life feature, which is meant to pay your beneficiary should you die during the term. For example, if you purchase an immediate annuity for "life and ten years certain," and you die soon afterward, your beneficiary will receive payments for ten years. If you die ten years after the purchase, your beneficiary gets nothing.

A Closer Look:

One Woman's Experience

A woman age 62 with annual living expenses of $52,000 was having a hard time managing her money. "Camille" had no pension and was concerned that she might spend or lose her $1.8 million inheritance. Her fear was that, absent some externally imposed controls, she could easily spend down her nest egg too quickly.

Based on current pricing, in exchange for a payment of roughly $1 million to an insurance company, Camille could expect to receive a monthly annuity payment of $4,334 ($52,000 a year) for as long as she lives. A few years ago (2009), the same annuity cost only $700,000.

If Camille dies before ten years after the purchase, her beneficiaries will continue to receive the monthly annuity payments for the remainder of the ten years. This type of policy is called "life with ten years certain."

Because Camille is still young (in her sixties), she should be concerned about inflation and taxes (see A Tax Advantage, page 113). This particular annuity does not pay increasing amounts to offset inflation. Had this annuity offered an annual 3 percent cost-of-living adjustment (COLA), it would cost Camille $1.4 million, leaving $400,000 to invest for capital appreciation for the future.

Sales of
Immediate Annuities
As discussed, it's important to understand how a salesperson presents a financial product to potential customers. A skeptic would say that his financial motivation, along with the anticipated ease of sale, may determine which financial instruments you are offered.

How Is an

Immediate Annuity Sold?   Retirees will be shown immediate annuities by financial advisers who are licensed to sell life insurance. Although an immediate annuity promises to solve the retiree's need for lifelong income, it is not a popular product for financial advisers to sell. Part of the reason is that, until recently, advisers were focused on selling accumulation products such as deferred annuities, not income products such as immediate annuities. Why? It's a question of demographics. Be sure to ask your financial adviser to explain your options regarding immediate annuities.

It is also possible to skip the visit to the adviser and purchase an immediate annuity directly from a vendor who sells products to consumers on a noncommission basis, usually online, through the mail, or by phone. Here are two examples (these are not recommendations or endorsements):

- Fixed Income Annuities offered by Fidelity Investments (www.fidelity.com)
- The Vanguard Lifetime Income Program® offered by the Vanguard Group (www.vanguard.com)

WARNING!

When researching immediate annuities, be sure to distinguish any product using the word "variable," as this refers to a different, more complex type of annuity that we will discuss in the next few chapters.

How Easy Is the Sale?

Selling an immediate annuity to a retiree would seem to be a piece of cake. After all, this product is a direct answer to the retiree's biggest fear—that of outliving his money. Yet immediate-annuity sales have not caught on.

Four factors affect sales of the immediate annuity: 1) because money can be tied up for life, the adviser has no opportunity to make subsequent sales; 2) commissions may be higher on other products; 3) retirees are reluctant to give up control over the money used to buy the immediate annuity; and

4) if interest rates at the time of purchase are low, payouts are low. Some more innovative products address these issues, as I discuss below.

Another factor is avoidance of immediate annuities based on the belief that you have to put all of your retirement savings into the product. That is not the case, of course. Consider an annuity purchase as a part of a larger retirement-income plan.

What Does the Salesperson
Make?   The financial advisor normally makes a one-time commission at the time of the sale. The amount (3 or 4 percent) is modest in comparison to other insurance products, such as the equity-indexed annuity.

Julie's Rating:
How Motivated Is Your Salesperson?
Not Especially. Between the minimal financial incentives offered to those marketing this product and its historical lack of popularity, the immediate annuity is hardly the star of the financial marketplace. This does not mean, however, that an immediate annuity should be overlooked. It simply means you'll have to ask your adviser if he doesn't bring it up, or do your own research; you can start with one of the direct sellers mentioned on page 109.

How Easy Is the Immediate Annuity
to Understand?   Of all the retirement-income products on the market, the immediate annuity is probably the easiest for retirees to understand, even if they are inexperienced investors. That's not to say that you can skip your homework; you need to compare competing products carefully. You have to be aware of pricing, the product's features (such as term and inflation), and, importantly, the financial strength of the issuer. Also be sure that you are not confusing annuity products—there are all kinds of annuities that promise lifelong income. Make certain that you are comparing like products.

Julie's Rating for Complexity

Easy to Understand. The immediate annuity is the least complicated of the retirement-income products that promise income for life. What you see—be sure to look—is what you get.

How Risky Is the Immediate Annuity?

The key to making a good choice in buying an immediate annuity lies in the company that stands behind the promise of lifelong income. That company's financial health is your major risk. If the company becomes financially distressed or goes out of business, you may lose the monthly stream of income. See Chapter 8 for a discussion of insurance failures, where to get information about the strength of your insurer, and state insurance guaranty funds.

Julie's Rating for Safety

Lets You Sleep at Night. An immediate annuity can be one of the safer retirement-income products, assuming the insurance company offering the annuity is in good financial health—and remains that way for as long as you live.

Costs and Taxes

Generally, when you buy an immediate annuity, there is no commission, or load, deducted from your purchase price—making your cost to buy zero. See "What Does the Salesperson Make?"

The cost to own an immediate annuity is embedded in the product. What do I mean by that? When an insurance company decides to sell you an immediate annuity, it has to find a way to pay for its own costs involved in delivering on its promises to you. Those costs are built into the product—you don't see them. The best way to judge costs is to do some competitive shopping among companies. By comparing terms and monthly payments, you'll get a sense of how the insurance company is pricing the immediate annuity.

There is no cost to sell an immediate annuity because normally, you cannot go back to the issuer to liquidate your annuity. (An exception is an annuity with a surrender, or "commutation," feature. Typically, there is a charge for commuting the contract.) You should be aware, however, that some annuity owners can find independent buyers for their annuities.

Taxes will depend on whether you use taxable or tax-deferred money to buy the immediate annuity. If you use your traditional IRA to make the purchase, the monthly check you receive from the immediate annuity will generally be taxable in full as income, as would withdrawals from a 401(k) plan at work. You will receive an IRS Form 1099-R at the beginning of each year from the insurance company showing the taxable amount that you need to report to the IRS on your prior year's tax return.

You will report a lot less taxable income if you buy the immediate annuity using money you've saved or invested in a taxable account (non-tax-deferred assets). The Form 1099-R you receive will report the taxable and nontaxable portions of your monthly payment. Only the taxable portion is subject to income taxes. How immediate annuities are taxed is explained in IRS Publication 575, "Pension and Annuity Income," which you can get online at www.irs.gov or by calling 1-800-829-3676.

For more information on how annuities are taxed, see Chapter 17.

Julie's Rating for Value

Good Value. An immediate annuity can be worth the price you pay for it, but be sure to shop around by comparing one immediate annuity to another with identical terms.

Important Considerations

With immediate annuities, there's more to consider than just how much you'll spend versus how much you'll receive. Some come with additional features to understand, such as withdrawals and death benefits; in addition, you should be aware of certain traps. Let's examine

A Closer Look:

A Tax Advantage

One attractive aspect of an immediate annuity is that the payments you receive are not fully taxable (assuming you did not use your IRA to buy the annuity), based on a concept called the "exclusion ratio." Essentially, part of the annuity payment is a return on investment, which is not subject to tax.

Recall Camille, the widow we met at the beginning of this chapter, who receives $52,000 a year from an immediate annuity. Her exclusion ratio—calculated by the insurance company to reflect a return of investment—is 80.40 percent. That means only about $10,200 of her $52,000 immediate-annuity income is subject to tax.

Assuming an income-tax rate of 20 percent, Camille's tax bill will be only $2,040 (20 percent of $10,200). What if she received the same amount of annual income from a different source, such as a corporate bond? The full $52,000 of income would be taxable at ordinary income-tax rates. If her tax rate were 20 percent, her tax bill for the bond interest would be $10,400 (20 percent of $52,000)—five times the $2,040 for the immediate annuity.

some important issues you should research before you purchase this retirement-income product.

What Happens If You Die While You Own
an Immediate Annuity?   Immediate annuities offer different pay-on-death features, and you need to be aware of your options. If you buy an immediate annuity for "life only," the annuity payments stop when you die—even if you die within days after you buy the annuity. (If death

occurs during the free-look period, the contract can be cancelled without penalty.)

If you have a family, don't buy a "life only" annuity: Nothing is left to pass on to your heirs unless you add a feature (such as the "ten years certain" option) ensuring that your beneficiaries will continue to receive payments. With a "joint life" annuity, you can cover yourself and your spouse. In that case, annuity payments continue to the surviving spouse after the first spouse dies. This works much like a pension with a "joint and survivor" option. Similarly, you can choose a 100 percent survivor benefit or a 50 percent (or lower) survivor benefit. With a 100 percent benefit, your survivor receives all of your payment; with a 50 percent benefit, your survivor receives only half of your payment.

If you buy an immediate annuity for a specified period of years ("period certain"), you will receive payments only during that time span and no longer. You can also buy an immediate annuity ("lifetime or longer") that continues to pay your beneficiary if you die before the guaranteed term. If you want your immediate annuity to serve as your personal pension plan, you need to consider a lifelong annuity (for example, "life with ten years certain," as opposed to just "ten years certain").

Make sure you understand all your options—and compare prices for each one—before you buy any annuity product. As you might imagine, the immediate annuity that terminates when you die (the "life only" annuity) is less costly than a life annuity with a guaranteed minimum term, such as "life with ten years certain."

Let's take a look at some of the options available to you, which you must select at the time you buy the immediate annuity.

- Single life: payments end when you die, even if you die right after you purchase the annuity. However, the contract can be cancelled if death occurs during the free-look period.
- Joint life: payments end on the death of the survivor. For example, you and your spouse can purchase a joint life immediate annuity that pays benefits until one of you dies, then continues to pay the same (or lesser) benefits until the surviving spouse dies.

- Period certain: payments are limited to a certain period of time, such as ten years. In this example, payments would be made to you (or your beneficiary) for ten years only, even if you live longer.
- Life with period certain: this option combines a life payment option with a period certain. For example, you can buy a joint life annuity for yourself and your spouse, with ten years certain. This means that even if both you and your spouse die before ten years have elapsed from the date of purchase, your designated beneficiary will step in to receive the payments that would otherwise have been made directly to you.

What Can Go Wrong?

The immediate annuity is a fairly straightforward insurance product that is easy to understand and hard to misrepresent. As a result, sales of immediate annuities tend to generate few complaints, unlike deferred, variable, and equity-indexed annuities, where misunderstandings can arise. (We'll discuss these products in the next few chapters.)

The press does not always distinguish among annuity types in negative articles about annuity sales practices. You can usually exclude the immediate annuity from most negative press that you see on annuities; the bulk of criticism is directed at other types of annuities that have more complex features.

Where can you get into trouble? You might misunderstand the terms of the annuity, especially if it combines features (see "Innovations," below). Or you could buy the wrong type of annuity if you don't realize the recommended product is a look-alike, such as those I discuss in the next few chapters.

Innovations

Some of the more recent innovations in immediate annuities address the need for increased flexibility. Here are examples of the features you can find. (Note that when you add a feature, the internal cost of the product is generally higher and your payout is lower.)

- Legacy benefits to provide for heirs. One such example is a "cash-refund guarantee," which works like this: if you die before your annuity payments equal your premium, your beneficiary will receive the difference between the premium and the payouts made up to that date.
- Inflation protection to increase the payout to offset inflation. This feature increases your payouts yearly—usually by a specific percent chosen at the time you buy the annuity.
- A survivor benefit. Some annuities allow you to choose to pay 100 percent (or a reduced amount) of your payout to a beneficiary for his lifetime. Others offer a percent of premium death benefit, which pays a single lump sum to your beneficiary.
- A feature allowing you to request withdrawals on a limited basis. For example, one annuity with a "cash-withdrawal feature" allows you to ask for a one-time-only withdrawal limited to a certain amount, which can be exercised on the 5th, 10th, or 15th anniversary of your first income payment. If this feature is used, future monthly payments are reduced.
- A payment-acceleration feature. For example, one annuity allows you to ask to receive six monthly payments in advance as a single lump sum; payments for the next five months are suspended.

Some annuities offer a combination of these features; for example, one annuity offers 1) guaranteed income for life, 2) survivor benefits for the owner's spouse, 3) legacy benefits that protect against both spouses dying too soon (through a period-certain feature), 4) inflation protection, and 5) withdrawal features (payment acceleration and a cash-withdrawal feature).

What Should You Read Before Buying
an Immediate Annuity?   You will have to read the immediate annuity contract to see how guarantees and other features work, how much of your payment is taxable, and what happens after your death. Conduct some research about the insurance company to determine its financial

strength. At a minimum, consult the resources discussed in Chapter 8 to assess the company's stability.

What Questions Should You Ask

Before You Buy? First, be sure to confirm that you are indeed being offered an immediate annuity and not another product. One way to tell is to ask for a prospectus; if the financial adviser hands you one, you are being offered a security, not an immediate annuity.

Then be sure to read carefully any material given to you by the financial adviser and any documentation he asks you to sign. Here are some important questions to ask before signing on the dotted line:

- How much will I receive each month?
- How long will these payments continue?
- What happens when I die? What happens if I die tomorrow?
- How strong is the insurance company issuing the immediate annuity, and how can I confirm that independently?
- What other options have you considered for me?
- Why are you recommending that I buy an immediate annuity?
- Why are you recommending this particular annuity?
- What do I need to read before making my purchase?
- What do I have to sign?

Buyer "Aware"

Here are some tips to consider before purchasing an immediate annuity:

- Do not buy an immediate annuity without considering your entire financial situation.
- Do not buy a life-only immediate annuity with money you want to leave to your heirs: this product is not intended to create a legacy. If you wish to leave a legacy, there are better ways. However, as discussed, do consider features that protect your heirs should you die prematurely (for example, period-certain or survivorship features).
- Do not buy an immediate annuity with a large portion of your savings. You need emergency savings for unanticipated expenses, such as

medical bills. In fact, you may want to limit your purchase of an immediate annuity to 40 to 50 percent of your savings at the most.

- You cannot "undo" the purchase after the free-look period—a short period of time during which you can cancel the purchase. This is a lifelong decision. Before agreeing to buy anything, take time to understand the pros and cons well enough to explain them to a friend.

- Consider limiting your purchase from any single company to an amount that falls below your state's insurance-guaranty fund (see Chapter 8).

- Do not buy an immediate annuity without considering inflation protection in the form of an annuity payment that increases over time. (Of course, there is a trade-off: an annuity that offers inflation protection will cost more to purchase than one that does not.)

- Know the financial strength of the issuing company. Because annuity payments are the obligation of the insurance company, it's imperative to research that company's financial stability.

- When comparison shopping, be sure you are comparing apples to apples. Make sure you are comparing like features. And don't compare a fixed immediate annuity to a variable immediate annuity or any other product.

Who Should Consider an Immediate Annuity?

Who Should Not? Immediate annuities can be quite helpful to both individuals of means and individuals with smaller amounts of savings. These retirement-income vehicles are particularly appealing because of their simplicity, especially to those who cannot (or prefer not to) manage their own finances.

I consider an immediate annuity to be a good option for retirees who are in the following circumstances:

1. You lack discipline. If you know you cannot control your spending— and therefore face the danger of running out of retirement savings prematurely—an immediate annuity will prevent you from outspending your capital. Immediate-annuity payments continue month after month, regardless of your spending habits. You can easily spend down

money in a bank account, an inheritance, or a large 401(k). Not so with an immediate annuity.

2. You lack a pension. If you have no pension, you might consider an immediate annuity to provide income for life in addition to your expected Social Security retirement benefit to help cover at least your Essential Expenses.

3. You lack time and/or experience. If you don't have the time required to manage your money—or you are simply averse to tackling the job yourself—consider immediate annuities. You don't have to monitor how investments are doing, because the insurance company is obligated to pay you the agreed-upon amount irrespective of how well its own investments perform. "The check is in the mail" in good markets and bad.

Even if you have other assets that you are turning into sources of income, the immediate annuity can smooth out your cash flow and improve your chances of maintaining your lifestyle in retirement.

Hint: Individuals with substantial assets typically hire their own money managers to help them create the lifetime cash flow they will need from their investment portfolios. (If you happen to be in that position, you may want to read my portfolio-management book, *Managing Retirement Wealth : An Expert Guide to Personal Portfolio Management in Good Times and Bad*.) Even affluent retirees, however, may want to consider immediate annuities in cases where cash-flow management is an issue, such as a divorce, widowhood, or the need to impose some financial discipline on a spendthrift.

Julie's Overall Recommendation

Consider. Plain-vanilla immediate annuities can be a simple, low-risk option for pension-less retirees who want to use a portion of their retirement savings to create their own personal pensions (adding features makes them more complex). In addition, the immediate annuity has the attraction of being "spendthrift proof." In contrast to a savings account or a 401(k), which you can liquidate, you cannot exhaust the assets behind your immediate annuity because you don't control them. As a result, you cannot outspend an immediate annuity (be sure to check your contract; cash- withdrawal features can work against you if you can't control spending). Moreover, payments continue regardless of the gyrations of the stock market.

Before you consider an immediate annuity, make sure you understand its risks (see "How Risky Is the Immediate Annuity?," page 111), features, and limitations, including the fact that the money used to buy a life-only annuity will not go to your heirs as an inheritance. Any time you add extra features, such as cash withdrawals, you have a different, more complex product that takes more care to understand fully and use wisely.

CHAPTER 10

The Promise of Gain with No Pain: Equity-Indexed or Fixed Annuities

Let me tell you about a reader I'll call Jane. She met a financial adviser at a free dinner presentation for retirees and later took him up on his offer of a one-on-one consultation. The adviser met with Jane, reviewed her finances, and made the following offer: "When you put your money in my hands, I will guarantee you stock-market returns without risking any of your money—plus you'll receive income you cannot outlive."

If you consider that a pretty intriguing offer, this chapter is for you.

Like most reasonable people, your first reaction might be, "What a deal! Where do I sign?" This chapter will keep you from signing on the dotted line long enough to see if the deal is really as good as it sounds.

Let me give you a preview of what you might experience in a sales presentation, as seen through Jane's eyes. You will be able to learn from her experience and judge for yourself whether this type of offer would be beneficial to you.

Let's start with the salesperson's presentation as I imagine it might have transpired, based on her story.

"Jane, I know you would like to make money in your retirement but, like many people, you are afraid of losing money," began the salesperson. "Remember those Enron employees who lost their life savings? What if I could promise you stock-market gains but protect you from losses? Would you be interested?"

"Of course. Who wouldn't be?" answered Jane.

"I thought so—most people I talk to are," said the salesperson.

The salesperson went on to explain his offer, a financial product he called a "fixed annuity." This term might give the impression that the buyer will receive fixed payments—not necessarily the case, as you will see.

During the presentation, the adviser wrote some notes, which you can see below. I'm sure you'll agree that the benefits sound compelling.

Salesperson's Notes

FIXED ANNUITY

100 percent guaranteed

No income taxes

No fees or upfront charges or commissions

No losses, just gains

Salesperson's Diagram

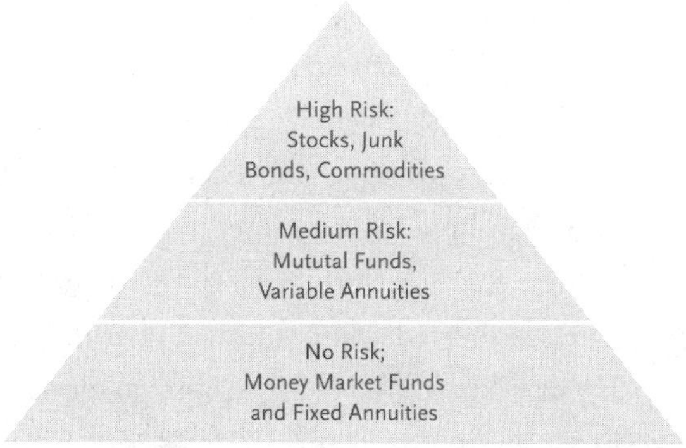

Figure 10-1

He also showed her a diagram in which he sorted selected investments and insurance products into three categories based on risk (see Figure 10-1).

At the top he placed "High Risk" vehicles (stocks, junk bonds, and commodities). In "Medium Risk" he placed mutual funds and variable annuities. Under "No Risk" he placed money-market funds and "fixed annuities." In addition, at each level he included percentages representing the amount of money he wanted Jane to use to buy the products shown in the diagram.

Hint: Some financial advisers use this type of diagram, known as an "investment pyramid," to help close a sale by guiding the customer to a particular decision. Advisers who use the pyramid write in risk categories and percentage recommendations to fit the situation.

The salesperson recommended that Jane put almost all (92 percent) of her retirement savings into "fixed annuities," which she understood from the diagram would be "No Risk."

At this point, Jane had no reason to question or to doubt this promise, as she was unfamiliar with the nuances of fixed annuities. In fact, as became apparent only later, this recommendation was for a certain type of fixed annuity, called an "equity-indexed annuity," or EIA (sometimes also called an "equity-linked annuity"). This term the adviser wrote on a separate page.

Go back to the salesperson's notes and you'll see the promise of "No losses, just gains." An EIA promises just that: all upside (gains) and no downside (losses), no matter how wildly the market may fluctuate.

Let's stop here for a moment. This is a critical point in the meeting. The salesperson introduced "indexed" annuities—something Jane had never encountered and could not possibly comprehend at this point. At such times, the tendency is to just go along, letting the salesperson lead you to a buying decision. It's far safer to stop here and ask a few direct questions before you find yourself buying something you don't understand or need.

Hint: Before getting too involved in a sales presentation, be sure to clarify:

1. Exactly when and what will I get for my money?
2. Under what circumstances will I not get what you're promising me?
3. Who is behind the guarantees, and how can I be sure they will live by their promises?
4. Who else offers this type of product, and how does it differ from yours?
5. What about my situation tells you I should buy this product?
6 Why is this the best income-producing product for me?

The Nuts and Bolts
of EIAs
If you're like Jane, you can easily understand the appeal of the equity-indexed annuity. Let's take a closer look now at just how this product works.

Why Are EIAs of Interest
to Retirees?
The EIA is a hot insurance product with record sales, largely because it directly addresses the retiree's conflict: the desire for high returns without the fear of loss. This product seems to solve this conflict by offering gains in up markets while protecting the principal from losses in down markets.

EIAs promise:

1. A minimum guaranteed interest rate
2. Possible interest above the minimum guarantee (as determined by a formula linked to an independent index)
3. No loss of principal or interest earned due to market declines
4. Possible availability of an income stream you can't outlive
5. Tax-deferral advantages

Let's see how these promises play out in practice.

What Is a Fixed Annuity?   First, let's talk about fixed annuities in general, then EIAs. A fixed annuity is a contractual obligation of an insurance company. You pay the company a premium. During the accumulation phase, the company credits your fixed annuity with interest at a specific rate (much like interest is credited to a bank account). Usually, there is an initial rate that is guaranteed for a period of time (three to six months or longer). After the initial period, the insurance company is at liberty to raise or lower the rate—unless there is a provision in the contract that prevents such a change.

Whereas the fixed annuity might remind you of a bank certificate of deposit (CD), it is not a deposit and it is not insured by the Federal Deposit Insurance Corporation (FDIC). A fixed annuity is usually tax-deferred, meaning no taxes are due until you withdraw money. Withdrawals before the annuity vests are usually subject to penalties.

Hint: When interest is credited, that doesn't mean you get paid. It simply means your interest is recorded on the books of the insurance company.

How Does the EIA Work?   An EIA is far from the typical fixed annuity I've just described. The EIA computes the amount of interest you will receive based on an index, such as the S&P 500. The insurance company credits your EIA some percentage of the index. The credit is called a "participation rate." For example, if the participation rate is 70 percent and the S&P 500 Index goes up 10 percent, your credit is 7 percent (70 percent of 10 percent). Periodically, the insurance company adjusts the value of the annuity to reflect the credit.

WARNING!

It's important to understand that the sponsor of the EIA can change the participation rate. For example, if you start out with 100 percent participation, you might find your rate lowered after a year. That's why you'll often see the participation rate referred to as the "initial participation rate" in the EIA contract. Some contracts spell out that the participation rate is "guaranteed for one year."

In addition, the EIA typically guarantees a minimum value (a "guaranteed floor"). A contract might provide, for example, that your value will not be less than a certain percentage of what you paid to buy the EIA, less withdrawals. This guaranteed value is the minimum amount available for withdrawals. Withdrawals without penalty or loss of interest and the guarantees can be taken after your annuity has vested, when you have converted your annuity to the periodic-payment mode, or if your contract has a death benefit.

The guaranteed floor is the basis of the no-risk guarantee. Most people would expect that "No Risk" means no losses of any kind at any time. That is not the case.

In Jane's example, the EIA's guaranteed value was 87.5 percent of the premium (or $87,500 on a $100,000 purchase) plus 3 percent, bringing her guaranteed value to only $90,125 (not $100,000).

The following year, Jane would earn another 3 percent, raising the guaranteed value to $92,829. In the next year after that, the value would be $95,614, and so on. It would take Jane five years for the guaranteed value to reach the original purchase price.

As you can see, the promise has a little more to it than initially meets the eye. Let's explore further.

When Do You

Get Your Money?   Now, this is a key question for any guaranteed product and one that needs to be addressed early on. With an EIA, you might have to wait to gain access to your money until your interest "vests," which means you have to hold the EIA until its term ends (commonly, six to ten years or longer). You will find the term in the contract—it's part of the deal offered by the insurance company selling the product.

If you need money earlier, consider these five potential barriers to getting your hands on it:

1. You may lose the benefit of the guarantee.
2. You may lose the promised interest.
3. You may have to pay a surrender charge, sometimes as high as 15 to 20 percent of the amount of your withdrawal.
4. You may not be permitted to make a partial withdrawal; some policies permit only full liquidations. Other, more flexible policies allow a penalty-free withdrawal of up to 10 percent of the value of the policy.
5. You'll have to pay income tax on any interest withdrawn.

Some EIAs offer a rider (an add-on to the EIA) that allows lifelong income withdrawals. In Jane's case, the withdrawals would be a set percentage of the EIA's "surrender value" (its value less surrender charges) based on her gender and age. In any case, you will need to read the contract to be sure you understand how to get money out of the EIA when you need it.

How Are EIAs

Sold? Expect to be introduced to EIAs by a financial adviser who is licensed to sell life insurance. An EIA can be one of the more profitable retirement sales a financial adviser can make. In addition to offering high commissions on the sale of an EIA (see below), the sponsoring insurance company might offer extra incentives such as trips or cash to the salesperson to boost sales.

It is also possible to purchase an EIA directly from a vendor who sells products to consumers on a noncommission basis. By purchasing online, through the mail, or by phone, you can skip the visit to the adviser—and, sometimes but not always, the necessity of paying his commission. Still, never use this purchase method without first understanding completely what you are buying.

Julie's Rating:
How Motivated Is Your Salesperson?

Eager to Sign You Up   This product can be one of the easiest conceptual sales, and one of the most lucrative. "When the market goes up, so will the value of your annuity. When the market goes down, you will not lose money." Who could pass up such a promise?

How Easy Are EIAs
to Understand?   Although the promised benefits of an EIA are easy to grasp, the product itself is one of the more difficult retirement products to understand because of its many moving parts—and, in some cases, the ability of the insurance company to change important features such as the "yield spread" (explained later) and participation rates.

I've discussed some of the nuances, but there are many others. For example, methods of calculating changes in the index differ (such as annual reset, point-to-point, high-water mark); some EIAs place caps on the index; participation rates can vary from 100 percent to less than 50 percent of the index; and some EIAs charge "spreads" while others charge "asset fees," "administrative fees," or "margin," all of which are costs that are subtracted from any gain in the index.

Remarkably, regulators caution that even the financial advisers who sell the product may not understand what they are selling. Nor does the marketplace make things any easier. The upside promise of the product hinges on how the insurer calculates interest during up-market periods. However, you can find more than three dozen interest-crediting formulas being used by different insurers today.

To find out whether you're getting a good deal, compare the product you're considering with the competition: how does the product that the adviser shows you stack up against other indexed annuities? Unfortunately, this comparison is easier said than done, according to a FINRA Investor Alert titled "Equity-Indexed Annuities—A Complex Choice." The FINRA report reads, in part,

> Although one insurance company at one time included the word "simple" in the name of its product, EIAs are anything but easy to understand. One of the most confusing features of an EIA is the method used to calculate the gain in the index to which the annuity is linked. To make matters worse, there is not one, but several different indexing methods. Because of the variety and complexity of the methods used to credit interest, investors will find it difficult to compare one EIA to another.

Where the regulators express concern about the complexity of this product, pay attention.

Julie's Rating for Complexity
For Ph.D.s   It is very difficult to understand what you're really getting.

What Does the Salesperson Make
If You Buy an EIA?   In Jane's example, the salesperson told her that his services were free to her. She didn't have to pay him a commission or any fee, he said, and no money would be deducted from her purchase price.

Your antennae should go up whenever any salesperson gives the impression that he is not getting paid. The sales commission on an EIA can be higher than the commission on other retirement-income products. (Note that the salesman shares part of this commission with his employer.) In fact, an EIA can earn the salesperson more than just about any other product. The product's sponsor sets and pays the commission, so in a sense it is not coming directly from your pocket. You pay for it indirectly, though, via fees embedded in the product. To find out the commission, just ask, "How much will you make if I buy the EIA you are recommending?"

How Risky Is the EIA? You have to be astute to figure out how you can lose money with an EIA—after all, the attraction is that the EIA is a "No Risk" product. But "No Risk" does not mean you cannot lose money. You can, as Jane's example illustrated.

Mindful that consumers may not understand the risks inherent in EIAs, the SEC has issued a special investor-protection warning about the nature of the guarantee:

> Even with a guarantee, you can still lose money if your guarantee is based on an amount that's less than the full amount of your purchase payments. In many cases, it will take several years for an equity-index annuity's minimum guarantee to "break even."
>
> You may also have to pay a significant surrender charge and tax penalties if you cancel early. In addition, in some cases, insurance companies may not credit you with index-linked interest if you do not hold your contract to maturity.

Risk of loss is real if you don't play by the EIA's rules. Even if you do, you may need to withdraw money before you anticipated, which can mean paying surrender charges, losing interest, and possibly losing guarantees. As a result, you (or your heirs) may not be entitled to a full return of principal.

Julie's Rating for Safety

Think Twice   With an EIA, safety is a question of avoiding surprises. Make sure you completely understand the deal you are being shown. Be sure to do your required reading (listed later in the chapter) before going forward.

How Good Is the Guarantee?

Before you buy an EIA, assure yourself that the company behind it is in good financial health. As the FINRA Investor Alert cited above makes clear, "While it is not a common occurrence that a life insurance company is unable to meet its obligations, it happens."

Costs and

Taxes Figuring out how much your EIA costs is not going to be easy for two reasons: 1) costs can be a moving target, as I explain later, and 2) you need to think of participation rates as a form of cost—the lower the participation rate, the lower your interest credit.

Cost to buy. Your cost to buy an EIA is normally zero; there is no commission, or "load," deducted from the purchase price.

Cost to own. You'll want to focus on your costs to own the EIA. One such cost, the "yield spread," is shown on the salesperson's "illustration," which you will receive at the sales presentation. The yield spread is an ongoing charge against the promised market-participation rate. For example, if the yield spread is 2 percent, the participation rate is 100 percent, and your index returns 10 percent, your credit is 8 percent. Yield spread can also be called a "margin," "administrative fee," or "asset fee."

Hint: What does yield spread mean to you? The higher the yield spread, the lower your potential return.

In Jane's case, the illustration showed a yield spread of a seemingly negligible 0.55 percent per year—which, the salesperson emphasized, was her only cost. That sounds like a great deal. But here is the potential trap: the contract provides that the yield spread is guaranteed for one year and *one year only*. It can increase after then, lowering your potential return.

Hint: Normally, EIAs adjust costs, participation rates, and other moving parts each year on the anniversary date of your purchase. If you don't like the new deal, some EIAs give you a thirty-day window during which you can choose to switch to another crediting formula, such as a fixed interest rate.

Cost to sell. To determine the cost to sell an EIA, look for penalties and surrender charges, which usually decrease gradually over time. Your EIA could have a surrender charge of 20 percent in the first year and

10 percent in the second through fifth years, declining over time to 0 percent after the tenth year.

Taxes   No taxes are due until you withdraw money. Then any earnings are taxed at ordinary income-tax rates, which are currently higher than capital-gains tax rates.

Julie's Rating for Value

Hard to Judge. Costs require careful analysis, but that analysis can be frustrated if the EIA's contract permits the insurer to change the cost structure (or lower the participation rate) after the first year. As a result, you will not know what you are getting until the change occurs. If you want to liquidate all or part of your EIA, you will be subject to surrender charges. These are all elements that can lower the interest credit and prevent this product from fulfilling your expectations.

Important
Considerations   Aside from the risks and costs we've discussed, there are several other factors to take into account when considering this purchase.

What Happens If You Die While You Own
This Product?   To answer this question, you will have to look at the contract for the particular product you are purchasing. Jane's contract specified that on her death her beneficiary would receive the greater of the "accumulation value" or the "minimum guaranteed contract value." The accumulation value is the value of the annuity after interest is credited, less withdrawals. A minimum guaranteed contract value provides that the value of your EIA will never be less than a percentage of what you paid for it.

Keep in mind that your EIA may adjust these values only once a year on the anniversary date of the purchase. If that is the case, beneficiaries will not receive any credit for interest after the adjustment (after the death). Surrender charges are usually waived in the event of death.

What Can Go Wrong? In a letter urging SEC oversight of EIAs, the Financial Planning Association pointed out the following issues:

- High commissions and other administrative charges that are not disclosed by sales agents
- Steep surrender changes in the early years of the policy
- "Returns that are typically capped below the market index's entire gain"
- Marketing literature that gives the impression that EIAs are investments in the stock market, even though they are not regulated as such

When you're considering purchasing an EIA, make sure you keep the above factors in mind.

What Should You Read Before Buying This Product?

Under a 2009 SEC rule effective January 12, 2011, most EIAs of the type we've discussed here are now treated as securities.

You will need to read, in descending order of importance: the prospectus, the contract, the disclosure statement, the illustration, the application, and the marketing literature. The contract is the most important document to read and understand, because it sets out the deal for you. If the agent or the marketing literature says something else, that won't usually help you. The contract is the final word.

Hint: Ask for a sample contract that you can read at your leisure before committing any money. Resist the salesperson's suggestion that you read the contract after the purchase. Even though you will have the right to a "free look" (usually ten days during which you can abort the purchase), it will take you a while to get comfortable with the contract. If after reading the contract you cannot explain how the EIA works to a friend, do not buy the EIA.

If you are considering buying an EIA, be sure to read "Equity-Indexed Annuities: Fundamental Concepts and Issues," published by the Insurance Information Institute, which you can find online at www.iii. org. This report is an unbiased view of EIAs and can supplement your understanding of the annuities. Another important resource is the NAIC's

"Buyer's Guide to Fixed Deferred Annuities with Appendix for Equity Indexed Annuities," which you can order online at www.naic.org. (search publications). Also make certain to read FINRA's "Equity-Indexed Annuities—A Complex Choice" online at www.finra.org.

What Questions Should You Ask before You Buy?

The following questions are based on those provided courtesy of The National Association of Insurance Commissioners. I've added a few of my own as well.

- What is the guaranteed minimum interest rate?
- What charges, if any, are deducted from my premium?
- What charges, if any, are deducted from my contract value?
- How long is the term?
- What is the participation rate?
- For how long is the participation rate guaranteed?
- Is there a minimum participation rate?
- Does my contract have a cap?
- Is averaging used? How does it work?
- Is interest compounded during a term?
- Is there a margin, spread, or administrative fee? Is that in addition to or instead of a participation rate?
- Which indexing method is used in my contract?
- What are the surrender charges or penalties if I want to end my contract early and take out all my money?
- Can I get a partial withdrawal without paying surrender charges or losing interest?
- Does my contract have vesting?
- Does my annuity waive withdrawal charges if I am confined to a nursing home or diagnosed with a terminal illness?
- What annuity-income payment options do I have?
- What is the death benefit?
- What will you make on the sale?

- What disclosure documents are you required to give me? Did you give them to me?
- Why are you recommending an EIA to me and why this particular EIA?
- What other products and investments have you considered for me?
- How sound is the insurance company offering the EIA?
- Why is this the best income-producing option for me?

Buyer "Aware" After every question on the list above, write the answer you think is correct based on your salesperson's presentation and the materials you reviewed with him. Do not buy the EIA until you have done all your reading and are confident that you have all the answers you need to fully understand what you are getting.

Keep in mind that you should not rely solely on verbal assurances. Do your homework; confirm your understanding in writing to avoid misunderstandings.

What If You Already

Bought an EIA? If you already purchased an EIA and now have a problem with it, contact the insurance commissioner of the state in which you live. You can find a list of insurance regulators online at www.naic. org or by doing an online search for your state and "insurance regulation." The regulator will investigate the situation; then, if the product was misrepresented to you, he will intercede on your behalf.

Even though the SEC does not currently regulate all EIAs, this federal agency would like to hear about the problem too. You can fill out a complaint form at www.sec.gov/complaint.shtml, or write to

SEC
100 F Street NE
Washington, D.C. 20549-5990

Who Should Consider an EIA?

Who Should Not? Consider an EIA under the following circumstances:

1. You are afraid of losing money in the stock market but want to participate in stock-market gains.
2. You want tax deferral.
3. You don't need to use this money for at least as long as the end of the vesting period and the surrender-charge period.
4. You don't anticipate needing this money for an emergency.
5. You are not using a large portion of your retirement savings to buy the EIA.
6. All your questions about the EIA being recommended have been answered.
7. You have read and understood the contract.
8. You can explain the product, including its drawbacks, to a friend.
9. You have shopped around, and this particular product is more desirable than others.

Julie's Overall Recommendation

Avoid unless you are an experienced investor who is prepared to do a lot of homework to understand exactly what you are getting with the EIA you are considering. Keep in mind that the NAIC, the SEC, and FINRA have all issued warnings about this product. That should send a strong message to retirees: if you are not willing to do the work necessary to understand the product, consider other options.

CHAPTER

11

It's Not Too Late to Catch Up: The Guaranteed Minimum Income Benefit

Picture this: you're reading this book on the beach and contemplating your future retirement, which is only ten years away. You decide to take a break.

You start walking along the beach, when you stub your toe. "Ouch!"

Bending down, you spot a brass lamp. You pick it up and rub off the sand. Whoosh! Out pops a genie.

The genie says, "You have three wishes."

With retirement on your mind, you sputter,

"I wish I had started saving earlier. I wish my investments would never decline in value. And I wish my money would last as long as I do."

The genie replies, "Your wishes are my commands," then disappears in a puff of smoke.

You go back to your beach towel and see that the wind has blown open your book to this chapter.

You jump for joy, shouting, "This is the answer!"

This fantasy is perhaps not all that far-fetched (absent the genie). GMIB stands for "guaranteed minimum income benefit." Created by the insurance industry to meet the needs of future retirees, it is especially attractive to boomers who need to play catch-up.

Why? Where else can you get this simple solution? Catch up on your retirement savings without fear of losing money (in adviser lingo: "all upside and no downside"), and in ten years retire on a lifelong income stream.

GMIB's are living benefits purchased as a "rider" or "add-on" attached to a variable annuity. A variable annuity is a financial product with investment and insurance features, sold by financial advisers who are licensed to sell both insurance and investments. When I use the term "GMIB," I'm referring to the whole enchilada—the rider and the variable annuity. More than 76 percent of the variable annuities sold today offer a "living benefit" rider such as the GMIB or the GMWB ("guaranteed minimum withdrawal benefit," the subject of the next chapter).

WARNING!

The issuer—that is, the company behind the product—is legally bound to explain GMIBs in writing to prospective buyers in a "prospectus." This document can be quite long. If you are interested in the GMIB, prepare to read a lot of disclosure materials. If you don't care to do so, keep in mind that you are "deemed" to know what's in the prospectus even if you didn't actually read it. There is nothing "plain vanilla" about GMIBs or other living benefits; there are many flavors and ingredients.

You don't want to buy a GMIB or GMWB without doing your homework. You will see some of the complexity behind the product when I walk you through how it works.

How Do Variable Annuities Work?

Before we can explore the mechanics of GMIBs, you first need to understand some basics about variable annuities. This type of product has two phases. During the first, the accumulation phase, your variable annuity acts like an investment—you make selections from a menu of investment options that are described in prospectuses. During the accumulation period, no income taxes are payable as long as you take no withdrawals, since the variable annuity is tax-deferred.

The second phase is annuitization. When you alert your insurance-company representative that you wish to annuitize, you're telling him that from that point on you want to receive regular payments. Once you do this, the insurance company sponsoring the product converts the amount that you (the contract owner) have built up (during the accumulation phase) into an income stream.

After annuitization, the variable annuity looks much like an immediate annuity, but with one big difference: the amount of the periodic payment you will receive at annuitization will normally not be known to you at the time you buy the variable annuity. You have to wait until you want to annuitize, then ask the insurance company to tell you what you will get before making a decision to start receiving payments. By contrast, at the time you buy the "plain vanilla" immediate annuity discussed in Chapter 9, you know exactly how much you will be paid and for how long.

The insurance company will weigh several factors to determine the amount of your payments at the time of your annuitization election. Factors include the account value on a specific day, your age on the date the income payments begin, the payment option chosen, and the performance of your investments during the accumulation period.

The Nuts and Bolts

of the GMIB As you can see, a variable annuity has both investment and insurance features. This type of annuity is a "variable" investment because your rate of return varies, or fluctuates, depending upon the performance of the underlying securities. As I mentioned, the GMIB is usually an add-on, or rider. When you purchase the variable annuity, you pay extra for this rider. The rider and the annuity are packaged together.

Hint: The way you choose investment options in a variable annuity may remind you of your 401(k) plan at work. In both cases, you can choose from a menu of investment choices. You cannot invest outside this menu. The 401(k) selections are prescreened for you by your employer, acting as your fiduciary.

Terms You Should Know

- The accumulation period is the first stage of a variable annuity, during which time your variable annuity acts like an investment—you make selections from a menu of investment options. Those choices are described in prospectuses. During the accumulation period, no income taxes are payable (unless you withdraw money), since the investment is tax-deferred. If you do make a withdrawal during the accumulation period, you may have to pay a penalty. (Note the withdrawal limitations for GMIBs below.)
- When you withdraw, or take out, money, technically you are "surrendering" all or part of your variable annuity.
- A surrender charge is basically a penalty for taking money out during a predetermined period of time.
- Annuitization. The above terms apply only during the accumulation period. Variable annuities have another phase—annuitization (that means you turn your variable annuity over to the insurance company in exchange for regular payments). That phase needs to be triggered by the investor, and historically most investors have opted not to do so. Why? Because they bought the product for tax-deferred growth, not income.

With more and more investors seeking an income stream, however, that may change.

Hint: For the GMIB guarantee to apply, you must meet some conditions. Most important, you need to "annuitize." Be aware that the amount of the annuity payments could be lower than those you would receive if you buy an immediate annuity, due to less-favorable annuitization tables, or "age setbacks." (If you see an "age setback" in your contract, be aware that a longer setback means a lower annuity payment.) Bottom line: be sure you understand how annuity payments are determined.

What the GMIB

Promises   Remember the promise: upside potential and no downside? Here is how that works. The GMIB provides a "floor," or minimum return, of, say, 5 percent during your accumulation period, during which time (usually ten years) there is a mandatory lock on your money. That means that if you make bad investment decisions or hit a bad market during the accumulation period, the insurance company will still credit your account 5 percent per year for each year of the accumulation period. It also means you can't take out money without jeopardizing the guarantee. If your investments generate more than 5 percent, you may—depending on certain factors—be credited with a higher number. (I discuss all of this shortly.)

Before we go any further, let's stop and exercise a "buyer aware" attitude, because here's something very important. Be sure to confirm whether the 5 percent guarantee applies to money you want to withdraw during the accumulation period.

Let me give you a quick example of how the 5 percent guarantee works.

Bob, age 53, pays $100,000 for a GMIB that guarantees 5 percent annual growth during the accumulation period. He makes no withdrawals or transfers during that time.

After twelve years, Bob decides he wants to retire and needs his money. And that's when he hits a major snag: because of poor investment performance, he discovers, his account is now worth only $85,000—far less than his original $100,000 investment. If Bob needs to cash out, he surrenders the GMIB for $85,000. Alternatively, he can annuitize based on a higher value ($179,585, which is $100,000 growing undisturbed at 5 percent per year for twelve years).

When Do You Get
Your Money?

To benefit from the guarantees of a GMIB, you are locked into a waiting period (say, ten years), after which you must annuitize. Therefore, GMIBs are for people who don't need their money for at least as long as the built-in waiting period. During that time, you can make withdrawals, but beware of two things: 1) surrender charges may apply if you withdraw more than 10 percent (usually) of your purchase price, and 2) by withdrawing any money, you risk interfering with the guarantee. So be sure you understand how withdrawals affect the guarantees offered by the GMIB you are considering buying.

After the waiting period, you annuitize in order to receive regular payments, much like the immediate annuity discussed in Chapter 9. The payment can be monthly for life, or for a certain period of time, such as ten or twenty years.

Remember that when you annuitize, you turn your money over to the insurance company. This act is normally irrevocable; you can't go back to the accumulation phase and take a withdrawal. In the example above, after Bob annuitizes, he receives his regular payments. However, he can't go back and get his $179,585—or even his $85,000.

Case Study: How the Company
Calculates Your Payment

To make an informed decision, you'll need to know how the insurance company calculates the value your policy gains during the accumulation phase, as well as how it sets the payment you receive for life once you annuitize. You'll find this information in the prospectus and in the contract. The following example shows you the workings of the particular GMIB I am reviewing here; others will have different features.

John, 60 years old, wants an investment to protect his principal for the next ten years. After he turns 70, he wants guaranteed income for life. He uses $96,000 to purchase a GMIB with a "life income with ten years certain" payment plan. That means that once John annuitizes, which he intends to do at age 70, he will be guaranteed income for life. If he dies before his eightieth birthday, his beneficiary will receive the income that John would otherwise have received from his death until he reached the age of 80.

Until he annuitizes, John will be directing his investments by choosing how to allocate funds to different "subaccounts"—the formal name for the investment options offered by the product. The subaccounts may be described in separate prospectuses. The subaccounts may remind you of mutual funds, but they are not offered outside the variable annuity. If the sponsor changes the subaccounts, it will send you a supplement to your prospectus to let you know.

Let me stress that there are all sorts of GMIBs. So that you can be more comfortable reviewing a GMIB shown to you by a financial adviser, I'll preview how one particular GMIB works in some detail here. Again, there are many other types of GMIBs; this is but one example.

Table 11-1 is an example of what you would find in the prospectus, which you would want to study carefully before buying a GMIB. The second column is labeled "Value of Accounts (Beginning of Year)." This reflects John's investment value during the accumulation period, which is $96,000.

The third column, "Transfers Made to Annuity Purchase Fund," refers to monies automatically transferred (in this example, $800 a month for 10 years for a total of $96,000, the original investment) into a special subaccount ("Annuity Purchase Fund") used to fund the annuitization. (John doesn't have to make the transfer himself—that's an automated bookkeeping function—but he has no say over whether or not a transfer will occur.)

In the fourth column, you'll see "Value of Accounts after Transfer," showing the account value after yearly transfers.

Next you'll see "Value of Annuity Purchase Fund (Beginning of Year)," representing the value of the annuity purchase fund before any transfers, followed by "Value of Annuity Purchase Fund (End of Year)," summarizing the total of the transfers, plus any accumulated investment gains at the end of each year.

Finally, in the last column, you arrive at the guaranteed minimum payment John will receive. Ten years after he purchased the GMIB with $96,000, John has created a guaranteed annual payment for himself of $9,563. That's the minimum payment he'll receive every year for the rest of his life, beginning the eleventh year of owning this product.

Year	Value of Investments (Beginning of Year)	Transfers Made to Annuity Purchase Fund	Value of Accounts After Transfers	Value of Annuity Purchase Fund (Beginning of Year)	Value of Annuity Purchase Fund (End of Year)	Guaranteed Minimum Annual Payment Accrued
1	$96,000	$9,600	$90,778	$0	$9,849	$956
2	90,778	9,600	85,303	9,849	20,173	1,913
3	85,303	9,600	79,565	20,173	30,995	2,869
4	79,565	9,600	73,551	30,995	42,339	3,825
5	73,551	9,600	67,247	42,339	54,230	4,781
6	67,247	9,600	60,639	54,230	66,695	5,738
7	60,639	9,600	53,712	66,695	79,761	6,694
8	53,712	9,600	46,452	79,761	93,457	7,650
9	46,452	9,600	38,841	93,457	107,814	8,606
10	38,841	9,600	30,864	107,814	122,863	9,563

Table 11-1: Sample of prospectus illustration showing John's experience during the accumulation phase

What you see in Table 11-1 is a summary of the accumulation phase. To secure the guarantee, John has to annuitize, the results of which are spelled out in Table 11-2.

The Calculated Payment, in the second column of Table 11-2, is determined by the insurance company based on the performance of the annuity's underlying investments. John will receive the higher of the Calculated Payment or the Guaranteed Payment, found in the third column.

For example, in the first year, the insurance company calculates that John should get $9,436, which is $127 less than he is guaranteed. John gets the Guaranteed Payment, and the $127 difference is recorded in his Adjustment Account Balance, found in the last column. The $127 is an advance, which he will have to repay only when his investments earn

Year	Calculated Payment	Guaranteed Payment	Payment to Owner	Adjustment Account Balance
11	$9,436	$9,563	$9,563	$127
12	9,557	9,563	9,563	133
13	9,679	9,563	9,563	17
14	9,803	9,563	9,786	0
15	9,928	9,563	9,928	0
16	10,055	9,563	10,055	0
17	10,184	9,563	10,184	0
18	10,314	9,563	10,314	0
19	10,446	9,563	10,446	0
20	10,579	9,563	10,579	0

Table 11-2: Sample prospectus illustration showing John's
annual payments after he annuitizes

enough to pay more than his Guaranteed Payment—that is, when his Calculated Payment exceeds his Guaranteed Payment.

What then happens is this: the amount that John makes over and above his Guaranteed Payment is used to repay the advances in his Adjustment Account Balance until the balance has been paid off. This provision is important to John in the end because even if his investments never perform well enough to repay the advances, he still gets his Guaranteed Payment every year—and doesn't have to repay anything.

How Is the GMIB
Sold?
GMIBs are sold by financial advisers who are licensed to sell both life insurance and mutual funds. The GMIB is described in a prospectus, which you will want to read. The adviser will show you marketing literature. You'll also want to wade through the prospectus and the contract to get the back story about how the product works.

The sales presentation will be the key to the sale, so take advantage of it. That is, take the opportunity to ask questions.

How Easy Is
the Sale?
GMIBs are easy to present because, as I've discussed, the product seems to be a win-win. It's a harder sell, however, if the potential buyer starts asking how the guarantees work, how much he can make during the accumulation period compared with other products, and how the annuity payments are figured.

What Does the
Salesperson Earn?
A salesperson who sells you the GMIB I've profiled in this chapter makes as much as 11 percent of your purchase price at the time of the sale, part of which he will share with the firm that employs him. On a $10,000 sale, that's $1,100. On a $200,000 sale, that's $22,000. Regardless of how much money is invested, an 11 percent

commission is substantially more than the salesperson will likely make compared to many other financial instruments.

To get a sense of whether the 11 percent payment is high or low, you need to do some comparisons. Take a load mutual fund, for example. Whereas a mutual fund lacks the guarantees of a GMIB, it pays to see how much more the salesperson might make if you buy a GMIB, particularly if you are investing a large sum of money. Table 11-3 shows the difference between buying a GMIB and buying a popular load mutual fund. Notice that for lower investments, the payment to the salesperson for the GMIB sale in this example is twice as much as that for the mutual fund. At the higher levels, it is ten times as much. That's because GMIBs (and variable annuities in general) may not offer discounts (reductions in commissions, also called "breakpoints") for larger purchases. For more information on payouts to salespeople, see Chapter 7. As I mentioned above, the salesperson shares part of this payment with the firm that employs him.

That raises a crucial point. If you are going to pay someone a lot of money, be sure you are getting the service you deserve. (That is to say, you don't want to buy a GMIB after only a short meeting with a salesperson;

Investment	Possible Payment to Salesperson for Sale of GMIB	Possible Payment to Salesperson for Sale of Load Mutual Fund
20,000	$2,200	$1,000
100,000	11,000	2,750
200,000	22,000	5,500
500,000	55,000	8,000
800,000	88,000	9,600
1,000,000	110,000	10,000

Table 11-3 Example comparing possible payment to salesperson
for sale of GMIB vs. popular mutual fund

instead, you want him to earn his pay by patiently addressing all your questions.)

The bottom line? Know what the salesperson is getting paid when you buy, and be sure you are buying the product because it's the best product for you to own.

Julie's Rating:
How Motivated Is Your Salesperson?

Eager to Sign You Up. While no ethical salesperson will be motivated by his compensation alone, this product will likely produce an attractive commission.

How Easy Is the GMIB

to Understand? The GMIB's promises are easy to understand, as we've seen. The conditions under which those promises are delivered or restricted and the product's other limitations—now, that's a different matter. That may take some work for you to uncover working with your salesperson.

It will be a challenge to ferret out the conditions on the guarantees, the true upside potential during the accumulation period, the costs, the limitations on accessing your money (as well as those on investment choices), and the risks of the insurance company going out of business during the annuitization phase.

Just understanding all the moving parts of a GMIB is a challenge: the terms are unfamiliar, and the information you need is buried in hard-to-read legal documents. Who wants to analyze hundreds of pages of legalese and then compare other similar products to get some perspective? (I'll give you an example of some additional prospectus disclosures shortly.)

For that very reason, buyers tend to rely on the salesperson's presentation, which by definition is not enough. Consider the comparison shopping you might do when buying an appliance or a TV. You need to do the same with a GMIB or any other retirement product.

Hint: If you are the type of person who doesn't read prospectuses (and contracts), you'll want to break that habit. A prospectus contains information that protects you from risking, expecting, or paying too much for a particular investment. The best way to learn how to read a prospectus is to compare two of them side by side. Familiarize yourself with the contents—you'll see that each document follows a pattern. Compare and contrast.

Julie's Rating for Complexity

For Ph.D.s. Compared with the immediate annuity discussed in Chapter 9, a GMIB is a complex product with many moving parts. Even if you have the patience to read everything you need to, you will still find it difficult to compare the GMIB to other retirement-income alternatives for the reasons explained above.

How Risky Are GMIBs?

How do you assess the risks of a GMIB? You must consider several factors:

- During the accumulation period, you bear the risk of gain or loss of the money you invest, unless there is a floor, or minimum guaranteed return, that kicks in.
- After annuitization, the insurer runs the risk that you will live a long life (longevity risk), but you bear the risk that the insurance company will go out of business or be unable to live up to its promises. A product's guarantee is only as good as the company behind it. The guarantees the GMIB makes are not secured obligations; they are merely contractual obligations, meaning there is no collateral behind the promises. Make sure you perform your due diligence—meaning, check out the company. (Chapter 8 tells you how to select a reliable company.)
- Think about the costs of owning the product as a risk as well: costs such as embedded fees, which I discuss shortly, reduce your returns.
- Whereas GMIBs typically offer a long list of investment choices, your options are limited to those offered by the product. Translation: you're stuck if you don't like your returns. Sure, you can get out by paying a surrender charge, but that's another risk.

- If you plan to annuitize, the GMIB's payout may not be as competitive as you could get on your own by buying an immediate annuity. There is no assurance that the GMIB will give you a favorable annuity rate.
- The sponsor can be subject to lawsuits or regulatory matters that can erode its ability to deliver on its promises.
- All GMIBs are not created equal. One insurance company's GMIB may be quite different from another's. Never buy a GMIB without doing some comparison shopping to make sure you are getting the best product for you.
- The biggest risk? Taking the easy way out and relying on the salesperson rather than judging for yourself whether the GMIB is a good deal for you.

Don't be influenced to buy the GMIB based on promises you don't understand.

Julie's Rating for Safety

Think Twice. After all is said and done, it's very easy to misunderstand what you are really getting. For that reason, you must proceed with caution. Read about, think about, and analyze your options. Compare the GMIB with other GMIBs—and with other investment products—before going forward with the purchase. Among other things, in most cases you must annuitize to gain the guarantee—and who's to say that the insurer's financial health will remain sound after annuitization for the duration of your life? Here is the key: avoid a GMIB if you can't explain its drawbacks to a friend.

Costs and Taxes

GMIBs are not cheap.

Cost to buy. As with other retirement-income products, there is usually no cost to buy a variable annuity with a GMIB—that is, no upfront commission or sales charge is deducted from your purchase price. That doesn't mean the product is free, however. There are costs to own and costs to sell.

Cost to own. The cost to own is high compared with the cost to own other investments, such as mutual funds. In the GMIB prospectus reviewed for this chapter, annual charges during the accumulation period can range as high as 3.7 percent. That's a big drag on performance. At that rate, if your investments return 8 percent, you will net only 4.3 percent after the fees are deducted. High fees can prevent you from benefiting from any upside potential.

Because costs to own are such an important factor with a GMIB, let's look at them more closely. This gets complicated, so let me take you through them step-by-step. Three types of annual charges go into figuring the cost to own, and they add up quickly:

1. The investment component (called "portfolio fees and expenses")
2. The insurance component
3. Optional riders, such as the GMIB

The investment fees in the prospectus under review here range from a low of 0.4 percent per year (quite attractive) to 1.75 percent (more than I like to pay).

The insurance component adds up to 1.45 percent and includes "mortality and expenses" (1.3 percent), administrative fees (0.15 percent), and an annual contract fee ($30).

There's also the cost of the guaranteed income rider (in this example, 0.5 percent per year), plus optional riders (in this example, 0.3 to 0.7 percent). Be aware that with some products, the cost of the rider is based on something other than the account value, which may mean an even higher cost.

Do the math: the minimum you'll pay per year is 2.35 percent and the maximum is 4.4 percent for this particular GMIB, based on the investment and rider options you choose.

Cost to sell. Variable annuities usually carry a surrender charge, which is a cost to sell. In other words, if you want to liquidate your GMIB during the accumulation period, you won't get all of your money back. A surrender charge of somewhere between 0 and 11 percent will be deducted from the value of your account. According to industry sources, surrender charges generally range from 5 to 7 percent of the amount withdrawn and decline to zero over time, typically five to seven years. Some products have no surrender charges.

A word of caution: retirees often ignore costs because they are so focused on the "guarantees." That's very dangerous. Sales literature showing graphs and numbers may not deduct the product's costs to own—and, of course, those costs will reduce your returns. Always compare costs to other similar retirement-income products.

Julie's Rating for Value

Hard to Judge. Comparison shop—remember, GMIBs are not all alike. Weigh the costs against the benefits of the particular GMIBs you are considering, and against other available retirement-income products.

Taxes

As long as you don't take any money out of the GMIB, you won't owe any income taxes. When you do start to withdraw money, however, each dollar above your "basis" is taxed at ordinary income-tax rates. Your "basis" is the amount of money you used to buy the variable annuity, unless you made the purchase with funds from an IRA or some other tax-deferred account. In the latter case, your basis is your nondeductible contributions to your IRA as reported on IRS Form 8606 (which you must file with your tax return when you make annual IRA contributions).

Important

Considerations   Because the GMIB is such a complicated product, you will need to know many additional factors before you purchase the product. Let's look at the most important of those now.

What Can Go Wrong?   Your expectations could be dashed if you don't dig deep enough into the GMIB's features and benefits. The best way to avoid surprises is to read the fine print, then re-read it, then read it again. The same warning holds true for any living benefit.

What Happens If You Die While You Own the GMIB?

Death benefits work differently based on whether you die before or after you annuitize, and contract terms vary on what happens in each case. If you die during the accumulation phase, your beneficiaries will receive a death benefit. Typically variable annuities offer optional riders (at a price) to have death benefits "stepped up," or increased, on anniversary dates.

After you annuitize, there is no death benefit unless you have chosen a term-certain period that has not expired by the time of your death. If a 70-year-old buys an annuity with a ten-year-certain period and dies before the end of the period, for example, his beneficiary will continue to receive payments until the tenth anniversary of the purchase.

WARNING!

Don't confuse your step-ups. The word "step-up" has different meanings in different contexts.

A stepped-up death benefit on a variable annuity means a bigger payment to beneficiaries upon your death. Say your policy allows you to step up from $10,000 (original purchase price) to $12,000 (value on anniversary date). Your beneficiaries would get $12,000 if you die that year.

But if you're talking estate taxes, there is no step-up for variable annuities. Whatever your beneficiaries receive at your death will not get the favorable tax treatment accorded stocks, bonds, mutual funds, and other assets that are not tax-deferred.

For example, if your child inherits $12,000 of a stock that you bought for $2,000, his cost basis will be $12,000—not $2,000—because of the stepped-up basis. If he then sells the stock at $12,000, he will owe no capital-gains tax because technically he realized no capital gain ($12,000-$12,000 = 0).

By contrast, if he is the beneficiary of your variable annuity with a $12,000 death benefit, there is no step-up in basis. The entire $12,000 will be taxed at ordinary income-tax rates—just as though he had received a paycheck for that amount.

What Should You
Read Before Buying a GMIB? The law requires the salesperson to provide you with the prospectus for the variable annuity and the GMIB rider associated with it, along with prospectuses describing the investment options offered with the product. You will also be given contracts to sign.

The lawyers who wrote the prospectus I studied for this chapter needed more than fifty pages to describe income payments, and another nine pages to disclose the charges and fees, including a description of charges for each rider and penalties for early withdrawals. I used to write prospectuses, but even with that background, it wasn't easy for me to read this prospectus. Any product that takes this many pages to describe is a very complex instrument indeed.

Before you buy a GMIB, be sure to read the prospectuses (no matter how daunting they appear), as well as any supplements (updates) to these prospectuses that you receive in the mail. You may find changes in fees or guarantees that can affect your contract. I recently read a supplement, for example, that changed a GMIB's annuitization features to make them less favorable than those in the original version.

You can also find cautions and alerts for investors at the following websites:

- www.sec.gov—the Securities and Exchange Commission (the securities regulators)
- www.finra.org—the Financial Industry Regulatory Authority (the largest nongovernmental regulator for all securities firms doing business in the United States)
- www.naic.org—the National Association of Insurance Commissioners (the insurance regulators)

Finally, you can (and should) ask your financial adviser to provide you with copies of reports prepared by independent parties on the product you are considering.

What Questions Should You Ask Before You Buy?

When you're offered a GMIB, keep in mind that you'll be speaking with a financial adviser licensed to sell securities who has to follow "suitability" standards, meaning he believes the GMIB is appropriate for you, given your financial situation and background.

Because you want to get your money's worth from the salesperson, prepare to put him through his paces. He will need to help you understand the product's features, benefits, costs, and risks, so get ready to ask a lot of questions.

Here is a list of questions to get you started.

- What will this GMIB do for me?
- How do the guarantees work?
- What conditions have to be satisfied in order for me to lock in the guarantees?
- Is there anything that can cause me to lose the guarantees in whole or in part?
- Who is behind the guarantees?
- What are the total costs I will incur when I buy this variable annuity with the GMIB rider? Specifically, what is the cost to buy, the cost to own, and the cost to sell? What are the costs of the rider based on?
- If I need to withdraw money at any time, are there any restrictions, penalties, or any other factors that I should consider?
- How will withdrawals during accumulation affect the guarantees?
- What happens when I die?
- How does annuitization work?
- How much income will I receive when I annuitize?
- What do you get paid if I buy this product? (Be prepared for the salesperson to say that you pay nothing, so it doesn't matter how much

he earns. You know it does matter, because it helps you identify potential motivation on his part to sell you a product that may be more lucrative to him. See Chapter 7 for more information on sales commissions.)

- Why do you think this product is suitable for me? (This refers to legal suitability.)
- What other products have you considered for me?
- Why is this the best income-producing option for me?
- Why are you recommending this product to me? (This goes beyond legal suitability and asks the adviser to explain all of his reasons for recommending the product.)
- How much would you recommend that I invest? What's your reasoning?

Finish up by asking for something in writing to confirm everything you've heard. Then say you'd like to think it over. Never under any circumstances should you buy this type of product until after you've had a chance to think things over.

Who Should Consider the GMIB? Who Shouldn't?

The GMIB can be a valuable investment for certain people for a small portion—30 percent, say—of their savings. The ideal GMIB buyer from my point of view is someone who has at least another ten years before he needs an income stream, is afraid of losing money between now and then, and is perhaps uncomfortable making his own investment decisions. If you are in that position, and you are not concerned about the limitations the GMIB places on you (waiting period, surrender charges, costs, unknown annuitization payment, limited investment choices), the GMIB might be a product to consider—again, for a fraction, but certainly not all, of your savings.

Hopefully, you will not buy a GMIB from a salesperson you meet at a free dinner seminar or during a quick visit to the bank. GMIBs and any other guaranteed lifetime benefits should never be purchased on a whim. Because GMIBs can be lucrative sales to the adviser, and because it's easy to feel inadequate or unprepared when dealing with so complex a product, you risk acting too quickly. Take your time. Assure yourself that the GMIB is good for you.

Julie's Overall Recommendation

Consider a GMIB only if you have a modest amount to invest, are new to investing, and worry about losing money between now and retirement (and retirement is some ways off and you have no need for the invested assets between now and then). Make sure to get answers to all your questions and understand all the drawbacks. Ask the salesperson to articulate why he is recommending the product to you, and get his reasons in writing before you buy. Then go talk to another financial adviser and repeat the process. Finally, I can't think of circumstances under which anyone would invest all (or a large portion) of their savings in a GMIB.

Guaranteed Withdrawals So You Don't Run Out of Money: The Guaranteed Minimum Withdrawal Benefit, or GMWB

One problem with managing finances in retirement is that it's difficult to grasp how much you can safely withdraw from retirement savings each year so that you don't run out of money. You can transfer to an insurance company the risk of living longer than your money lasts by purchasing an immediate annuity, as discussed in Chapter 9, or by converting a variable annuity into an income stream ("annuitizing"), as discussed in Chapter 11.

What if you could get lifelong guaranteed income without having to annuitize? That's the innovation behind the guaranteed minimum withdrawal benefit (GMWB), another type of rider attached to a variable annuity that you purchase from an insurance company.

The Nuts and Bolts of GMWBs   Let's take a look at exactly how this product works, and how it may serve your retirement-income needs.

Why Is This Product of Interest to Retirees?   Think of the GMWB as a cousin of the guaranteed minimum income benefit (GMIB). First, you receive guaranteed payments for life, but they are withdrawals instead of annuity payments. (This can be seen as a significant advantage over the GMIB and the immediate annuity because you may still have access to your money should you need it. You should be aware, however, that some companies are developing GMIBs under which the contract owner will retain access to the cash value of the contract.) Second, you have the opportunity to increase the amount of those withdrawals over time if your investments work in your favor. Finally, you have the flexibility to receive money now or in the future.

Like many retirement income products, however, it may have potentially high fees and restrictions that you must abide by in order to preserve the product's guarantees. Ultimately, if you misunderstand how a GMWB works, the product's promises may not meet your expectations. So if you are presented with the opportunity to invest in such a product, proceed with "questions."

How Does the GMWB Work?   Like the GMIB discussed in Chapter 11, the GMWB is a living-benefit rider to a variable annuity. When I use the term "GMWB," I'm referring to the variable annuity and the rider attached to it. (Some new GMWBs are incorporated into the variable annuity, so there is technically no rider.)

As with the GMIB (or any variable annuity), you invest your assets in different options (subaccounts) that the insurance company sponsoring the GMWB makes available to you. Unlike the GMIB, however, you don't annuitize a GMWB. Instead, the insurance company guarantees that you can withdraw (not annuitize) a certain percentage (typically 3 to 7 percent) of your purchase payment each year. The older you are at the time of purchase, the higher the percentage you can withdraw. You get to withdraw that amount even if the value of your investments in the variable annuity subaccounts drops below your original investment—provided you meet certain conditions outlined in the prospectus and contract for that particular GMWB.

What Does the Product Promise?   The real selling point here is that poor investment performance does not reduce the amount you can withdraw. As long as you meet specified conditions (conditions differ depending on the GMWB you buy), you will be eligible to make withdrawals that are at least equal to the amount of the purchase payments you made to the contract, even if your subaccount investments fall to zero. See below for examples of what could happen to your account in both good markets and bad.

When Do You Get Your Money?   You can begin your withdrawals right away or wait until a future date. How much you can take out seems straightforward, but it is not, due to various product features. You can trip yourself up if you don't understand the product features' twists and turns, all of which are explained in the prospectus and contract. Make sure to dig for details.

WARNING!

The conditions you have to meet in order for the guarantees to work vary from contract to contract. In the product reviewed for this chapter, to receive the full "withdrawal limit" (the maximum dollar amount you can withdraw each year) you must invest all purchase payments a certain way. If you fail to do so, your withdrawal limit could be reduced by 50 percent, even though you continue to pay the full amount charged for the GMWB rider.

Now, let's look at two illustrations to compare poor investment performance against good investment performance. Watch for the product features and limitations. (Again, I give you an example of only one product here—others will have different features.) Keep in mind that the terms I use below are product-specific (other sponsors may use different terms to explain the same features).

Illustration #1: Poor Performance   Here is an illustration in which you'll see how all the factors I've discussed affect the amount of money you can withdraw over your lifetime. As you read through this illustration, refer to Table 12-1. This illustration comes from the prospectus for the product.

Jimmy is age 65 when he buys a GMWB for $100,000, with the intention of receiving $5,000 a year for life. At age 65, the percentage Jimmy can withdraw each year (his "Withdrawal Factor") is 5 percent, and the amount available to him (his "Withdrawal Base") is $100,000, guaranteeing him $5,000 a year for life.

Jimmy chooses, as he must, the specified investment strategy in order to qualify for the guarantees promised by the GMWB, but his investments don't perform well. They lose 2 percent yearly after expenses.

But for the GMWB, Jimmy would have run out of money by the time he turned 81, as shown in Table 12-1. Fortunately, the GMWB protects him from becoming destitute; as you can see, he continues to receive $5,000 a year until his death at age 90.

In Table 12-1, watch for two factors that can change the guarantee you are expecting: "Withdrawals Taken (End of Year)," which stays stable at 5 percent of the purchase payment, and "Contract Value (End of Year)," which declines because of investment performance, withdrawals, and costs. You'll see that in the first year, Jimmy withdraws $5,000 even though the value of his annuity's investments (his "Contract Value") drops to $93,000. The Withdrawal Base ($100,000) does not change over time. But notice that the last column in the table ("Rider Death Benefit"), which is the benefit payable to Jimmy's beneficiary in the event of his death during the time he owns the product, eventually drops to zero.

Age	Contract Value (Beginning of Year)	Withdrawals Taken (End of Year)	Contract Value (End of Year)	Withdrawal Base (End of Year)	Rider Death Benefit (End of Year)
65	$100,000	$5,000	$93,000	$100,000	$95,000
66	93,000	5,000	86,140	100,000	90,000
67	86,140	5,000	79,417	100,000	85,000
68	79,417	5,000	72,829	100,000	80,000
69	72,829	5,000	66,372	100,000	75,000
70	66,372	5,000	60,045	100,000	70,000
71	60,045	5,000	53,844	100,000	65,000
72	53,844	5,000	47,767	100,000	60,000
73	47,767	5,000	41,812	100,000	55,000
74	41,812	5,000	35,945	100,000	50,000
75	35,945	5,000	30,197	100,000	45,000
76	30,197	5,000	24,563	100,000	40,000
77	24,563	5,000	19,041	100,000	35,000
78	19,041	5,000	13,631	100,000	30,000
79	13,631	5,000	8,328	100,000	25,000
80	8,328	5,000	3,131	100,000	20,000
81	3,131	5,000	0	100,000	15,000
82	0	5,000	0	100,000	10,000
83	0	5,000	0	100,000	5,000
84	0	5,000	0	100,000	0
85	0	5,000	0	100,000	0
86	0	5,000	0	100,000	0
87	0	5,000	0	100,000	0
88	0	5,000	0	100,000	0
89	0	5,000	0	100,000	0

Table 12-1 Illustration #1: Poor performance

As the table makes clear, even though Jimmy is still able to withdraw $5,000 a year until his death at age 90, his Contract Value starts dropping in the year of purchase and falls to zero after age 81. The same can be said of the Rider Death Benefit value. His heirs receive nothing if he dies after age 83. (Important: Although this particular illustration shows the death benefit going to zero, other GMWBs continue to offer death benefits to later ages.)

Illustration #2: Good Performance

Illustration #1 showed the effect of Jimmy's subaccounts' performing poorly. In the next illustration (Table 12-2), let's consider how a "reset" can help lock in profits. A reset is a more expensive option that permits Jimmy to benefit from the positive performance of his subaccounts. In this example, Jimmy chose a three-year reset. He may (but is not required to) reset his Withdrawal Base, raising it to a new, higher value. This option can come at a cost: in this case, the cost of resetting can be up to 2 percent of his Contract Value, which is charged at the time of the reset.

Again, other contracts offer different terms. This is why it's hard to make apples-to-apples comparisons of GMWBs. In contrast to the example in Illustration #1, the Withdrawal Factor is subtracted from the Contract Value (End of Year) instead of from the Withdrawal Base.

As you look at Table 12-2, watch for changes in the "Withdrawal Base" column. Jimmy resets the Withdrawal Base every three years (upon the anniversary of his contract). When he resets, he locks in the investment gains of his subaccounts, which increases the value of his Withdrawal Base—which in turn increases his available end-of-year withdrawals. Remember, Jimmy's guaranteed Withdrawal Rate is 5 percent of the previous year's Contract Value (End of Year). So looking at age 66, we see that the previous Contract Value (End of Year) is $103,000, and a 5 percent withdrawal of $103,000 is $5,150.

But at a certain point, the death benefit goes to zero, which means that Jimmy's heirs will not receive anything if Jimmy dies after the age of 80, in this case.

Age	Contract Value (Beginning of Year)	Withdrawals Taken (End of Year)	Contract Value (End of Year)	Withdrawal Base (End of Year)	Rider Death Benefit (End of Year)
65	$100,000	5,000	$103,000	$100,000	$95,000
66	103,000	5,150	106,090	100,000	89,850
67	106,090	5,305	109,273	100,000	84,546
68	109,273	5,464	112,551	109,273	79,082
69	112,551	5,628	115,927	109,273	73,454
70	115,927	5,796	119,405	109,273	67,658
71	119,405	5,970	122,987	119,405	61,688
72	122,987	6,149	126,677	119,405	55,538
73	126,677	6,334	130,477	119,405	49,204
74	130,477	6,524	134,392	130,477	42,681
75	134,392	6,720	138,423	130,477	35,961
76	138,423	6,921	142,576	130,477	29,040
77	142,576	7,129	146,853	142,576	21,911
78	146,853	7,343	151,259	142,576	14,568
79	151,259	7,563	155,797	142,576	7,005
80	155,797	7,790	160,471	155,797	0
81	160,471	8,024	165,285	155,797	0
82	165,285	8,264	170,243	155,797	0
83	170,243	8,512	175,351	170,243	0
84	175,351	8,768	180,611	170,243	0
85	180,611	9,031	186,030	170,243	0
86	186,030	9,301	191,610	186,030	0
87	191,610	9,581	197,359	186,030	0
88	197,359	9,868	203,280	186,030	0
89	203,280	10,164	209,378	203,280	0

Table 12-2 Illustration #2: Good performance (reset every 3 years)

How Is the

Product Sold? Financial advisers will present GMWBs to you by emphasizing their benefits and showing you illustrations, marketing literature, and a prospectus. If you are interested in the product, ask lots of questions so that you understand the potential benefits, limitations, and risks of going forward. As with any retirement-income investment, do not make a quick decision. Study the prospectus and sample contract, and sleep on your decision. Don't forget to review the questions at the end of this chapter.

How Easy

Is the Sale? Retirees can be convinced by the promises the product offers, but a careful retiree will be wary. Any product that promises to be the solution to all of a retiree's problems deserves to be well understood. Kick the tires. Ask hard questions.

What Does the Salesperson Make

If You Buy the GMWB? Commissions vary with each product. With the product we are reviewing here, the commission payable to the salesperson at the time of purchase is 11 percent of the initial purchase payment. As with other variable annuities, this payment does not reduce your investment. Although the adviser's commission is paid by the sponsor of the annuity, it comes from you indirectly through ongoing fees and charges embedded in the product. To give this arrangement some context, review Chapter 11, on GMIBs, and Chapter 7, on advisers, for a more complete discussion of how salespeople are paid.

A vendor who sells directly to the consumer may be in a position to offer lower-cost products. That's because such "direct sellers," as they are called, have no need to compensate financial advisers acting as middlemen.

Julie's Rating:
How Motivated Is Your Salesperson?
Eager to Sign You Up. Let's face it. The commission a salesperson makes

on a GMWB could be a motivator, especially if you have a lot of money to invest.

How Easy Is the Product to Understand?

The GMWB seems simple enough in concept. But, as we saw in the last chapter, we need to look deeper. When it comes to understanding how the withdrawal feature works, this is what a sample prospectus says:

> While the rider is designed to provide lifetime withdrawal benefits and the return of purchase payments, these benefits are guaranteed only to the extent that you comply with the limits, conditions and restrictions set forth in the contract [emphasis added]. There can be no assurance that you will receive more than a return of purchase payments.

Let's pause here. Note the reference to "limits, conditions and restrictions set forth in the contract." Be sure to read the contract terms. If you don't, and you find out later that you don't qualify for the guarantee—which is, after all, your motivation to buy the product—your goals may not be met.

Before you invest any of your retirement savings, make sure you know how the product you are buying works. The conditions vary from one product to the next.

The bottom line is that you have to understand enough of the contract's fine print to be able to make an informed decision about the benefits offered by the GMWB (or any living benefit). To fully evaluate the product, you need to understand the value of the guarantee compared with its cost. That's why I conclude that these products are complicated, and that puts the consumer at a distinct disadvantage in assessing whether this product is a good deal for your situation.

Julie's Rating for Complexity

For Ph.D.s. To understand the value of the product and, of course, its drawbacks, you have to do a lot of reading, analyzing, and comparison shopping—not just with other GMWBs, but with other retirement-income products as well. Given the way these products are structured, though, that may not be easy. Most important, you have to understand the circumstances under which your expectations for guaranteed payments will not be met. This is true even with newer GMWBs, some of which have fewer moving parts.

How Risky
Is the Product?
How do you assess the risks of the GMWB? Pay attention to several factors:

The withdrawal factor is guaranteed at a certain percentage, but the guarantee depends on the continuing ability of the insurer to make payments for as long as you live.

Whether or not you achieve returns above the guaranteed amount is another matter, which you will need to assess by studying the particular product you are considering.

Critics question whether you can make any headway, considering the potential costs associated with the product—a concept called "fee drag." That is, the potential upside can be jeopardized because the internal costs of the product are higher than those of other, nonguaranteed products. (See "Costs and Taxes," below.)

Another risk to consider is the effect of taking additional withdrawals above the guaranteed limit, should you need to do so. Withdrawing more than your guaranteed limit can cause a permanent change in how your yearly Withdrawal Benefit is calculated. (In the prospectus I reviewed, the Withdrawal Benefit is normally calculated on either the Contract Value or the Withdrawal Base, using the higher of the two numbers. However, withdrawing more than the guaranteed limit can result in the permanent use of the lower of the two numbers to calculate the benefit.)

Finally, be aware that regulators review whether insurance companies issuing these guarantees will be able to live up to them—specifically, whether the insurers have adequate reserves, have priced benefits properly, and have proper risk management in place.

How Good
Is the Guarantee?   All guarantees are based on the claims-paying ability of the insurance company making the promise. Be sure you check out the company's financial stability (discussed in Chapter 8) before considering this product.

As with other living benefits, it's important to understand the GMWB's limitations and conditions, especially when the GMWB permits guaranteed payments to be lowered or terminated if certain conditions are not met. But, you may protest, "By definition, you cannot lower or terminate a guaranteed payment." Not so. That would be an "unconditional guarantee," which I have yet to see in any financial product. When you're dealing with guarantees of any sort, assume that all guarantees are conditional. If you don't meet the conditions, you don't get the guarantee.

Julie's Rating for Safety
Think Twice. The biggest risk of a GMWB lies in not understanding what you are getting. Avoid GMWBs if you can't explain the benefits and drawbacks of a GMWB to a friend.

Costs and Taxes
Because the GMWB rider is built on a variable-annuity product, you need to understand the annuity's cost structure. (See Chapter 11 for the costs to buy, own, and sell variable annuities.) Typically, the sales literature for this type of rider does not mention all the fees that apply—only the cost of the rider.

The GMWB rider in this particular example is a little more expensive (0.6 percent of Contract Value per year) than the GMIB rider (0.5 percent) discussed in the last chapter. If the GMWB is purchased for a couple, the rider is more costly (0.85 percent). But again, that's only a fraction of the total cost, which is as high as 4 percent per year for this particular product. You'll find these costs in the prospectus and the contract.

Once you begin to receive withdrawal payments from the GMWB, your payments will be taxed on each dollar above your basis (original investment) at ordinary income-tax rates. For example, if your effective income-tax rate is 25 percent, your $5,000 withdrawal will be worth $3,750 after taxes, assuming a zero cost basis. For more information on taxes, refer to Chapter 11.

Julie's Rating for Value

Hard to Judge. Given that GMWBs are not all alike, you'll have a hard time weighing the costs and benefits of the particular GMWB you are considering. Comparison shop by getting proposals from more than one adviser.

Important
Considerations
Here are some considerations you should take into account when weighing the pros and cons of a GMWB.

What Can
Go Wrong?
As with a GMIB, a GMWB could easily surprise you some day in the future if you don't fully understand the terms and features of the one you are buying. This product demands homework and comparison shopping.

What Happens If You Die
While You Own a GMWB?
The death benefit I discuss above (Tables 12-1 and 12-2) is payable to your beneficiary. In the example I use for this chapter, if your beneficiary is your spouse, he has the option of continuing the contract as the new owner. If the beneficiary is not your spouse, the death benefit will be payable to the designated beneficiary. If you live beyond a certain age (again, see Tables 12-1 and 12-2 for examples), the death benefit dissipates and the beneficiary gets nothing.

What Should You Read
Before Buying a GMWB?   You must read the contract, the riders, and the prospectus.

What Questions Should You Ask
Before You Buy?   If an adviser recommends a GMWB to you, that doesn't mean you should buy it. Remember from Chapter 7 that a sales-person licensed to sell a GMWB (Series 6 or 7 plus an insurance license) needs to believe that the GMWB is suitable for you when you buy the product.

Understand what you are getting, the risks you are taking, and what you will receive in return.

Here is a list of questions to get you started.
- Why are you recommending this product to me?
- What will this product do for me?
- What do I have to do to receive these benefits?
- Is there anything that I do that can void, lessen, or lose these benefits?
- How is my money invested and at what risk level?
- How much will this product cost me?
- When can I get my money?
- What happens when I die?
- What do you get paid if I buy this product?
- What other products have you considered for me?
- Why do you think this product is suitable for me?

As with other retirement-income products, ask for something in writing to confirm everything you've heard. Then say you'd like to think it over.

Buyer "Aware"
Because these products are fairly new, the sales literature may show an illustration that does not reflect actual performance. If you see the word

"hypothetical," be alert. Do not buy a product—any product—based soley on an illustration or a glossy brochure.

Who Should Consider the GMWB?
Who Shouldn't?   The promise of guaranteed withdrawals that you cannot outlive may be appealing to people who are unsure of how to invest for themselves. It may also be appealing to people who are approaching retirement with a large 401(k) or other company retirement plan, but no investment experience. These individuals are buying peace of mind, but the real question is whether that feeling is deserved. One can know the answer with certainty only in hindsight, and then it can be too late to change course.

Julie's Overall Recommendation
Consider, but proceed with caution: make sure you do some comparison shopping.   Avoid if you are not willing to do the work necessary to fully understand the drawbacks of the particular GMWB you are looking at.

If you can do that, then I recommend the following:
Under no circumstances should you invest all of your money in this product (or any other).
Do not buy this product (or any other) based on a single sales presentation.
Take care to understand how you can withdraw money, for how long, and if there is anything you or anyone else could do that would interrupt, diminish, or stop the withdrawals.
Consider other retirement-income alternatives and compare them.
Because it is easy to misunderstand what you are getting, take a friend with you when you talk to the adviser. Ask lots of questions. Take notes.
Consider writing a letter to the adviser telling him what you understand you are getting, and ask for a written response before you make a purchase. He has a legal duty to ensure that his recommendation is suitable

for you, given your financial circumstances and goals. If something is amiss, the adviser can correct the misunderstanding before you buy. If he doesn't, you have a record of his response that you can use to lodge a claim against him if promises don't pan out. If the promises are too good to be true, be sure to get a written response from your financial adviser's compliance officer as well.

13

Certificates of Deposit: Not All CDs Are Created Equal

As children, we first learned about earning interest by opening a savings account at a bank. Because of these childhood experiences, banks are familiar ground for most people. So it's not surprising that many retirees turn to savings deposits, such as certificates of deposit (CDs), when they are ready to retire. CDs usually pay slightly higher interest than savings accounts because you have to leave your money on deposit at the bank for a specified length of time, until the CD "matures."

Why else do people choose CDs in retirement? They do so because CDs are easy to understand and offer safety. If the bank goes out of business, your deposit is safe because of FDIC insurance. These factors make CDs suitable for retirees with little or no investment experience; in fact, of all the financial products a retiree can use for income, the traditional CD is perhaps the only one that retirees seek out on their own initiative—normally without the help of a financial adviser.

Longer-term CDs usually offer potentially higher yields, and some retirees stagger maturities to benefit from those higher rates. But CDs offer relatively low income compared with other investments, and they are not the best choice for retirees with substantial income needs. Nor are CDs good inflation hedges.

Today's CDs are not the plain-vanilla bank CDs you may remember from your youth. This chapter examines these look-alikes, which are sold by certain financial advisers, so you can understand your options and avoid surprises. Because I compare different types of CDs here, this chapter departs somewhat from the question format in the prior four chapters. However, it does provide you with an overall recommendation for each type of CD that is discussed.

Hint: The Federal Deposit Insurance Corporation (FDIC) insures CDs—up to FDIC limits. You are protected for up to $250,000 (per depositor per institution) if the bank holding your deposit goes out of business. Additionally, the FDIC insures bank deposits held in IRA accounts up to $250,000.

WARNING!

The FDIC protects you only against bank failures, not losses of any sort, including those due to penalties or having to liquidate a CD before maturity. For more information about federal deposit insurance, visit the Federal Deposit Insurance Corporation's website (www.fdic.gov) and read its publication *Your Insured Deposit*. Call the FDIC's Consumer Information Center (877-275-3342) to find out whether a specific bank is FDIC-insured.

How Do Traditional CDs Work?

When you deposit money in your bank account in the form of a CD, you are in effect lending money to the bank in exchange for a fixed interest rate for the term of the CD. For example, you might deposit $10,000 in a CD that pays you a fixed percentage per year for five years. Interest might accrue to you monthly, quarterly, semiannually, or yearly.

You can get your money back before the CD matures, but you'll pay a penalty for early withdrawal. For example, a five-year CD might have a penalty of twelve months of interest. The penalty on a one-year CD might be six months of interest. Longer-maturity CDs (ten years or longer) can have substantial penalties. Penalties are not standard among banks and institutions—you have to ask.

When you shop for interest rates, you must be specific. To get an apples-to-apples comparison of the rate you will actually earn, you need to ask the bank for the annual percentage yield (APY), not the annual percentage return (APR). APY takes into account compounding, which is basically interest on interest. APR does not.

Julie's Recommendation for Traditional CDs

Consider. The traditional CD can have a place in the portfolio of a retiree who wants safety, backed by FDIC insurance. People who buy CDs sometimes "ladder" them, meaning they buy CDs with different maturities. This way, they can cash out CDs that mature earlier for current spending needs and hold on to those that mature later.

CD Look-Alikes

The CD we have been talking about, which I will call the "traditional CD," is simple to understand and safe. But some CDs aren't what they seem—and that is raising regulators' concerns. Time and time again, regulators have warned retirees to make sure they ask questions about what they are really buying.

Consider the following types of CD offers and how they differ from

A Closer Look:

A Matter of Interest: Know Your APY

Watch for APY: Let's say you have a $10,000 CD that accrues interest annually (let's use 5 percent, even though rates are lower in 2017) and compounds only once per year. In this scenario, the APY is 5 percent. You earn $500 interest in a year.

However, if interest compounds semiannually (twice a year), after the first six months, you accrue $250 in interest (5 percent of $10,000, divided by two, for half a year). At the end of the year, you'll receive $256.25 (5 percent of $10,250). So you earned a total of $506.25 in interest ($250 plus $256.25)—making the effective rate of interest (the APY) 5.063 percent.

But what if interest compounds daily? The APY will be even higher, 5.127 percent, earning you interest of $512.71 in the first year.

The Federal Truth in Savings Act requires disclosure of the APY, as well as the CD's maturity date and any applicable minimum deposits, penalties, or "call" features. A call feature allows the bank to pay your deposit back to you early, usually with interest accruing to that date. Why would the bank want to pay you earlier than the maturity date? If your CD's interest rate is higher than current interest rates, your bank may find it more profitable to pay newer depositors lower rates than the one it is paying you.

So, to summarize: in comparing traditional CDs, ask about penalties for early withdrawal, as well as the timing of interest payments (are they made monthly, quarterly, semiannually, annually, or at the maturity date of the CD?). To help you, I provide a questionnaire at the end of this chapter to use when you shop for a CD.

By the way, when your CD matures, don't be surprised if the bank teller suggests you see the investment representative sitting in the bank lobby. Banks may pay tellers a cash bonus for sending you to a salesperson who can turn your cash into a commissioned product sale.

the traditional CD discussed above. In each case, there is no assurance that you will get your principal back if you need your money before your CD matures. Not only that, but the penalties for early withdrawal may be more severe than those for traditional CDs. In some cases, the CD may be illiquid—meaning you may not be able to cash it in when you wish.

Callable CDs

Callable CDs are being marketed through newspaper ads, telephone solicitations, and direct mail. Regulators have warned that retirees are being misled into buying CDs with up to thirty-year maturities that can be "called away" by the issuer before the CD's maturity date.

For example, a "two-year callable CD" may be called by the bank after two years, even if the CD has twenty-eight more years before it reaches maturity. What's wrong with that, you might ask?

A bank won't call a CD unless interest rates decline, which leaves you searching for another source of income in a lower-interest-rate environment. You won't be able to find a replacement at the same interest rate unless you're willing to invest in higher-risk instruments—not a good idea for retirees. (Chapter 16, on investing, talks about the relationship between risk and reward. For now, be aware that a higher return usually means more risk.)

Hint: If a low-risk CD is called away, that usually means interest rates declined after you bought your CD. You won't be able to find another low-risk CD to replace the CD at the same interest rate.

Julie's Recommendation for Callable CDs

Consider, as long as you know that a callable CD can be called away from you. This can leave you scrambling for substitutes, possibly at a lower interest rate.

Step-Up or Step-Down CDs   The interest on CDs with a "step-up" or a "step-down" is fixed for a period of time, usually one year. A CD with a "step-up" is sold at a lower interest rate to begin with, but the rate increases after the fixed period. A CD with a "step-down" pays a higher rate of interest, but the interest decreases after the fixed period. My view of step-ups or step-downs? I don't like unknowns. It's better to buy a fixed-term CD with a known rate.

Julie's Recommendation for Step CDs
Avoid, unless you can come up with a very good reason to buy a product with uncertainty built into it.

Brokered CDs
As you know, banks sell CDs. You need to be aware that CDs are also sold by brokerage firms—but these CDs are different.

A brokerage firm can arrange a higher rate on a large CD, then offer a fractional interest of the CD as a "brokered CD" to its customers. When the brokerage firm makes the sale, it will charge a "concession," which is essentially a commission.

Many people think that if they buy a CD from a brokerage firm (a "brokered" CD), they can get all their money back at any time. Not necessarily so. The brokerage firm is not obligated to buy back the CD from you for your purchase price. If you want to liquidate (cash in) your brokered CD before maturity, the brokerage firm will attempt to sell it on the "secondary market," meaning it will try to find someone who wants to buy your CD from you. Most CD buyers, however, are more interested in new issues sold on the "primary market" than those sold on the secondary market, so there are fewer buyers. As a result, when you sell you may get substantially less than you paid.

As the SEC points out, "Don't be embarrassed if you invested in a long-term, brokered CD in the mistaken belief that it was a shorter-term instrument—you are not alone." If you have been actually misled about terms, do complain to the broker and the branch manager, and write to the SEC (SEC, 100 F Street NE, Washington, D.C. 20549-5990).

WARNING!

When you buy a CD that is FDIC-insured, you need to be sure that your coverage isn't limited because of other deposit accounts you may have at the same bank. Also find out if the brokered CDs are carried only on the books of the CD broker, or whether they are registered with the Depository Trust & Clearing Corporation (DTCC) as "master CDs." Because master CDs enable the brokerage firm to clear and settle buy-and-sell transactions more easily, they are potentially safer than those not registered with the DTCC should a CD broker become insolvent.

Julie's Recommendation for Brokered CDs

Proceed with Caution. Be sure you understand the terms of the CD. You may not get all your money back if you need to cash in the CD before its maturity.

Variable Interest Rates and Index Participation CDs

You may not realize that some CD interest rates are variable, as opposed to fixed. You can buy a CD that offers returns linked to an index (the consumer price index or the S&P 500 Index, for example), or to a basket of securities (equity-linked CDs).

Purchasers of such CDs give up a portion of the upside, or potential for gain, in exchange for principal protection. The upside is limited with either a cap, a ceiling, or a "participation rate." For example, if the participation rate is 70 percent and the S&P 500 goes up 10 percent, your return is 7 percent.

There is some debate about how effective equity-linked CDs can be in delivering on their promises; an even bigger question is how the investor can adequately evaluate and compare one equity-linked CD with another. Faced with so many variables—time to maturity, participation rates, market indexes, guaranteed coupon (interest) rates, and minimum deposits—how does one begin to make reasonable comparisons?

You can't. Here's why.

Equity-linked CDs are "structured products" because they are constructed using derivatives, which are financial instruments derived from others; for example, a stock option derives from a stock. You would need a graduate-level course in financial engineering to fully understand whether an equity-linked CD being recommended to you is a good deal. So unless you plan on signing up for such a course, it's probably best to avoid this product.

A Closer Look:

"Do Equity-Linked CDs Have Equity-Like Returns?"

When asked this question, some academics respond: "The simple answer is 'no'." They conclude that equity-linked CDs generally offer returns no higher than a five-year U.S. Treasury Note. You can do better by constructing your own do-it-yourself ("synthetic") equity-linked CD. Here's how: buy zero-coupon bonds and stock-index call options. Zero-coupon bonds don't pay interest—instead, they are purchased at a discount and the interest is accrued. A stock-index call option is a right to buy the underlying stock index at a certain price before the expiration date.

Julie's Recommendation for Equity-Linked CDs
Avoid. Why buy a product that even the experts can't figure out?

Your CD Checklist
If you are approaching retirement or are already retired, be aware that when a bank or financial adviser offers you a "CD," you must be alert. You will need to know more to see whether this product is suitable for you. How can you know? By making sure it meets your needs, after fully understanding how the product works.

Use this checklist (adapted with permission from the NASAA's "Callable CD Checklist") to take notes when speaking with your banker, salesperson, or adviser about CDs. Be sure to record details of the recommendations you receive and the instructions you give. Make copies of this form to have handy, and keep all notes in your files. (Do not accept any unsolicited phone calls from salespeople.)

Don't go chasing higher interest rate CDs in retirement. Here's why: if you do, you're likely to come across a financial instrument that is not the traditional, safe CD. You might buy a look-alike that doesn't deliver on the promise of higher interest—or loses you money. Safety should come first in retirement.

The CD checklist appears on the following pages.

CD CHECKLIST

Getting Information

Date: _____   Time: _____

Salesperson's name: _____   Phone: _____

Organization: _____   Phone: _____

Address: _____

About the Salesperson

Why did you contact this salesperson?

❏ He/she is my financial adviser

❏ I responded to an ad in the paper (attach ad)

❏ Other _____

About the Bank & FDIC Insurance

Who is the issuer of the CD? _____

❏ I checked with the FDIC to make sure the issuer was FDIC-insured by calling 1-877-275-3342 or checking online with FDIC's "Bank Find" at http://www3.fdic.gov/idasp/main.asp.

❏ I ran the EDIE estimator (https://www.fdic.gov/EDIE/index.html) to make sure this CD will be covered by FDIC insurance in my particular case.

About the CD

Dollar Amount of Intended Purchase: $ _____

Interest (APY): _____   ❏ Fixed ❏ Variable

Payments: ❏ Monthly ❏ Quarterly ❏ Yearly

Maturity Date: _____   Penalties: _____

Risks: _____

Type of CD:

❑ Traditional Bank CD

❑ Callable CD

❑ Step-up CD

❑ Equity-linked CD

❑ Brokered CD

❑ Step-down CD

❑ Other _____

About Your Needs

What is your objective in buying this CD?

_____

When do you need your money back? _____

How much will you get if you hold the CD to maturity? _____

What happens if you have to surrender (or sell) the CD before it matures?

_____

Why did the salesperson recommend this particular CD to you?

_____

Does it meet your objectives?

_____

CHAPTER 14

Cashing Out of Your Home

Consider this scenario: you are fast approaching retirement and haven't saved enough to support yourself, but you do own your home. There are several ways to use the equity in your home to generate retirement income.

You can scale down and either rent or purchase a smaller, less expensive home, freeing up cash that you can use to create retirement in-come. Or you can stay in your home and arrange a reverse mortgage.

Reverse mortgages may be an option for retirees who find themselves needing more money than they had anticipated. A reverse mortgage allows you to use the equity in your house to fund some of your retirement expenses.

As with many of the financial products discussed in earlier chapters, you should be aware that there are risks and costs to a reverse mortgage. It's essential that you consider these before committing yourself to the arrangement.

Before we begin, I'd like to thank the subject matter experts at the U.S. Department of Housing and Urban Development (HUD) for their help with this chapter.

What Does a Reverse Mortgage Offer?

As with a typical mortgage (a "forward mortgage"), you must meet a number of requirements to qualify for a reverse mortgage. In 2015, the U.S. Department of Housing and Urban Development tightened lending criteria for the reverse mortgages it insures. Borrowers must be 62 years of age or older, own their property outright or have paid down a considerable amount, and occupy their property as a principal residence. Additionally, you must not be delinquent on any federal debt, have financial resources to continue to make timely payments of ongoing property charges, and participate in an information session given by a HUD-approved HECM counselor. Your property must also meet certain requirements, and your income, assets, living expenses, and credit history will all factor into your ability to qualify for a reverse mortgage. Requirements will vary for reverse mortgages not insured by HUD.

Lenders will tell you that you don't have to pay the bank back as long as you live in the house, maintain it, insure it, and pay its real-estate taxes. (As you will see shortly, the reality is otherwise.)

The economics of this deal can stump even the most astute mathematician. Just how can the promise of lifetime payments be honored when it is based on the value of an asset that can appreciate, depreciate, or incinerate?

A reasonable person would ask if there is a catch of some sort. Where does the bank get the money to pay you as long as you live in your home? What if you live so long that the monthly payments to you eventually exceed your home's value? Won't the bank evict you if your mortgage debt outgrows the value of the house? If not, does the bank lose money on the loan it made to you and others who outlive their life expectancies? Which brings us back to our first question: where does the money come from to pay you? Are your heirs responsible if your house decreases in value or your mortgage debt grows beyond the value of the house because you live longer than expected?

These are all good questions—the type you should be asking when reviewing a lifetime offer of any sort.

Here are the answers.

Home Equity Conversion Mortgages (HECMs)

A government program insures certain reverse mortgages—those called HECMs, or Home Equity Conversion Mortgages. HECMs are insured by the Federal Housing Administration (FHA), a branch of the U.S. Department of Housing and Urban Development (HUD).

Hint: The common usage among lenders and counselors in this market is to say "a HECM," which they pronounce "hek um."

The linchpin of the HECM program is insurance that you are obligated to purchase as a condition of the loan. This insurance, paid by each borrower in the form of a "mortgage insurance premium" (MIP), protects you by funding promised payments to you if the lender is unable to make a loan advance to you. It also guarantees your right to stay in your house for life. The MIP shields the lender as well: it protects the lender from losses should the loan balance be greater than the proceeds from the sale of your home.

The cost of the MIP is steep: a onetime upfront fee of either 0.50 percent or 2.50 percent, based on the disbursements to the borrower, or disbursements made on their behalf, during the first 12-month disbursement period. The borrower will pay 0.5 percent of the maximum claim amount

(MCA) when the initial disbursement limit or borrower's advance is 60 percent or less of the principal limit. The borrower will pay 2.5 percent of the MCA when the initial disbursement limit or borrower's advance is greater than 60 percent of the principal limit. A monthly fee of 0.104167 percent (which equals 1.25 percent on an annual basis) is also charged on the mortgage balance.

Let's look at an example. Keep in mind that your mortgage balance increases every time you borrow—that is, every time you receive a monthly or periodic payment from the bank. (The amount of interest and MIP are added to the balance, in addition to advances made to the borrowers.) That's why this product is called a "reverse" mortgage: you are not paying a mortgage down, you are increasing it.

Assume your home is worth $500,000 and your principal limit is $250,000. You could borrow $150,000 (60% of your principal limit). In this case, your one-time up front MIP will be $2,500 or 0.5 percent of $500,000. Had you drawn more than $150,000 in the first 12 months in this example, your initial MIP would have been $12,500 or 2.5 percent of $500,000. Your monthly MIP (0.104167 percent per month) will be charged against your total loan. So in the first year of the loan, your total monthly MIPs would be $1,875 ($156.25 monthly).

A Closer Look

The HECM loan is a "nonrecourse" loan, meaning neither you nor your heirs can be held personally liable for the loan beyond the value of your house, so long as it is sold to repay the loan. If the house is not sold and you or your estate repays the loan, the full amount of the loan must be repaid—even if it is greater than your house's value.

WARNING!

You can default on your reverse mortgage during your lifetime if you violate any of its conditions. The home must be your principal residence. Generally, you may not sell the home or give it to your children or a trust; that you must continue to live in and maintain the home; and that you must pay real-estate taxes and home insurance when due. The loan becomes immediately due and payable if you default. Loan defaults are covered on pages 194-197. There are exceptions: For example, you could transfer title to an eligible living trust without triggering a default.

Non-HECM Loans

HECM is not the only game in town. Other types of reverse mortgages are available through other lenders. Some are insured; others are not. (The latter are known as uninsured private reverse mortgages, or "proprietary" reverse mortgages.) Generally, people choose a non-HECM mortgage if the HECM doesn't meet their needs—if, for example, one's home is worth substantially more than the HECM limit of $636,150. A HECM is usually the first choice for the simple reason that HECM loans are normally less costly.

How Much

Can You Borrow? That's the big question. Just how much money can you expect to borrow through a reverse mortgage? As you might imagine, lenders look at several factors, including the age of the youngest borrower (who must be 62 or older), the type of reverse mortgage you select, the current value of your home (subtract liens and mortgages), the location of your home, and current interest rates. The older you are and the more equity your house has accumulated, the more the lender will allow you to borrow. If the reverse mortgage is a HECM loan, these factors go into figuring your "maximum claim amount," which is the total amount of equity against which you can borrow.

To get an idea of how much you might be able to borrow under a HECM, use a free calculator online or download HUD's reverse mortgage calculator at

https://portal.hud.gov/hudportal/HUD?src=iprogramoffices/housing/sfh/
hecm.

Let's go through an example together. (If you try to reconstruct this
example online, you'll likely see different results, reflecting changing
interest rates.)

Mary has a home in Cuyahoga County, Ohio, valued at $200,000.
Since she has no mortgage, her equity is $200,000. She is single and age
62 in January 2017. Using the AARP calculator, Mary learns that she can
expect to receive a monthly loan advance of $546 for as long as she lives
in her home. Alternatively, she can set up the reverse mortgage as a line of
credit, with a starting balance of approximately $105,000. Mary can then
draw upon this LOC if and as she needs it, but leave it untapped when
she does not. While other payment options are available, most adjustable
rate reverse mortgage borrowers choose the line of credit option, which is
not available for fixed rate HECMs. It provides more flexibility to pay for
a variety of unanticipated financial needs in the future.

John, who lives down the street from Mary, likewise has a home that is
appraised at $200,000, but because he is older—82—he could receive $962
a month for as long as he lives in the home, or set up the reverse mortgage as
a line of credit with a starting balance of approximately $135,000.

If your home is worth more than $636,150, the maximum value limit
that goes into the formula to determine how much you can borrow in
most of the U.S. is $636,150. If your home is worth a lot more than the
HUD limit, you may be able to borrow a higher amount via a proprietary
reverse mortgage. Be sure you understand all costs, however; they could be
higher than those of a HECM. At this time, there are very few proprietary
reverse-mortgage loans.

The amount you can borrow is based on the value of your home and
your age, expressed as your "principal limit factor." This factor usually
ranges from 45 to 85 percent—the older you are, the higher the percentage. Again, the older you are, the higher the amount. The bank uses
HECM software to calculate the monthly or periodic payment amount,
based on actuarial assumptions for longevity.

You can ask for money to be advanced to you monthly, all at once in a lump sum, or in the form of a reverse-mortgage credit line, letting you borrow when and as you need to. You can also arrange for a combination of these options. The credit line is by far the most popular payment plan selected by HECM borrowers.

How Much Will the Loan Cost?

The lender may say to you, "We're paying you for as long as you remain in your home. We'll even lend you the money to pay most of the closing costs and fees." (The loan needs to be "closed" even though you own the house.) So, should you be concerned about costs?

That statement may have merit on the surface, but it contains a deep-seated flaw: reverse mortgages are expensive.

The borrower is paying for the advantage of having a non-recourse loan, which does not have to be currently repaid.

During the life of the loan, interest accrues; interest is not paid incrementally and directly by the borrower, but rather it is added to the outstanding loan balance, as is the recurring MIP.

As to closing costs and fees, a lender may absorb them (but be sure to ask), thereby eliminating or significantly reducing their impact on available funds. Servicing fees, when charged, are accounted for in the origination process by establishment of a set-aside account.

All of these factors can affect you personally if the loan becomes due during your lifetime because of a default, causing your equity to be lower or even nonexistent. (See "Loan Defaults: A High Price to Pay," page 197.) If you stay in the house, costs directly affect your heirs. When the loan becomes due after your death, depending on circumstances there may be little or nothing left for your heirs once they pay off the loan.

Here's what you can expect in terms of upfront closing costs and fees on a $500,000 HECM loan.

Upfront mortgage insurance premium (MIP) of $2,500 (½ percent) or $12,500 (2.5 percent) of the loan amount, depending on the disbursements to the borrower.

Origination fee paid to the lender of 2 percent for the first $200,000 and
1 percent of the annual in excess of $200,000 (origination fees cannot
exceed $6,000)

Other closing costs, such as legal and recording fees, that vary by state but
generally range from $2,000 to $5,000

The total approximate loan costs range from $7,000 to $13,500, but
could be substantially higher. You will also pay the monthly MIP discussed
earlier in this chapter plus monthly servicing fees, which can be as much as
$35 per month for the life of the loan.

Although the MIP is nonnegotiable, HECM lenders can negotiate the
amount they charge for origination and servicing fees. Other variable costs
include the appraisal fee and the closing costs for title insurance and attor-
neys' fees. It therefore pays to ask about all fees when considering any type
of reverse mortgage; some may be negotiable.

Hint: One reliable way to compare costs and fees is to ask for a TALC statement, which
stands for "total annual loan cost," as required by the Truth-in-Lending Act. The TALC shows
the projected annual average cost of a reverse mortgage, including all itemized fees. To learn
more, visit www.reverse.org/talctuto.htm. Also ask for an "amortization schedule," which
shows you a projection of how much your home might be worth (assuming certain appreciation rates) and how much you could owe on your reverse mortgage loan over time.

Can the Loan Default? When the loan becomes due, three factors—
loan advances, loan costs, and leftover equity—will determine what
remains for you or for your heirs after the lender is paid off.

1) Loan advances are the amounts that were paid to you by the lender.

2) Loan costs include ongoing interest accruing on advances, monthly servicing fees, upfront and monthly MIP charges, origination fees, and closing
costs (unless you paid those costs out of your own pocket at the time of the
closing). Most HECM loans have variable interest rates, not fixed. Lenders
who offer fixed-rate HECMs require that you take all of your available loan
funds as a single lump sum of cash at closing. But unless you happen to need

all of that money to spend right now, that's a sure formula for escalating your loan costs because you are charged interest on the total lump sum.

Together, your loan advances and costs make up the total amount you owe (the lender refers to this as your "outstanding balance").

3) Leftover equity: As time goes on, the outstanding balance grows as advances are paid out to you and interest and costs accrue. Home equity declines (assuming your home does not appreciate). When it's time to pay off the loan, all of the advances and costs are deducted from the proceeds of the sale of the house to find your leftover equity; this is what you (or your heirs) have left over after paying off the loan. The maximum pay-off amount is 95 percent of appraised value if the loan is in default.

What Will Your Heirs

Receive? Let's return to our earlier example of Mary, who received a HECM loan at age 62. Assume Mary lives in her home until she dies at the age of 82. Her heirs sell her home for $400,000 and use that money to pay off the reverse mortgage balance in full.

How much will her heirs receive? Over twenty years, Mary borrowed a total of $131,040 ($546 a month for twenty years). Servicing costs came to $30 a month, or $7,200. Her initial loan fees, which she borrowed at the time she received the loan, came to $7,223.

In this example, the total due, including advances, interest of $58,356 (assuming current rates never rise), and costs, comes to approximately $211,960, which Mary's heirs must repay when the house is sold, leaving them $188,040 ($400,000 minus $211,960).

There is no capital-gains tax on the sale of the home because the heirs receive a "stepped-up" basis at the date-of-death value of $400,000. (In other words, the heirs' cost basis is $400,000—the value of Mary's home at the date of her death, not Mary's original purchase price of the home.) Depending on the value of Mary's total assets, including her house (less the amount paid to the bank), an estate tax may be due. For a discussion of estate taxes, see Chapter 17.

Note: When you are considering whether your estate might be subject to estate taxes, be sure to check with your lawyer for current exemptions.

Hint: The reverse mortgage becomes due and payable when the last surviving borrower no longer lives in the home.

Under What Conditions Can the Loan Default?

If you get a reverse mortgage, you don't want to trigger a default. A default that is not cured on a timely basis may cause the loan to become due and payable. Rarely do reverse-mortgage sales agents discuss the conditions that could prompt such a calamity. You'll have to read the loan documents carefully to uncover the conditions of default for the loan you are considering. Typically, any one of the following can trigger a default:

- You declare bankruptcy
- You fail to pay homeowners' insurance when due
- You fail to pay property taxes when due
- You abandon your home
- You fail to keep your home in good repair
- You give away your home without retaining a legal right of use and occupancy.
- You commit fraud or misrepresentation in the loan application
- A government agency condemns your property for public use or for health or safety reasons (If this occurs, however, you may receive sufficient compensation from the government agency to satisfy your loan.)
- The zoning changes from a residential area to a commercial area

Again, default means that you have to repay the loan and all interest and costs immediately. That's not to be taken lightly.

WARNING!

A reverse mortgage may look like a great deal on the surface, but it is one of the more complicated financial products you'll come across. How complicated? So complicated that federal regulators require you to receive one-on-one counseling from a HUD-approved counselor. Not only that, but you must provide the lender a certificate proving you have received this counseling before the lender can complete your reverse-mortgage application.

What the Salesman Won't Tell You

Products that promise lifelong income tend to be complicated. The reverse mortgage is no exception. As CFP Jeffrey Voudrie notes in *The Ins and Outs of Reverse Mortgages*, "The complexity of reverse mortgages makes it difficult for the average senior to separate myth from reality."

If you are considering a reverse mortgage because you want to fund a vacation or buy another financial product with the advances, don't. Never pursue a reverse mortgage without undertaking a lot of research—and a lot of thought. Use of HECM funds should be carefully considered by the borrower over the life of the loan, as a source of funds remain in the property, maintain property condition, provide an emergency source of funds for illness, and so on. The bottom line is the money is yours to spend as you wish.

A Closer Look:

Loan Defaults: A High Price to Pay

What would it cost if you defaulted on a reverse-mortgage loan? A lot.

Let's take another look at Mary's situation. If she were to default on her loan after three years, she would have been advanced $19,656 ($546 a month for three years). However, the amount she must repay comes to $29,374—taking into account closing costs of $7,232, servicing fees of $1,080 ($30 a month for thirty-six months), interest of $1,020 (assuming her interest rate did not rise), and total monthly MIPs of $395. That means that her costs are about 50 percent of what she borrowed—and thus a very bad deal for Mary. Because of the high cost of defaulting early, you should generally consider a reverse mortgage only if you plan to remain in your home for many years into the future.

Know Your Facts

What do you need to know before getting a reverse mortgage?

• Educate yourself about reverse mortgages by reading consumer guides published by federal regulators. You'll save a lot of time if you start with the bible: the ninety-six-page Fannie Mae booklet called A Guide to Understanding Reverse Mortgages, available at www.efanniemae.com. You can also get a copy by calling the Fannie Mae Resource Center at 1-800-232-6643. Also read the Federal Trade Commission's publications, such as "FTC Facts for Consumers: Reverse Mortgages—Get the Facts Before Cashing in on Your Home's Equity," available online at www.ftc.gov. AARP is another resource: you can call the organization at 800-209-8085 and ask for "Reverse Mortgage Loans: Borrowing Against Your Home." Or, to download a copy (or order a printed version) online, you can find it at www.aarp.org/revmort. Also be sure to read "Reverse Mortgages: Avoiding a Reversal of Fortune," a FINRA Investor Alert that was last updated in 2014 (www.finra.org).

• Before signing anything, ask for a sample of all the loan documents you will be asked to sign upon closing the loan. Take these home and review them carefully one by one.

• Ask for a sample of the monthly account statements the loan servicer will be sending you once you close on the loan.

• Make sure you understand how to read the statement: do you understand how the outstanding loan balances and interest-rate calculations work? This is especially relevant if you will receive monthly payments and also have a credit line.

• Meet with a HECM counselor, even if you are considering a private loan. (You'll be given a list of counselors when you inquire about a loan.) HECM requires counseling from an independent, HUD-approved housing-counseling agency. The intention here is to make sure that you understand the financial implications of a reverse mortgage—and any alternatives that may be available to you.

• The use of HECM loan advances may affect social programs such as SSI (Supplemental Security Income) or Medicaid benefits. To determine if

HECM payments will affect your situation, consult your local SSI or Medicaid office.

- Before going forward, talk your decision over with the lawyer who drafted your will to make certain that a reverse mortgage does not conflict with your estate plan. You might want to involve your children as well, given that the remaining equity in your home is likely to decline.

Be sure to consider the following questions before going ahead:

- What are the benefits of getting a reverse mortgage right now? In the future? (Loan options are changing; better products may be available in the future.)
- What are the drawbacks, including the costs and the mortgage's effect on the equity in your home?
- Do you understand what conditions can cause a reverse mortgage to default? Can you live with those conditions?
- Do you know who will service the loan after it closes?
- Which lender is best suited to your needs?
- What have you learned from speaking with a HECM counselor about the pros and cons of a reverse mortgage for you? Are there other alternatives to explore?

Julie's Overall Recommendation

Proceed with caution. What I mean by caution here is this: A reverse mortgage can be a lifelong commitment that should not be entered into without an objective analysis—and that takes effort.

In some circumstances, a HECM can enhance the longevity of retirement and assist in preventing the "outliving of retirement assets." That is perhaps THE most critical component of the decision making process.

As with many complicated financial planning tools, there can be pitfalls for the uninformed participant. The reverse mortgage is no different. Never make a significant financial decision without having all the relevant information. As with all the retirement decisions, knowledge is the key to a sound decision.

PART III

Investing in Your Future: Retirement-Income Planning and the Markets

15

Tax-Deferred Account Decisions

If you work for a company that offers a savings plan such as a 401(k), or if you are retired and still participate in such a plan, this chapter is for you—as well as Individual Retirement Account (IRA) owners.

As you'll notice, the chapter is divided into three decisions. The first decision (how much you should contribute) deals specifically with 401(k) plans; however, the points also apply to other company-sponsored retirement plans that offer to match a percentage of your contributions, such as 403(b)s. The second and third decisions (how to invest and what to do after you retire) apply to all tax-deferred accounts, including traditional IRAs, or individual retirement accounts.

The Retirement Plan

Landscape More and more Americans now hold a significant amount of money in retirement accounts such as 401(k)s and other employer-sponsored retirement plans and IRAs. In fact, reports the Investment Company Institute (ICI), by the end of 2016 Americans had amassed $14.9 trillion in both IRAs and defined-contribution plans such as 401(k)s. By comparison, $8.4 trillion was held in private and governmental pension plans, including $5.5 trillion in federal, state, and local pensions. If you include annuities (both immediate and variable), that's an additional $2.0 trillion, for a grand total of $25.3 trillion in retirement assets. (For a breakdown of the U.S. retirement market, see Table 15-1.)

IRAs	$7.9
DEFINED-CONTRIBUTION PLANS	$7.0
PRIVATE DEFINED-BENEFIT PLANS	$2.9
FEDERAL, STATE, AND LOCAL PENSIONS	$5.5
ANNUITIES	$2.0
TOTAL	$25.3

Table 15.1 Breakdown of U.S. retirement market
in trillions of dollars (2016)
Courtesy of the Investment Company Institute (ICI)

The 401(k)

Advantage Let's turn to 401(k)s. A 401(k) is a retirement-savings plan that an employer sponsors for its employees. More than 94.6 million Americans participate in 401(k) plans at work, and the assets they have accumulated in these accounts total almost $4.8 trillion.

Before we dig into the details of 401(k)s, you should first familiarize yourself with some lingo you're likely to encounter. A "defined-contribution plan," such as a 401(k) or a 403(b), is a retirement plan to which employees can contribute through payroll deductions ("salary deferrals"). A traditional pension plan is known as a "defined-benefit plan." Today, many employers offer defined-contribution plans in place of traditional pension plans. When you leave the employ of a company, you can transfer, or "roll over," the amount you have invested in a 401(k) to an IRA, called a "rollover IRA."

Your 401(k) plan offers you the opportunity to become financially self-sufficient in retirement. Your job as a 401(k) investor is to understand how to manage your account wisely. After all, 401(k)s and other tax-deferred retirement plans are wonderful tools for accumulating retirement wealth even in declining markets, but unless you learn how to manage them after you retire, they can trigger unnecessary taxes.

Decision #1:
How Much Should I Contribute? If you are eligible for a 401(k), the burden of funding your retirement does not rest on your shoulders alone. Your company may help you fund your 401(k) with a company match or a profit-sharing contribution. Both are employer contributions. A match is tied to what you contribute; a profit-sharing contribution is not. In addition, when you choose to contribute to your 401(k), you enjoy valuable pretax advantages.

Hint: Employees aren't required to contribute to 401(k) plans. It's optional. That's why your paycheck contribution is called an "elective" contribution. To encourage as many employees as possible to capitalize on the tax-savings and matching-contribution benefits of employer-sponsored 401(k)s, more and more employers are introducing "automatic 401(k)s": the salient feature here is that employees must opt out, not in.

The Pretax Advantage
When you contribute to your 401(k) through payroll deductions, you are setting aside part of your paycheck to help fund your future retirement. Most plans provide that this contribution is "pretax," which means your

contribution is not taxable W-2 income. When it comes time for you to pay your income taxes for the year, you pay no taxes on your pretax 401(k) contributions.

When your company gives you a match or profit-sharing contribution, that money does not show up on your W-2 as taxable income. So if you contribute $10,000 in pretax money to your 401(k) as an elective contribution and you receive a $10,000 match, that's $20,000 of earnings that is not counted as W-2 income. That's the powerful pretax advantage of a 401(k).

Hint: Some plans allow only pretax contributions. Others also allow after-tax contributions and Roth 401(k) contributions. (Pretax contributions do not appear on your W-2; after-tax and Roth contributions do.)

However, Roth contributions provide certain advantages—most important, that earnings are income-tax-free for you and your heirs if you meet certain requirements (see below). You can roll over your Roth 401(k) into a Roth IRA after you retire and even continue to accumulate money after age 70.5 if you have earned income. Proper beneficiary designations can stretch out tax benefits for heirs.

Company Match

There is no requirement for a company to offer a match (or a profit-sharing contribution). Because matches are usually tied to a percentage of your contribution and capped at a certain percentage of your salary, you have to figure out how much to contribute in order to derive the maximum benefit from the match.

Hint: Generally, the size of your match is directly tied to how much you contribute to the 401(k). For example, your plan may provide that the company will contribute 50 cents for every $1 you contribute (a pretty common match, up to a cap).

A profit-sharing contribution, by contrast, is ordinarily independent of your contributions—the company determines how much each employee is to receive, usually at its sole discretion.

Are You Saying "No" to Money?   If your goal is to grow your retirement savings as quickly as possible, there is no better way than to maximize your employer match. In the case of a 100 percent match, you are doubling your investment instantaneously (vesting occurs later)—for every dollar you contribute to your 401(k), your employer puts in another dollar. Talk about compounding. It would take you seven years to do that on your own with an investment that earned 10 percent per year.

Remember, your match is excluded from W-2 income, so taking advantage of a match is like getting a tax-free raise. For that reason, it pays to maximize that match.

Let's look at an example.

Janie, who is single, has a 401(k) with a dollar-for-dollar match that caps at 6 percent of compensation. She earns $100,000 in salary, before withholding for taxes and FICA (the Federal Insurance Contributions Act mandates that money be withheld from your pay for Social Security and Medicare).

Assuming Janie doesn't currently contribute anything to her plan, how much money is she losing by not maximizing her match?

Let's see. When you contribute to your 401(k) pre-tax, your taxable income is reduced by the amount of the contribution. If Janie did not participate in the plan, her tax bill would be $18,190, assuming a federal tax rate of 18.19 percent. By participating in the plan at 6 percent ($6,000), her W-2 income is reduced from $100,000 to $94,000; her federal tax bill is reduced to $16,690. That's a federal tax savings of $1,500.

Thinking as an investor, Janie realizes that the tax savings reduces her "cost" of participating in the 401(k) from $6,000 to $4,500 ($6,000 less her tax savings of $1,500). But that's not all. Because her contribution triggers the company match (subject to vesting), her $6,000 contribution "buys" a 401(k) balance of $12,000. Janie's cost of investment ($4,500), compared to her 401(k) balance ($12,000), puts her ahead by $7,500. You can think of that as an immediate return on investment of 167 percent.

Annual	0% Contribution	6% Contribution
Salary (Annual)	$100,000	$100,000
401(k) Salary Deferral	0	6,000
Match ($1 for $1) (Must Vest)	0	6,000
Total 401(k) (Salary Deferral + Match)	0	12,000
Taxable Income	100,000	94,000
Federal Taxes (18.19 Percent)	18,190	16,690
Tax Savings Due to 401(k)	0	1,500
Cost of 401(k)	0	4,500
401(k) Balance (Match Must Vest)	0	12,000
Ahead By	0	7,500

Table 15-2: Cost benefit of maximizing company match in 401(k)

That's a tidy windfall if you take advantage of it—and a big loss if you don't. As a general rule, you never want to make a decision about how much you should contribute to your 401(k) before you calculate the effect of maximizing your match.

WARNING!

When your company pays a match or profit-sharing contribution, that money is not yours to keep if you leave your job before the company contribution "vests." How long do you have to work before vesting? That depends on your plan. The longest vesting period permitted by law is six years.

So, how much should you contribute? Your best decision will be to contribute at least enough to trigger the maximum match (in dollars) that your company is willing to pay. That gives you a positive return, even if you do nothing else.

You may be thinking that you would love to maximize the match, but there's just one small problem: you can't afford to reduce your paycheck by even a penny.

Depending on your circumstances, there may be a way to maximize your match *without* decreasing your take-home pay substantially, if at all. Let me take you through an illustration.

How to Earn Your Match without
Reducing Your Paycheck If you are not maximizing your 401(k)'s match—or, worse, if you are not participating at all—because you believe you can't afford to do so, drop everything. Find last year's tax return. Check to see if you got a refund. If you received a refund last year, you're in luck. You can "use" your refund to earn that match. Let me give you an example.

Let's go back to Janie. Last year, Janie received a federal tax refund after claiming zero withholding exemptions on the Form W-4 she submitted to her personnel department. (IRS Form W-4 determines tax withholding; *zero exemptions give you the highest withholding and the biggest potential tax refund.*)

By running a tax calculator for payroll deductions on Bankrate.com's website (www.bankrate.com; click on "Calculators"; go to "Tax," then "Payroll Deductions Calculator"), Janie discovered that if she raised her 401(k) contribution from 0 percent to 6 percent and raised her withholding allowances from zero to two, she could fund part of her contribution. Increasing her allowances will cover $2,300 of the $6,000 contribution. Her tax savings cover another $1,500, so she just has to save an extra $2,200 per year, or $183 a month. If you compare the "before" and "after" pictures in Table 15-3, you'll see that this simple change will put Janie ahead by more than $7,500 a year.

Decision #2:
Which Investments Should I Pick? The investments you select will determine how well your assets will grow during your working career—and, by extension, what sort of retirement income you are able to create for yourself.

Annual	Before	After	Difference
Salary (Annual)	$100,000	$100,000	$0
Take-Home Pay (Annual)	79,660	77,360	(2,300)
Withholding Allowances	0	2	
401(k) Salary Deferral (%)	0%	6%	
401(k) Salary Deferral ($)	0	6,000	6,000
Match	0	6,000	6,000
Total 401(k) (Salary Deferral + Match)	0	12,000	12,000

Table 15-3: Increasing withholding and salary deferrals to fund your 401(k).

Warning: this could result in taxes being owed at the end of the year.

When you are working and growing your assets, you need to ask yourself:

What investments should I choose to reach my objective of building my retirement nest egg?

Later, when you are retired and living off your 401(k) savings, you will need to ask yourself a second question: What investments will help me create an income stream?

Warning: This could result in taxes being owed at the end of the year.

By knowing the risk and reward characteristics of the selections offered by your plan, you will be able to choose investments that offer the greatest potential for long-term accumulation. (I go into more detail on this topic at the end of the chapter.) Positioning yourself in the more aggressive, and potentially more rewarding, investments during the growth phase of your 401(k) is a good strategy for the early stages of your 401(k) plan. Conversely, you'll want to seek more stable investments as you move closer to retirement and when you are seeking retirement income.

Hint: Study your investment options to make the most of your 401(k). Here's a hint to start you in the right direction: the key is the prospectus for the investment. Look up the "investment objectives" in the prospectus for each available investment option. This is where you will discover if the goal is to create income or growth ("capital appreciation") or both. This is more useful than making decisions based on recent performance, because past performance does not guarantee future results.

The 401(k) Life Cycle

The secret to managing your 401(k) investment portfolio is what I call "the 401(k) life cycle." The life cycle has three phases, which flow from how far away you are from retirement. Each phase is governed by a different set of investment objectives. Your job is to properly line up the investment objectives to your stage in your 401(k) cycle.

The three 401(k) phases are accumulation, rebalancing, and withdrawal. These stages and the primary investment objectives that govern them are defined below.

The Accumulation Stage

When you enroll and begin to participate in your plan, you are in the beginning stages of the accumulation phase. During this stage, your purpose is to accumulate and grow 401(k) assets by funding your plan with contributions and allowing the plan to develop through capital appreciation and the reinvestment of dividends, capital gains distributions, or interest.

The length of the accumulation phase varies from one individual to the next. If you are 25 years old, your accumulation phase will last decades longer than if you are 40.

You can have secondary objectives, depending on your particular situation. For example, if your plan pays a match in the form of company stock, you may need to have diversification as your secondary objective in order to lower your risk in case your company stock takes a nose-dive. Another example of a secondary objective is to add one or more investment vehicles that can reduce the volatility of your accumulation portfolio. An income fund is a possibility, for example.

Consider the case of Jennifer, who is 40 years old and in the accumulation phase. She chooses to invest 60 percent of her 401(k) contributions in an S&P 500 Index fund, 20 percent in an international stock fund, and 20 percent in a bond fund. That means her allocations are 80 percent in stocks, which is an aggressive but acceptable allocation for someone who has another twenty-five years before retirement.

The Rebalancing

Stage   The rebalancing phase of your 401(k) life cycle is the time period between accumulation and withdrawal. This phase prepares your portfolio for the production of income. How long should this phase last?

The primary investment objective is to move from a capital-producing portfolio to an income-producing portfolio. The speed at which you rebalance will depend on your circumstances. For example, if you are holding a high concentration of company stock because of a company match, you may need to move more quickly in order to diversify your holdings.

For example, Jennifer, now 50, has no investments other than her 401(k). She changes her 401(k) salary deferrals so that she is now investing 80 percent of new contributions in a bond fund and 20 percent in a balanced fund (a combination of stocks and bonds). Importantly, she also assesses the growth holdings she acquired in the accumulation stage to see if she should switch them to less-aggressive balanced or income holdings. This helps prepare her for the final phase of her 401(k) life cycle.

The Withdrawal

Stage   Every action you take in your plan leads up to the withdrawal phase. When you are in this phase, you want to be able to provide yourself with a monthly "pension" check out of your 401(k) or IRA rollover. This stage can last twenty or thirty years, and occasionally longer. During this stage, your primary investment objective will be to produce income. Your secondary objective will depend on your particular circumstances. For example, if your 401(k) is not large enough to support you throughout retirement, your secondary objective may be to commit some percentage (for example, 30 percent) of your 401(k) portfolio to capital growth.

Returning to our example: Jennifer has now retired. Based on how much cash flow she needs to create, she restructures her 401(k) portfolio to create income. Most likely, she will roll over her 401(k) to an IRA first. After this rebalancing, she might have 70 percent in income-producing investments in her IRA and 30 percent in growth investments. The actual allocations will depend on her lifestyle, her Social Security benefits, her cash-flow needs, and her ability to manage risk.

Another issue in retirement is managing taxes, which we'll discuss in Chapters 17 and 18. Optimally, you should hold off taking any money out of your 401(k) or rollover IRA until you must, by law. With few exceptions, withdrawals must begin at age 70.5. No matter how old you are when you take them, usually withdrawals are taxed as ordinary income, much as a paycheck would be taxed. An early withdrawal penalty may apply if you are under 55 (401(k)) or 59.5 (IRA).

Decision #3:
How Do I Transition to Retirement? If you were to liquidate
your 401(k) account at retirement, a large chunk of retirement assets would be lost to income taxes. If your 401(k) was worth $500,000 and you asked for a check for that amount, you would also get a Form 1099-R for $500,000 of taxable income. Every dollar you take out of your pre-tax 401(k) is subject to income taxes at ordinary income tax rates.

Consider rolling over your 401(k) into an IRA (individual retirement account) and continuing to let your savings grow tax deferred for as long as possible. Then, at mandatory distribution time (beginning at age 70.5), you can choose to get advice on how to keep your taxes low while maintaining a high after-tax income stream, a topic I touch on in Chapter 18, on IRA distributions.

There are many potential pitfalls to be aware of when rolling over a 401(k), so don't do this without consulting an adviser. Be especially careful if you have employer stock—stock of the company you work for—in your plan or if your 401(k) is substantial in size. You don't want to botch up a rollover and get a Form 1099-R at the beginning of the following year showing the entire 401(k) as taxable income. Also, be aware that pre-retirees are favorite clients of all advisers, both with and without experience, so take care to find someone who understands retirement plans. (Be sure to read Chapter 20, on choosing an adviser.)

Hint: If you made after-tax contributions to your 401(k), that money is not subject to income taxes when you make a withdrawal.

Characteristics of Investment
Selections
Your plan likely provides you a range of investment options, usually mutual funds that offer growth and income possibilities. Each of these selections has a different set of investment characteristics, most notably, the difference between growth of capital (building wealth) and creating income you can live on. These characteristics define whether or not there is a fit—that is, whether or not the investment moves you toward your objective.

Investment selections appropriate for income production are typically less suited for capital growth. For example, a bond fund may be better suited for the production of income in your withdrawal phase than for the growth of capital in the accumulation phase. Conversely, an investment selection appropriate for capital growth may not be best suited for income production. For example, by definition, a growth fund such as a small-cap fund does not produce income and would therefore not be suitable as the primary holding in your withdrawal phase. However, the growth fund may meet a secondary objective of building capital in any phase.

Generally, you will be able to assess the investment objective of any particular selection and match it to the primary and secondary investment objectives of your particular phase.

Hint: Do not choose investments based on performance; instead, choose based on the investment's objective to match where the investment's objective to match you are in your 401(k) life cycle.

To give you an example of how these considerations might come together, imagine the following scenario. You are 25 years old, with thirty-five to forty years of accumulation ahead of you. Let's say you have a generous match of 100 percent that is paid in cash (not company stock), and that you have done your research regarding your investment selections. You understand the volatility of your investment options, you are willing to live through down markets, and you are confident of your ability to make good investment choices.

In such a case, there would be little reason for you to contribute monthly into money-market instruments or bonds. All of your salary deferrals could justifiably be directed into the stock market. If the 401(k) offerings include a broad market instrument, such as a fund that mimics the S&P 500 Index, you might put 60 percent in the broad market and 40 percent in a stock fund with a "growth" objective. As you invest each month, you will continue to add to these holdings through good and bad market periods until you are about ten years away from retirement.

If you intended to retire at age 65, then at age 50 or so you could start adding a third asset class to your holdings: an income or balanced fund that invests in both stocks and bonds. When you reached age 60, you would direct a percentage of your contribution into appropriate shorter-term, high-quality bond funds in order to further diversify in anticipation of retirement.

If you did not intend to use your 401(k) assets until mandatory distribution begins at age 70.5 (or later if you are still working), you would hold onto all of your positions, reinvesting dividends all the while, until you were age 67 or so. At that time, you would reassess your holdings and the market and begin to rebalance your portfolio in anticipation of minimum withdrawals beginning at age 70.5 or later. Ideally, you would limit withdrawals to those minimums required by law, in order to take maximum advantage of compounding and tax deferral for as long as you live.

I'm not going to suggest how to make those withdrawals at this point because your 401(k) should not be considered in isolation. You can get more of a feeling for how to do this in Chapter 18. Ultimately, though, this is what your adviser needs to do with you, because how you withdraw will depend on your other holdings, your need to cover essential expenses, and how you want to live in retirement.

You have every opportunity to do well with your 401(k) investments—or other tax-deferred accounts—as long as you keep your objectives in sight. As a 401(k) investor, your overall strategic objective is to accumulate an asset base large enough to create adequate retirement income. Depending on where you are in your 401(k) cycle, your current objective may be to grow capital, produce income, or rebalance in preparation for producing income. To be successful, you have to do only one thing: make certain that each decision to buy, hold, or sell aligns properly with your current target. If you can do that, you will be on the path to achieving your retirement goals.

16

Making the
Stock Market Work for You

In the last chapter, we talked about investing through a retirement plan at work—a sheltered environment, when it comes to investing, because your company screens your investment options for you and you needn't interact with a salesperson. Once you roll over your retirement-plan assets to an IRA, however, you are on your own. Outside the work environment, the marketplace is vast, and you are in a very different position. You are now responsible for your own due diligence, and you can't afford to make mistakes—not with your retirement savings. There is simply too much at stake.

Let's build on what we talked about in earlier chapters so that you will be more comfortable managing your money before and after you retire. To lay the groundwork for how to structure and monitor a retirement portfolio, let's discuss different asset classes, diversification, and how different holding periods affect results. Then, at the end of the chapter, we'll go through some examples of how to approach a portfolio based on size and income needs, as well as a balanced strategy. But first let's set the stage by talking about risk and reward.

Risk and Reward

Why do people put their money at risk in the stock market? Why don't they just pick safe choices, such as savings accounts, CDs, or money-market funds?

It comes down to this: safe investments such as savings accounts and money-market funds will earn a little interest for you and help you sleep at night—for a while, until you start to notice that your money isn't going as far as it used to. Savings accounts don't hold up to inflation very well, and at some point your money starts to lose its purchasing power.

As you can imagine, rising prices are harder to deal with after you retire than before. This is especially true if you are living on a fixed income from a fixed pension. Most pensions do not adjust for inflation (although Social Security does).

Types of Asset Classes

Stocks are one of three asset classes we'll discuss in this chapter. (By "asset class," I mean simply a group of investments with common characteristics.) The other two asset classes we'll discuss are bonds and cash equivalents.

Stocks: Investing for Growth

Stocks are financial instruments that represent ownership interest, or "equity," in a company. People buy stocks with the goal of selling them at a higher price at some point in the future—and possibly earning some dividend income along the way.

Hint: Your "investment objective" defines what you are seeking to accomplish with your investments. Someone who invests in stocks has a "growth" investment objective. By contrast, a person investing in bonds has an "income" objective. And those investing in cash equivalents, such as CDs, are seeking "safety" or "stability of principal."

Stocks are expected to move in price (up or down). Rather than looking for safety, the stock investor wants growth—enough growth to achieve meaningful returns that outpace inflation over time. He is willing to accept the ups and downs of the stock market.

Besides potential gains, some stocks offer potential income in the form of dividends. A "dividend" is a payment made to stockholders from the company's earnings. Dividends can be an important source of income for you after you retire.

Bonds:

Investing for Income Bonds represent a company's debt. When you buy a bond, you are lending money to the company in exchange for interest payments and the company's promise to repay the debt at a particular time in the future when the debt becomes due (the "maturity date").

The goal behind buying bonds is to earn interest, or—to put it another way—to "create income."

Bonds deliver a series of interest payments to the investor, usually once every six months until the bond matures. For example, a $100,000 bond with a 5 percent coupon will pay you $2,500 every six months ($5,000 annually).

Cash Equivalents: Providing Some Income and Stability of Principal

Cash equivalents represent short-term debt (maturities of one year or less) and include savings accounts, U.S. Treasury bills, CDs, and money-market funds. Having a savings account or a traditional CD earns you some interest while protecting your principal, making your investment objective "stability of principal."

Money managers typically use cash equivalents to park money on a temporary basis while waiting for better investment opportunities. Another use is to add a stable element to a portfolio: cash equivalents normally do not fluctuate in price. Individuals might use cash equivalents for safety, especially if they are not experienced investors.

Taking Stock

You can think of the stock market as a place where investors can make money by buying a stock at one price and selling the stock to another investor at a higher price (and potentially earn dividends during the holding period). As discussed, the objective with stocks is growth—building the nest egg you hope to live on in retirement.

Implicit in every stock purchase is the anticipation of a profit on its sale (and a loss, if you sell the stock at a price that is lower than your purchase price). Over the long term, however, stock prices tend to rise, thanks to increases in productivity, corporate earnings, and economic expansion.

Diversification

As you prepare for and enter retirement, you want to carefully manage the risk in your portfolio; one way to do that is to diversify your holdings.

As a general rule, there is far greater risk investing in a single stock than investing in a collection of stocks of companies in diverse businesses. Any single company can run into problems—increased competition from lower-cost or better-positioned companies, a change in the demand for its products or services, or other factors or events that can cause the company to perform poorly (or even fail). To lessen these risks, investors diversify their portfolios among fifteen or more stocks in different industries to adjust their risk to what is called "market risk."

It needs to be understood, however, that a diversified stock portfolio does not protect you from losses when the market declines, as it did during the Financial Crisis in 2008. Imagine that you had invested your retirement savings in an S&P Index fund (an example of a diversified stock investment) at the beginning of 2008. Your investment would have dropped by 37 percent to $63,000 by the end of the year.

To further lessen your risk, you can add bonds and cash equivalents to your portfolio. You can even add other asset classes, such as real estate or gold and other commodities. (More "exotic" instruments such as inverse exchange-traded funds, which go up when the stock market goes down, are beyond the scope of this book.)

A Closer Look
Terms of Investment

A "portfolio" is a collection of securities managed to meet certain objectives. "Market risk" is the risk associated with the broad market, as measured by the S&P 500 Index, or a segment of the market, as measured by the stocks of large companies, midsize companies, small companies, or sectors, such as energy or technology.

Hint: When selecting a mutual fund, avoid the common mistake of choosing a fund based on its recent returns—the kind of fund you will find on lists of "Hot Funds to Buy Now." Though picking a mutual fund is a topic for another book, here is a starting point: select based on what the fund is seeking to accomplish—for example, "capital appreciation over the long-term"—which you will find in the prospectus. Then, find out how the fund is doing compared to others with the same objective. To research funds, go to the public library reference desk or consult a source such as Morningstar (www.morningstar.com).

A Closer Look:

Here Today, Gone Tomorrow

A rising stock market can turn into a declining market quickly, so you need to make sure you don't speculate with your retirement savings. A retired couple in their early seventies, for example, came to me in January 2000. It was the peak of the Internet "bubble" market, and with their (perfectly sound) stock-and-bond portfolio underperforming the Nasdaq by quite a bit, the couple felt left behind: their friends were making a lot of money in Internet stocks, so they wanted to invest their entire portfolio likewise. I politely declined to take them on as clients—but suggested that they not make any changes at all. Luckily, they took my advice: had they made the move into Internet stocks at that time, the couple would have lost more than 80 percent of their retirement assets.

Investing for Income

Many people mistakenly believe they can't lose money in bonds. That is not true. Before we talk about how to use bonds, let's discuss an important concept: credit risk.

Credit Risk

Bonds are IOUs. When you buy a bond, you are really lending money to the issuer in exchange for the company's promise to repay the loan, plus interest. If the company gets into financial problems, it may not be able to keep up with interest payments; worse, it may go out of business. As the owner of a bond issued by that company, you have the rights of a creditor in a bankruptcy proceeding, giving you higher standing than a stockholder. If there are insufficient funds to pay off creditors, your bond may not be worth much of anything.

This concept is called "credit risk." To get an assessment of how creditworthy an issuer is, investors turn to resources such as Moody's (www.moodys.com), Standard & Poor's (standardandpoors.com), and Fitch (www.fitchratings.com). See Chapter 8 for sample ratings.

U.S. government bonds are the highest-quality bonds, because they are backed by the U.S. Treasury. Corporate bonds reflect the creditworthiness and safety of the corporation issuing them.

Market Risk (Also Called Interest Rate Risk)

You might think that you can't lose money in U.S. government bonds because they are the most creditworthy. Indeed, the U.S. government guarantees your principal and income stream. But this does not make government bonds devoid of risk if you can't hold them until maturity.

If you have to sell the bonds before they mature—to pay for medical expenses or a grandchild's college tuition, for instance—you expose your bonds to market risk. (And even if you do hold your bonds to maturity, inflation risk can erode the value of the income stream, and reinvestment risk can leave you with less income when it's time to buy a new bond.)

To see how interest rates affect market prices, we can look at an example from a period of rising interest rates.

Let's assume you paid $50,000 for twenty-year U.S. government bonds in 1976, maturing in 1996 with a coupon of 8.5 percent. Now imagine that the year is 1982 and you need your $50,000 to pay for an unexpected expense, such as nursing-home care.

You will need to sell those bonds (you can't return them for a refund). How much money will you get when you sell them? $50,000? More? Less?

That depends on how interest rates have changed since you bought the bonds. Between 1976 (when you bought the bonds) and 1982 (when you want to sell them), interest rates rose substantially. In 1976, these bonds were issued at an 8.5 percent yield. By 1982, you could buy 13 percent U.S. government bonds with the same maturity (1996).

So there you are selling your 8.5 percent bonds when the government is selling 13 percent bonds. No one would be willing to pay $50,000 for bonds yielding 8.5 percent when they could get the same quality bonds yielding 13 percent.

In fact, the market would discount your bonds to about half of what you paid for them to give the buyer a yield of 13 percent. That means you would receive only about $25,000 for bonds you originally purchased for $50,000.

Conversely, you can sell a bond for a profit if yields fall and your bond pays a higher yield than the market currently offers. In this scenario, you recoup the full amount you paid for the bond, and then some—but you sacrifice receiving a higher income stream than is available in the current

A Closer Look:
What Are Treasury Bills?

U.S. Treasury bills, a type of cash equivalent, represent the most secure part of the debt market. Known as T-bills, these assets are short-term U.S. government debt with maturities of one year or less. They are usually issued in four-, thirteen-, or twenty-six-week increments. T-bills are considered risk-free investments. Some money-market mutual funds that invest in short-term (maturing in less than one year) T-bills and other money-market instruments have prices per share figured at a stable $1 and normally experience no volatility in price.

market. For that, the market pays you a premium over the face amount of the bond. The bond-market rally, beginning in 1982 and ending in early 1994, made bond investing profitable as interest rates fell. As interest rates rose in the balance of 1994, however, great sums of money were lost.

The effect of the changing interest rates that we've just talked about also affects bonds held in a mutual fund. This means that as a mutual-fund investor, you will see your shares fluctuate in value due to changes in bond prices, which in turn are due in part to changes in interest rates.

Mutual funds that invest in U.S. government bonds buy and sell bonds for a portfolio at different prices as the markets change over time. They are required to price their holdings daily, which is reflected in the daily price (net asset value) of your mutual-fund shares.

As a general rule, the longer the maturity of a bond, the higher its volatility. Bonds with the longest maturities are most exposed to the risk of being sold at a loss during rising interest-rate markets. Conversely, the shorter the maturity of a bond portfolio, the lower its volatility.

Investing as You
Approach Retirement
As you near your retirement date, you'll need to shift your thinking from growth to creating retirement income.

If you are heavily invested in stocks, you will want to consider what you will be doing with those stocks when you retire. If you intend to use your portfolio to create income (which I discuss shortly), you will want to start making some changes slowly over time to lessen the risk of having to sell stocks in a down market.

A good strategy is to reallocate your portfolio from stocks to bonds over time, which will shift your portfolio from growing capital to producing income. Essentially, you will make a transition from a "growth" investment objective to a "growth and income" investment objective by adding income-producing investments—bonds and bond mutual funds—to your portfolio. (There is no hard-and-fast rule governing how much to transfer, or how quickly to transfer it.)

Holding

Period What effect does your holding period—the number of years you expect your stock investments to work for you—have on volatility, risk, and ultimately your results? You will need to manage decisions related to your holding period regardless of your age, even if you are retired.

Although you can choose from thousands of stocks and mutual funds, let's see what a broad market investment in an S&P 500 Index mutual fund can do for you over longer periods of twenty, thirty, and forty years. We'll then compare those returns to a shorter, ten-year period.

If you are 35 years old and want to retire at 65, pay particular attention to the thirty-year holding period. If you are ten years away from retirement, focus on the ten-year holding period.

If you are retired, don't ignore these lessons. You could be 70 and still have a ten- or twenty-year holding period ahead. After all, you most likely will continue to invest in stocks after you retire—most people need some growth in their retirement portfolios. The difference is that the retiree will probably not be investing new savings. Instead, he will be moving money from one asset class to another.

Let's see what lessons we can draw from the following market data. Let's assume you are making investments in the S&P 500 Index of $100 each month for different periods of time (ten, twenty, thirty, and forty years). What I share with you here are the best, worst, and median experiences in all market periods going back to 1928. The dates in the tables are the actual periods that produced the returns we will review.

As you read on, note the worst return for each period. Let me emphasize this point: you always learn the best lessons from the worst-performing periods.

For a ten-year period, you are making 120 monthly investments of $100 each ($12,000 in total) in an investment that replicates the S&P 500 Index. Table 16–1 shows the results:

Invested	Rank	Return for Period	End Value	Period
$12,000	Worst	-3.8%	$9,900	1999–2008
	Best	22.0%	38,300	1946–1955
	Median	11.1%	21,500	2005–2014

Table 16-1 S&P 500 Index comparison of worst to best 10-year periods
(investing $100 a month) from 1928 to 2016

The median reflects the middle of the range. There are as many periods with returns above the median as there are periods below. Again, focus on the lowest percentage returns for each period—the worst market periods.

The results of making 240 monthly investments of $100 over a twenty-year period ($24,000 in total) are shown in Table 16-2. Compare that to a thirty-year period in which you made 360 monthly investments of $100 ($36,000 in total), shown in Table 16–3:

Invested	Rank	Return for Period	End Value	Period
$24,000	Worst	4.0%	$36,500	1955–1974
	Best	18.4%	203,000	1980–1999
	Median	11.6%	88,900	1968–1987

Table 16-2 S&P 500 Index comparison of worst to best 20-year periods
(investing $100 a month) from 1928 to 2016

Invested	Rank	Return for Period	End Value	Period
$36,000	Worst	8.5%	$156,000	1952–1981
	Best	15.8%	663,000	1970–1999
	Median	11.7%	294,000	1962–1991

Table 16-3 S&P 500 Index comparison of worst to best 30-year periods
(investing $100 a month) from 1928 to 2016

Note that the lowest performance ended in 1981 (not 1974, as before). In case you're wondering, the thirty-year period ending in 1974 had an 8.69 percent return.

The results of investing for a forty-year period are shown in Table 16–4, with 480 investments of $100 per month ($48,000 in total), and with the lowest returns occurring in the period ending in 1974:

Invested	Rank	Return for Period	End Value	Period
$48,000	Worst	9.6%	$504,000	1935–1974
	Best	13.5%	1,480,000	1960–1999
	Median	11.2%	785,000	1941–1980

Table 16-4 S&P 500 Index comparison of worst to best 40-year periods
(investing $100 a month) from 1928 to 2016

Intriguingly, the lowest percentage return for a ten-year horizon was a loss of 3.8 percent, but over a twenty-year period the lowest return was a gain of 4 percent. For a thirty-year horizon, the lowest return was 8.5 percent; for a forty-year period, it was 9.6 percent.

You can draw some revealing conclusions from these numbers.

First, the longer your holding period, the higher the potential return. Why? Because markets have an ebb and flow, and the longer you devote to investing, the more time you have to make it through different economic periods and take advantage of compounding (a concept discussed in Chapter 5).

Second, it doesn't take much money to become wealthy. It takes a little money, some time, an understanding of investment fundamentals, and persistence. As we saw earlier, investments of $100 a month for thirty years ($36,000) grew to $294,000 during the median period, for an 11.7 percent annual return. That's a very good return, and a reasonable expectation for a long investment horizon.

Third, the more time you have, the likelier it is that your return will be positive. Our data show that even the worst returns in the longer holding periods were positive. Only the shortest holding period ended with a loss.

Fourth, even if you find yourself ending your investment period with a bad market, the best thing to do is to be sufficiently flexible that you needn't liquidate at a time like that.

Let's go back to the worst ten-year holding period (-3.8 percent ending 2008; see Table 16-1). This ten-year period started with three down years (-9 percent in 2000; -12 percent in 2001; -22 percent in 2002) as a result of the bursting of the Internet Bubble; during that time, you were investing monthly as the market was declining. Then, positive years followed in 2003 (29 percent); 2004 (10 percent); 2005 (5 percent); 2006 (16 percent); 2007 (5 percent). The final year of the 10 year period ended with the 2008 decline of 37 percent.

The market hit bottom in March of 2009. If you had held onto your investments after the 10 year period ending 2008 through 2016, your average annual return would have been about 7 percent annualized, which includes the original 10 year period ending 2008.

In comparison, if you had not invested monthly during the decade ending 2008, your average annual return ending 2016 would have been 5.4 percent. But, your average annual return during the 10 year holding period would have been -1.4 percent (you were not buying as the market was declining) instead of -3.8 percent.

You may also be wondering about the longer holding periods that ended in 2008. While the ten year holding period return was -3.8 percent the twenty-year period was 5.2 percent, the thirty-year was 9.3 percent, and the forty-year was 9.8 percent in 2008.

You cannot normally achieve 9.3 and 9.8 percent results with bonds or cash equivalents, such as CDs or savings accounts. You can do that, however, with a diversified portfolio of well-selected stocks or stock mutual funds—given time and the right market conditions, that is.

If you are an experienced and confident investor with a lot of time between now and retirement, there is little reason to have a high allocation of bonds. If, on the other hand, you are inexperienced, close to retirement, investing a large sum of money, or beginning a relationship with a new adviser, you might want to increase your percentage of high-quality bonds.

Using Your Portfolio to Create Retirement Income

In earlier chapters, we discussed how to examine your expenses to determine your needs in retirement. Your portfolio should be structured to cover the gap between what you need and what you receive in Social Security and pension income.

How do you fill the gap using your portfolio? As discussed in Chapter 5, there is no one-size-fits-all formula. This part of the puzzle has to be custom-fit to (and by) you, based on all the factors that go into making decisions about your portfolio. These include your age, marital status, dependents, lifestyle, expenses, and expectations. Also take into consideration your investment experience and risk profile, your assets and the current market conditions, the proportion of your tax-deferred to taxable accounts, and your desire to leave a legacy.

Hint: To arrive at the correct allocations for yourself, talk to your adviser or follow the example of the case study in Appendix D. This appendix, used as training material for advisers who want to help retirees create retirement income, shows how different advisers make allocation recommendations to their clients.

Goal: Create Income and Protect Legacy for Substantial Assets

People with substantial assets often have two countervailing goals: to create income for their own retirement and preserve an estate for their heirs. To achieve that result for my clients, I use a "demands-based" formula to structure a portfolio that can meet income needs while preserving principal for heirs. I start at the end—the desired income from the portfolio—and work backward to the appropriate stock and bond allocations.

Let me illustrate the concept. Assume you have $5 million in retirement savings, and imagine that you need $90,000 of income from your portfolio this year to supplement your Social Security and pension income. Further assume that you can buy $3 million of good-quality bonds yielding 3 percent to produce $90,000 to satisfy your first year's income goal.

The remaining $2 million would be invested in stocks for growth and in short-term money-market instruments for stability of principal. The percentage allocation between stocks and money-market instruments would depend on market conditions, your age, and your risk profile. Because dividends and interest payments meet your income needs, there's no need to liquidate principal—instead, the principal can grow over time, offsetting inflation while you're alive and leaving a legacy for your heirs once you're gone. For more details on how to structure such a portfolio (and how to manage large portfolios in general), consult *Managing Retirement Wealth: An Expert Guide to Personal Management in Good Times and Bad.*

Smaller Accounts
and Income Needs This next technique works well if your assets are more modest, but only if your income needs are equally modest. For example, assume once again that U.S. Treasury bonds are yielding 3 percent. You have $100,000 to invest and need $2,500 of annual income, in addition to Social Security benefits (and pension payments, if applicable). You can achieve your income needs while protecting your principal, because you would need to invest about 80 percent of your savings in bonds. If you need $5,000, however, you cannot generate that income, since you would need more than $100,000 to produce $5,000 in income. In that situation, you might be tempted to invest in high-yielding bonds (called "junk bonds")—which, by definition, will have lower creditworthiness and therefore higher risk. Unless you are an experienced investor, in almost all cases that would be foolish.

If you have higher income needs that cannot be met through this method, you have other options—but they will not protect your principal and legacy in quite the same way.

For instance, in Chapter 5 we discussed withdrawing money from your portfolio. This technique involves selling some stocks or bonds when you need money, or taking money out of your savings account—a very difficult process to manage. I have watched people struggle with the dilemma: what should I sell when the bills come in?

There is another approach that may work for you, if you are willing to use some principal. Unlike the earlier technique, in which we do not sell any holdings to "create" income, here we sell a modest amount each year from a well-diversified portfolio of high-quality stocks and bonds—let's call this a "balanced strategy."

Let's briefly consider some historical data that may help you understand how a balanced strategy can work. Using the Thomson index for "balanced" mutual funds, I considered all twenty-year periods from 1933 through 2016. Balanced funds invest in both stocks and bonds, which approximate an allocation of 60 percent stocks and 40 percent bonds. (To find a balanced fund that may be appropriate for you, conduct some research of your own at www.morningstar.com, a free website offered by Morningstar.)

What would happen if an investor withdrew 4 percent of the initial investment in the first year, increasing the withdrawals by 3 percent yearly to help offset inflation? My findings are summarized in Table 16-5, which assumes $100,000 invested at the beginning of the year in a balanced fund (represented by the Thomson Balanced Index), with the first year's

		Withdrawals Increasing by 3 Percent per Year		
Period	Performance	Ending Balance	Annual Return	Amount Withdrawn
1937–1956	Worst	$81,800	4.6%	$107,481
1979–1998	Best	880,000	13.7%	107,481
1967–1986	Median	308,000	9.0%	107,481

Table 16-5 $100,000 "invested" in Thomson Balanced Index, all 20-year periods from 1933 through 2016, with withdrawals of $4,000 per year increasing by 3 percent

withdrawal of $4,000 (4 percent of $100,000), followed by withdrawals that increase by 3 percent yearly.

As you can see from Table 16-5, there were no negative periods. You would not have run out of money if you had invested in a balanced fund that replicated this index during these market periods. After investing $100,000, an investor could have withdrawn $4,000 the first year, and could have increased that withdrawal by 3 percent a year to offset inflation for twenty years without running out of money (year one = $4,000; year two = $4,120 [$4,000 inflated by 3 percent]; year three = $4,244).

To replicate these results, an investor could purchase a well-selected, balanced fund and hold on to it. The stock-bond mix of these funds typically makes for a much less volatile holding than the S&P 500 Index and can serve as the core holding of a retirement portfolio for many retirees.

How you actually set up your portfolio will depend on your adviser's recommendations, which in turn will be based on your assets, your age, your experience and risk profile, your desire to leave a legacy—and, importantly, your cash-flow needs.

PART IV

Pulling It All Together: Uncle Sam, Your Adviser, and You

17

Taxes
in Retirement

At the height of the Internet bubble, a financial adviser convinced a retiree that his heirs would be facing large tax bills because his IRA would be worth a huge sum by the time he died. So the retiree agreed to buy an insurance policy—and to pay the annual premiums with money withdrawn from his IRA. When the bubble burst, the retiree found his IRA dwindling fast. Not only was he suffering market losses because of the high-risk investments in his IRA, but each payment he made to the insurance company from his IRA required an additional withdrawal to pay the taxes triggered by that withdrawal.

(Just about any time you withdraw money from an IRA, the withdrawal is taxable.) That was one very expensive insurance policy.

Hint: When I refer to a traditional IRA (one from which distributions are generally taxable as income), I simply say "IRA"; when I refer to a Roth IRA (one from which distributions are not taxable, provided certain conditions are met), I use the term "Roth IRA."

Before we begin, let me thank tax attorney Bob Rywick, primary author of *Tax Age*, published by the Tax and Accounting business of Thomson Reuters (previously Thomson RIA), for his assistance with this chapter.

When you are retired, nothing is more vexatious than having to worry about taxes every time you pay a bill. As you move into retirement, be sure you understand the actions that trigger a tax. Some sources of income are taxed in full or in part at ordinary income-tax rates; others are taxed at capital-gains tax rates; still others are not taxed at all.

Assume that your taxes, federal and state combined, equal 25 percent of your income (that's your "effective income-tax rate"). Say you need $100 to pay your doctor. If you use money from your IRA or other tax deferred retirement accounts, such as a 401(k), at the 25 percent rate you'll need $133 to pay that bill—$100 for the doctor, and an extra $33 for taxes. IRA withdrawals are taxed as ordinary income, as explained below. To calculate your rate, divide the amount of the expense ($100, in this scenario) by 1 minus your tax rate (1 − 0.25). In this example, that's $100 divided by 0.75, or $133.

If, however, you use money from after-tax sources (money you've already paid taxes on, distributions of after-tax contributions to your 401(k), or distributions from a Roth IRA), you won't have to worry about that extra $33, and your cost is $100—no more.

Why the difference? Because some sources of income are taxable, and some are not. That's the topic covered in the first half of this chapter. In the second half, I address some of the key tax concerns retirees often face, such as taxes on annuities, Social Security, and home sales, as well as estate taxes.

Hint: Your "effective income-tax rate" is the percentage of your income that goes to paying taxes. For example, if your taxable income is $50,000 and your federal and state income tax bills total $5,000, your effective income-tax rate is 10 percent.

Income Tax Up to this point, I've been talking about IRAs, 401(k)s, and other retirement accounts in terms of the benefits of tax deferral. When you start withdrawals, the money you take out of tax-deferred accounts is subject to income taxes.

Likewise, payments you receive from company pensions, Social Security retirement benefits (if the recipient's income exceeds certain levels), immediate and variable annuities, and tax-deferred fixed annuities are taxable as income, in whole or in part.

With few exceptions (notably the interest on municipal bonds, distributions from Roth IRAs, and distributions attributed to after-tax contributions to retirement accounts), every dollar that you receive in retirement income (or withdraw from IRAs and other tax deferred retirement accounts) is taxable as income at ordinary income-tax rates.

Taxes on Long-Term
Capital Gains
Some retirees expect to live on the gains from the sale of their investments. These gains are also taxable, but a slightly different tax structure applies.

If you sell an investment that you've held for more than one year, you figure your tax on the gains at the long-term capital-gains tax rate. On the sale of most assets, the long-term capital gains rate is determined as follows: If the gains would be taxed at a rate below 25 percent if they were taxed as ordinary income, they are taxed at a zero rate, i.e., they would not be taxed at all. If they would be taxed at a rate about 15 percent but below 39.6 percent if taxed as ordinary income, they are taxed at a 15 percent rate. If they would be taxed at a rate of 39.6 percent if taxed as ordinary income, they are taxed at a 20 percent rate.

So if you are taxed at a rate of 15 percent on gains from the sale of a stock, bond, or mutual fund, and you need to sell property to pay that $100 doctor's bill we discussed, you will need to determine your capital gain on the sale of that property, in determining how much property you must sell to be able to pay both the bill and the tax. If you pay tax on long-term capital gains at a rate of 15 percent, and your gain equals 50 percent of the amount you receive for the property, you will have to sell property worth $108 to pay the $100 bill plus $8 of tax (25 percent of $54 [half of $108]).

If, however, your holding period is one year or less, you will be taxed at ordinary income-tax rates. If your effective income tax rate is 25 percent, paying that $100 doctor bill will cost you $114 ($100 to pay the bill, plus $14 (25 percent of $57 [half of $114]).

Note: The maximum long-term capital gains tax rate on the gain on the sale of certain assets is higher than set out above. Gain on the sale of collectibles (e.g., art work, antiques, etc.) is taxed at a maximum rate of 28 percent, and unrecaptured section 1250 gain (gain attributable to depreciation taken on real property) is taxed at a maximum rate of 25 percent.

Tax-Free Sources
of Income
There are three sources of tax-free money:

1. "Qualified" withdrawals from Roth IRAs are free of tax during your lifetime, so long as the Roth was set up at least five years previously and you are age 59.5 or older (or younger, if you are disabled or are buying a home for the first time).

2. Tax-free municipal-bond interest is free from federal and state income taxes, if the bond is issued by the state in which you live. However, if you sell the bond for a profit, the profit is taxed at long-term capital-gains tax rates if held for more than a year, or at ordinary income-tax rates if held for a year or less. In addition, the interest you receive from certain municipal bonds called private activity bonds is taken into account in determining whether you are subject to the alternative minimum tax (AMT). For more information on bond investing, visit www.investinginbonds.com, an educational website

for individual investors maintained by the Securities Industry and Financial Markets Association.

3. Money that has already been taxed is not subject to tax again. Here is an example: when you were working, you paid income taxes on your paycheck and your earnings. Now you use your savings to pay that doctor's bill in our example. You need $100—no more—since you already paid taxes on the $100.

Hint: If you meet certain eligibility requirements, you can "convert" your tax-deferred IRA or 401(k) into a tax-free Roth IRA. Let's say you have taxable income of $50,000. You tell your broker you'd like to convert your $20,000 IRA to a Roth IRA. The conversion triggers a taxable withdrawal of $20,000, meaning you will be taxed on $70,000 ($50,000 plus $20,000). Everything you earn in your Roth from that point on will be free of income taxes, so long as you satisfy the qualification period.

You want to make absolutely certain a conversion is right for you. So talk to your tax adviser to decide whether or not you should convert to a Roth. Converting may be beneficial if a) you can afford to pay the tax on the withdrawal from another source, not your IRA; b) you are ten to twenty years or more away from retirement; or c) if you would like to leave an income-tax-free IRA to your heirs. You can find eligibility and qualification requirements in IRS Publication 590-A, available free by calling 800-829-3676.

Uncle Sam and Your Retirement Assets

Taxes are an integral part of retirement-income planning, yet they are frequently overlooked.

Note: You might wish to skim this chapter first, then return to it when you are facing a decision that involves annuities, Social Security, selling a home, or estate planning.

Immediate Annuities

Immediate-annuity payments (see Chapter 9) can offer some of the lowest-taxed income payments that you can arrange for your retirement. Although no tax deduction is allowed for amounts you use to purchase an immediate annuity, the annuity payments you receive from the insurer are taxable as income at the time of receipt. If you use tax-deferred assets such as your IRA to buy an immediate annuity, your taxes will be governed by IRA rules.

But here is the tax advantage for non-IRA annuities: a part of each payment is excluded from taxable income because it is a return of investment.

Consider this example: Jessica, age 65, pays $516,600 for an immediate annuity that pays $41,000 a year for life. Her life expectancy is twenty-one years, so her "expected return" is $861,000 ($41,000 x 21). Of that amount, $516,600 is her purchase price, which can be excluded for tax purposes. The ratio between the two gives you an "exclusion ratio" of 60 percent ($516,600 ÷ $861,000). This means that 60 percent of each annuity payment Jessica receives is not subject to income taxes. In this example, 60 percent of her expected annual return, or $24,600, can be excluded, which exposes to income taxes only $16,400 of the $41,000 that Jessica receives each year.

You might be wondering if the exclusion ratio continues beyond the time that it takes to recover the purchase price. The answer is no.

If Jessica lives more than twenty-one years (when her full investment in the contract is recovered), 100 percent of the $41,000 is taxable, because the exclusion ratio is no longer operable. However, if she dies before twenty-one years pass, the unrecovered amount may be claimed as a deduction on her final income-tax return.

For a variable annuity, the part of the investment in the contract that is taken into account each year is determined in the same way, but the amount that is received each year may differ. This means that the exclusion ratio has to be re-determined each year. Thus, if the annuity in the above example were a variable annuity, and $49,200 was received in a year, the exclusion ratio for that year would be 50 percent ($24,600 ÷ $49,200).

Social Security
Social Security benefits are tax free for some and partially taxable for others, based on your other income and the size of the Social Security check. For

A Closer Look:

Know Your Lingo

Here are some terms you will come across when factoring Social Security into your tax planning:

Adjusted gross income (AGI): Your gross income less certain deductions and exclusions (above-the-line deductions) such as the amount of a deductible IRA contribution and one-half of your self-employment tax. Simply put, your AGI is the amount shown on the bottom line on the first page of Form 1040.

Modified adjusted gross income (MAGI): MAGI for Social Security purposes is your AGI after adding in tax-exempt interest on municipal bonds and certain deductions, such as student-loan interest.

Provisional income: The sum of your MAGI plus one-half of Social Security benefits received that year.

Base amount: The amount of provisional income over which Social Security benefits will be taxed. The base amount is $32,000 for married individuals filing a joint return, zero dollars for a married individual filing a separate return (unless he lived apart from his spouse for the entire tax year), and $25,000 for all other individuals.

many individuals, up to 50 percent of their benefits are taxable. However, up to 85 percent can be taxable if your income (including one-half of your Social Security benefits) is more than $34,000 ($44,000 if you are married filing jointly; or zero if you are married but filing separately and have filed with your spouse for any period of time during the tax year).

Here is an illustration. Wayne and Wanda, a married couple who file jointly, have a modified AGI of $31,000. They receive $14,000 from Social Security between the two of them. How much of their Social Security benefit is taxable? The answer is only $3,000. Here's how you get to this number:

Step 1: Determine the couple's provisional income. In this case it's $38,000 (MAGI of $31,000, plus $7,000—one-half of $14,000).

Step 2: If the provisional income ($38,000) exceeds the base amount ($32,000), use the lesser of:

1. One-half of the Social Security benefits received that year ($7,000); or

2. One-half of the excess of the provisional income over the base amount (one-half of the difference between $38,000 and $32,000 = $3,000).

Compare step 1 and step 2. Since $3,000 (step 2) is less than $7,000 (step 1), only $3,000 is included in their gross income.

For more information on the taxation of Social Security benefits, get IRS Publication 915 online at www.IRS.gov or by calling 800-829-3676. The publication contains a valuable worksheet to determine how much of your Social Security benefits will be taxed.

Retirement and the Home-Sale Exclusion

Whereas some retirees who owned their homes before they retired will stay put after they retire, others will want to sell their homes and move. Any prospective retiree who plans to sell his home should be aware of the home-sale exclusion rules. These allow an individual to exclude up to $250,000 ($500,000 for married taxpayers filing a joint return) of any gain realized on the sale of his principal residence, so long as certain requirements are met.

Generally, an individual taxpayer qualifies for the home-sale exclusion if he both owned and used the property as his principal residence for at least two years during the five-year period ending on the sale date. (You don't have to own the home for five years.)

The required two-year ownership and use periods need not be continuous over the five years. You meet this requirement if you can show that you owned and lived in the property as your main home for either twenty-four full months or 730 days (365 x 2).

For example, Ed and Edna bought a house in 1990 that they used as their principal residence until Ed's employer transferred him on July 1, 2012. While Ed and Edna were away, they rented the house to a friend.

Ed and Edna returned to the house on June 1, 2015, and used it as their principal residence until they sold the house on August 1, 2016, shortly after Ed's retirement. They met the two-out-of-five-year ownership test because they owned the house for the entire five-year period before they sold it. They also met the two-out-of-five-year use test because they used the house as their principal residence for at least twenty-four months during the five-year period before they sold it.

What if you don't meet these requirements? A partial home-sale exclusion is allowed in some circumstances. Generally, you can qualify for the partial exclusion if your failure to meet either rule occurs because you must sell the home due to your health, a change in your place of employment, or other unforeseen circumstances, such as a move to a nursing home occasioned by a sudden illness.

Surviving Spouses   If you sell your home after you are widowed, you may still be able to use the exclusion for both spouses if you don't remarry. A surviving spouse can qualify for the up-to-$500,000 exclusion if the sale occurs no later than two years after the other spouse's death, if the ownership and use requirements for the $500,000 exclusion were met immediately before the first spouse's death, the survivor hasn't remarried before the sale, and neither spouse was ineligible for the benefits of the exclusion with respect to the principal residence by reason of the one sale every two years rule.

Regardless of when the home is sold, the surviving spouse's basis in the decedent's half of the property is stepped up to its date-of-death or alternate-valuation-date value.

Gains Greater than Exclusion   What if gain on the sale of a principal residence is more than the allowable home-sale exclusion?

Gain on the sale of a principal residence will sometimes be more (and in some cases substantially more) than the allowable home-sale exclusion. To the extent the gain exceeds that exclusion, it will be taxed at long-term capital gain rates. Some taxpayers can offset all or part of this gain with capital losses from the sale of other assets, such as stocks and other securities. But these losses should be taken only if it makes economic sense to do so. Consult your financial or tax adviser before taking such a step.

Estate Planning When someone dies, two types of taxes can come into play: income taxes, which affect everybody, and estate taxes, which affect the wealthy. By "wealthy" I mean those with assets in excess of the applicable exclusion amount ($5,490,000 for decedent dying in 2017). All assets owned by you at death are counted, including your house, furnishings, personal items, savings, IRAs, Roth IRAs, 401(k) plans, life insurance, etc.

Individual income taxes are payable for the year in which you die. Your executor will file your final Form 1040 by April 15 of the year after your death. For example, if you die on June 1, you will owe income taxes on any income received through that date. Income received after June 1, such as interest, dividends, and capital gains from all sources, will be included on the estate's income-tax return (Form 1041).

Whether federal estate taxes will be due depends on the law in place in the year of death. For example, if you die in 2017, no federal estate tax will be owed if your taxable estate is not more than $5,490,000, the federal applicable exclusion amount for that year. (Note, however, that if you made any taxable gifts during your lifetime, the applicable exclusion amount available to your estate will be reduced by any part of that amount applied against those gifts.)

The tax rate for estates valued above the applicable exclusion amount is 40 percent in 2017. While many states (including large states such as California, Texas, Florida, and Ohio) no longer have estate taxes, states have their own sets of laws regarding estate taxes, and it is possible for more than one state to claim such taxes on your estate. This could happen if, for example, you owned property in more than one state with an estate tax. Each state could tax the property within its borders and the income attributable to that state.

Leaving Assets
to Your Spouse   If you are married to a U.S. citizen, everything that you leave to your spouse will be free of federal estate taxes. There is no

limit—even if you have $1 billion. (Special rules apply, however, to spouses who are not U.S. citizens.)

Assets you leave to your spouse fall under the "unlimited marital deduction." The effect of this deduction is to exclude from your taxable estate any assets you leave to your spouse. Essentially, the marital deduction defers the payment of estate taxes on those assets until your spouse dies. In addition, any part of your applicable exclusion amount that is not used in calculating your estate tax can be used by your surviving spouse.

Consider the following example. To simplify the example, assume both deaths occur in 2017.

First Death Say you and your spouse jointly own $10 million of property with "right of survivorship" ("JWROS"), meaning in 2017 the property passes to your spouse without having to go through probate. At your death, the entire estate passes to your spouse free of federal estate taxes. Because there is no federal estate-tax liability, your applicable exclusion amount of $5,490,000 goes unused.

Hint: Probate is the court process that makes after-death transfers possible. If you own property with your spouse jointly, with right of survivorship, the property passes to your spouse without having to go through probate.

Second Death When your surviving spouse dies, his or her estate-tax-applicable exclusion amount includes your unused applicable exclusion amount so that the total amount available is $10,980,000 ($5,490,000 plus $5,490,000). Accordingly, no part of the $10 million estate will be subject to federal estate tax.

Best Use of Both Spouses' Applicable Exclusion Amounts

It's possible that your heirs could receive more if your estate uses your applicable exclusion amount instead of allowing that amount to be carried over to be used by your spouse's estate. This could be done by using a bypass trust (sometimes called an applicable exclusion amount trust and formerly called a credit shelter trust).

Here is a simplified example of how a bypass trust works: your lawyer creates a bypass trust in each of your wills. He directs you to transfer $10 million of the joint property into two separate $5 million accounts, one owned by you and one owned by your spouse. When the first spouse dies, the $5 million in the deceased spouse's name becomes the property of the bypass trust.

Bypass trusts, which are used in conjunction with the marital deduction, are set up to pay income to a surviving spouse and to pass family assets to one's heirs after the death of the second spouse. This trust is not taxable in the estate of the first spouse because its value is less than the applicable exclusion amount. It will not be taxable in the surviving spouse's estate no matter how much it increases in value before that spouse dies. For example, if the value of the bypass trust doubles in value to $10 million before the surviving spouse dies, the full amount in the trust can be distributed to your other heirs without any estate tax being paid. The unused part of the full applicable exclusion amount can be carried over to be used by the surviving spouse.

Nonspouse Beneficiaries and Unmarried Decedents

If you are married and leave property to someone other than your spouse, or if you are single, your estate gets to claim your estate-tax-applicable exclusion amount in computing your federal estate tax. Thus, your estate will be subject to federal estate tax only to the extent it exceeds the available applicable exclusion amount.

Your Tax Adviser

As detailed as this chapter is, there is no substitute for meeting with your accountant, attorney, or tax adviser. Situations differ and laws change. Also, in addition to the estate tax, a decedent's estate may be subject to a generation skipping transfer (GST) tax in addition to an estate tax when property is left to individuals two generations below the decedent, e.g., to grandchildren. The GST tax rules are very complex, and need to be discussed with a competent tax advisor. Accordingly, be certain to review your personal circumstances with your tax adviser before taking any action based on something you may have read or heard.

Taking Money Out of IRAs and Other Tax-Deferred Accounts

Retirees have successfully saved trillions of dollars in tax-deferred savings accounts at work, in 401(k)s, 403(b)s, and other company savings plans, as well as on their own in IRAs and tax-deferred financial vehicles, such as tax-deferred variable annuities held in IRAs.

Tax-deferred accounts are tax advantaged in that no taxes are due while the money stays in these accounts. In fact, the law discourages you from withdrawing any money before age 59.5 by assessing a 10 percent penalty on such withdrawals.

After age 70.5, by contrast, the law discourages people from keeping too much money in their tax-deferred accounts. There is a whopping 50 percent penalty on money that you should have withdrawn but did not. That's what this chapter is primarily about—the rules on post–age 70.5 withdrawals, or "required minimum distributions" (RMDs). (The chapter touches on a few other withdrawal types as well.) A quiz at the end of the chapter invites you to test your RMD knowledge.

Before we begin, let me thank CPA Ed Slott (irahelp.com) for his assistance with this chapter.

Hint: When do tax officials celebrate your birthday? If you turned 70 this year and your seventieth birthday falls somewhere from January 1 to June 30, inclusive, the tax rules consider you to be 70.5 this year. If your seventieth birthday falls somewhere from July 1 to December 31, however, you will be deemed not to have reached 70.5 until next year (that is, in the calendar year when you actually turn 71).

Hint: As in prior chapters, we'll use the term "Roth IRA" when referring to the tax-free IRA. The term "IRA" denotes the traditional IRA, which is the tax-deferred IRA.

Let me give you five key rules on how taxes work when you withdraw money from your tax-deferred accounts.

Withdrawals Trigger Taxes

Rule 1: When you withdraw money from a tax-deferred account, expect to pay income taxes on those withdrawals. For example, if you need to take $1,000 out of your IRA, you will pay taxes on $1,000 because it is considered taxable income. If you take that withdrawal in 2017, you will receive IRS Form 1099-R in early 2018 showing a taxable "distribution" from your IRA of $1,000. If you are taxed at a rate of 25 percent, that withdrawal will cost you $250 in income taxes. (If you are under age 59.5, you'll also be facing an early-withdrawal penalty.)

Rule 2: Sometimes, the withdrawal is not taxable at all—when you withdraw after-tax contributions to your 401(k) or nondeductible contributions to your IRA.

Rule 3: A special rule applies if you own employer stock in your 401(k). There may be advantages to transferring the stock directly to your brokerage account (called an "in-kind transfer") instead of rolling it into an IRA. If you have employer stock, be sure to get tax advice before rolling over your 401(k) to an IRA.

Rule 4: There is no income tax on money you withdraw from a Roth IRA or Roth 401(k), since those are not tax-deferred accounts. They are tax-free—assuming you meet the conditions for tax-free withdrawals, such as the five-year holding period discussed in Chapter 17. See IRS Publication 590-B for more information.

A Closer Look:

Special Considerations for Employer Stock

If you own employer stock in a 401(k), there can be tax advantages to moving the stock out of the 401(k) "in-kind" into your brokerage account, as opposed to rolling it over into an IRA. (Your 401(k) administrator will need to make arrangements.) When employer stock is transferred out of your 401(k) in-kind as part of a "lump-sum distribution," you will receive a taxable distribution in the amount of the cost basis of the stock—the stock's cost at the time you acquired it, not the value it has reached since then. (Your employer will tell you the cost basis.) A lump-sum distribution essentially means you are withdrawing the entire balance from the 401(k) within a single tax year. For more information, read IRS Publication 575.

The difference between the cost basis of the stock and its value at the time of the transfer is known as "net unrealized appreciation" (NUA). The NUA is not taxed until you sell the stock. When you sell, the gain is taxed at capital-gains tax rates, which are currently lower than income-tax rates. If you own employer stock in your 401(k), be sure to ask your employer about NUA before rolling over your 401(k) to an IRA.

Rule 5: Always talk to your tax adviser before making any decisions on a tax-deferred account. Why? Because things change. Rules evolve. And there are exceptions to almost every rule. For example, in response to the 2008 financial crisis, Congress passed a law that suspended all RMDs for 2009.

RMD Rules

for Owners
Under RMD rules, generally, you (the owner of the IRA) must begin to withdraw money from your tax-deferred accounts in the year in which you reach age 70.5. You have to take out a minimum amount each year, as I discuss shortly. If you wish, you can add up the RMDs for all of your IRAs and withdraw that sum from any one of the IRAs, or from a combination of them. If you have multiple 401(k)s, you can't lump the payments together—you need to take an RMD from each one. For more information, check IRS Publication 590-B.

The penalty for failing to take your RMDs is 50 percent of the amount that should have been withdrawn but was not. I'll discuss penalties in further detail in a moment.

Hint: Only one individual can own the IRA; there is no such thing as a jointly owned IRA. This is not to say that you can't have multiple beneficiaries—people who inherit the IRA after your death.

The only type of retirement plan that exempts the owner from RMDs is the Roth IRA. If you inherit a Roth IRA, however, you are required to take RMDs as a beneficiary (not an owner), but no income tax is triggered on those withdrawals. (Read the section on beneficiaries at the end of this chapter.)

Owner's Manual:

Applying RMD Rules
You may think that your RMDs take care of themselves—that the custodian of your IRA account is responsible for calculating and withdrawing the correct RMD for you. Not so. You, as

the IRA owner, are responsible if the amount withdrawn is insufficient to meet RMD requirements. You will need to report the insufficiency on IRS Form 5329 and calculate the penalty (50 percent of the amount that should have been withdrawn, but was not). For instance, if you were required to withdraw $20,000 and you did not, your 50 percent penalty would be $10,000. The penalty carries over from your Form 5329 to your Form 1040.

If the custodian does calculate your RMD, as some offer to do, be aware that if there is an error, you need to correct it within the distribution year. Don't wait until the last minute.

Note, however, that if you have an RMD shortfall due to "reasonable error," and you take "appropriate steps to remedy the shortfall," you may be able to get a waiver of the penalty from the IRS. If you miss all or part of your RMD, be sure to get your accountant's advice.

Important: If you miss your RMD, call you tax advisor right away.

Calculating Your RMD

To calculate the RMD, you will need three pieces of information:

1. Your date of birth (and your spouse's if he/she is a beneficiary).
2. Your December 31 (last year) balances from each tax-deferred account. Make sure to keep a copy of each year-end statement.
3. The correct IRS table to find the divisor that applies to your situation. All of the tables are printed in Appendix C to IRS Publication 590-B. Most people will use Table III, the Uniform Lifetime Table. If you have a spouse who is more than ten years younger than you, use Table II (Joint Life and Last Survivor). If you inherit a tax-deferred account from an owner (you are the beneficiary), Table I (Single Life Expectancy) is for you.

Hint: Remember to keep all your year-end statements for your tax-deferred accounts—all your RMDs are based on your previous year-end balances.

Table 18-1 is an excerpt from Table III, which is published in IRS Publication 590-B.

Age	Distribution Period	Age	Distribution Period
70	27.4	80	18.7
71	26.5	81	17.9
72	25.6	82	17.1
73	24.7	83	16.3
74	23.8	84	15.5
75	22.9	85	14.8
76	22.0	86	14.1
77	21.2	87	13.4
78	20.3	88	12.7
79	19.5	89	12.0

Table 18-1: Table III, the Uniform Lifetime Table

Let's look at a couple of examples.

Example 1:   Assume Edward was born on January 1, 1947 and that it is now 2017, making Edward age 70 and age 70.5 in 2017. He has only one IRA and no other tax-deferred accounts.

To use Table III correctly, he needs to look up his age (70) as of the end of 2017, the year in which his distribution is due (the "distribution year"). Then he can find his distribution period (27.4). This is the number he uses to figure his first RMD.

Assuming Edward's December 31, 2016 balance was $100,000, he divides that balance by 27.4 to get his RMD for 2017 of $3,650. That's the amount Edward must withdraw for his first RMD. (He must withdraw that amount before his "required begin date," which is April 1, 2018. To find out more about this exception, read "The April 1 Rule," opposite.)

What about the following year? Let's assume Edward's December 31, 2017 balance is $101,168. In 2018, he must withdraw $3,818 ($101,168 divided by 26.5). Each year, his RMD is recalculated based on his previous year's balance and the divisor in Table III.

Hint: You can withdraw more than your RMD. Your RMD is only the minimum amount you are required to withdraw each year after age 70.5.

Example 2: Note that Edward was born in the first half of the year (January 1). If you were born in the second half of the year (from July 1 to December 31), the tax rules treat you as not reaching 70.5 until the following year (2018, in this case).

Imagine for a moment that Evelyn was born on July 14, 1947, making her 70.5 in 2018. At the end of 2018, she will be 71 years old and her divisor will be 26.5. If Evelyn's December 31, 2017 balance is $105,000, her RMD for 2018 will be $3,962.

Hint: Some 401(k) participants can delay their RMDs past age 70.5 to age 75 if they are still working. To find out how you can do this, contact your 401(k) administrator.

The April 1
Rule
Here is an RMD wrinkle: you can delay taking your first RMD until April 1 of the year after you turn 70.5. But if you do, you must then take two RMDs in that year.

Let's look at an illustration. Evelyn can delay her RMD for 2018 until 2019. In that case, she will have to take two RMDs in 2019: her 2018 RMD that she delayed until April 1, 2019 ($3,962), plus her 2019 RMD, which is calculated based on her December 31, 2018 value. Keep in mind that she will be paying taxes on both withdrawals when she files her 2019 tax return.

April 1 of the year following the year in which you turn 70.5 is called your "required beginning date."

RMD Resources

Brentmark Software, which provides pension and RMD programs, maintains an informational website about RMD rules at www.newrmd.com.

An RMD Quiz

The mandatory withdrawal rules I discuss above all deal with the "owner" of the tax-deferred account (that's you). In the following quiz, you can review some of the owner rules and see how they differ when a young spouse or a beneficiary enters the picture.

This quiz is adapted with permission from The Retirement Savings Time Bomb. . . and How to Defuse It by Ed Slott. This book is an excellent resource, especially if you have a large tax-deferred account.

All of the following questions assume that "Seth" is the IRA owner. He is 74 years old in 2017 (date of birth: July 14, 1943). His December 31, 2016 IRA balance was $425,000.

What is Seth's 2017 RMD in each of the following scenarios?

scenario 1: Assume that Seth's sole beneficiary is his wife (age 72).
Answer: $17,857. Use the Uniform Lifetime Table (Table 18-1) to look up the distribution period for age 74, which is 23.8. Divide the $425,000 balance by 23.8, which gives you $17,857, the amount that Seth must withdraw from his IRA before December 31, 2017.

scenario 2: Assume that Seth's sole beneficiary is his wife (age 45).
Answer: $10,842. Why is this result different from the first? A spousal exception applies because the spouse is younger than the IRA owner by more than ten years. Instead of using the Uniform Lifetime Table, use the IRS Joint Life and Last Survivor Expectancy Table. Look up the joint life expectancy of a 74-year-old and a 45-year-old (39.2 years). Divide $425,000 by 39.2 to get $10,842.

scenario 3: Assume that Seth's beneficiaries are his spouse (age 55) and his son (age 30). Under Seth's designation, the spouse will receive 90 percent of the IRA when Seth dies. The son will receive the remaining 10 percent.

Answer: $17,857. Even though the spouse is more than ten years younger than the IRA owner, the spousal exception does not apply because she is not the sole beneficiary. The Uniform Lifetime Table applies, as in the first example above.

scenario 4: Assume that Seth's sole beneficiary is his spouse (age 53). She dies in November 2017, and Seth names his son as beneficiary in December 2017.

Answer: $13,199. Even though the spouse died during the year of the distribution, the spousal exception still applies for 2017. Using the Joint Life Table, the joint life expectancy of a 74-year-old and a 53-year-old is 32.2 years. Divide $425,000 by 32.2 to get $13,199.

scenario 5: Following up on scenario 4, Seth does not remarry and keeps his son as the sole beneficiary for 2018, when Seth is 75 and his 2017 year-end balance is $450,000.

Answer: $19,651. The Uniform Lifetime Table applies. The life expectancy for a 75-year-old is 22.9 years. Divide $450,000 by 22.9 to get $19,651.

scenario 6: Seth (age 74) names his alma mater as his sole beneficiary.

Answer: $17,857 (calculated as in scenario 1). For someone past his required beginning date, the identity of the beneficiary does not matter (exception: a spouse younger by more than ten years). Even if there is no beneficiary, the RMD is calculated using the Uniform Lifetime Table.

scenario 7: Seth dies in 2019 at the age of 76 before taking his RMDs for the year. His December 31, 2018 balance is $429,273. His son (age 28) is the owner's sole beneficiary.

Answer: $19,512. In the year of death, the RMD is calculated using the Uniform Lifetime Table and the age of the deceased owner. Divide $429,273 by 22.0 to get $19,512. The son will need to withdraw this amount before the end of 2019 and pay income tax on the withdrawal.

scenario 8: In the last scenario, what is the beneficiary's RMD for 2020, assuming the account balance is $430,249 at the end of 2019?

Answer: $7,924. In 2020, the son is 29. The factor for a 29-year-old (using the Single Life Expectancy Table) is 54.3 years. Dividing $430,249 by 54.3 gives him $7,924. In 2021, the son will use the same factor (54.3) reduced by one (53.3). In 2022, the divisor will be 52.3, 51.3, 50.3, and so on.

These examples hint at some of the nuances of RMDs. They are hardly a full review of the RMD rules. Notably, they do not touch on those that apply to beneficiaries who inherit an IRA from someone who hasn't reached his required beginning date. (If you have inherited an IRA, you may want to read Inherited IRAs: What Your Family Needs to Know by Seymour Goldberg.)

The rules surrounding RMDs and beneficiary planning are a complex area of the law. If you are thinking of taking money out of your tax-deferred accounts, be aware of the tax consequences, and don't forget your RMDs. Above all, don't assume that every financial adviser knows all the rules—especially those for beneficiaries, which can affect your planning. Always consult your accountant or tax adviser when making RMD decisions.

CHAPTER 19

Sales Tactics, Scams, and Bad Advice: A "Perfect Storm" of Disaster for Retirees

Being a knowledgeable investor may not insulate you from harm. Being alert to persuasion techniques almost certainly will.

So test yourself here and now. How would you react to the following phone call?

This is Steven from American Income Corporation and I have a potentially lucrative investment opportunity for you.

Have you ever heard of biodiesel? It is made by American farmers from soybeans and it's the latest rage in alternative fuel sources. We have confidential information about a company named BioFuel Inc. that is gearing up to produce biodiesel and whoever invests now will make 15 to 20 times their investment back.

Now I have a packet of information that I am willing to send to you about this offer at absolutely no charge. But in order to ensure that you are serious about this, I will need to get some information from you. I will need to know a couple of quick facts about your investment portfolio and write down your date of birth and Social Security number to verify your identity.

If you received this call and did anything other than hang up, you may be susceptible to persuasion and identity theft.

The above script comes verbatim from the "Investor Fraud Study Final Report," an investigation of consumer fraud among older Americans, released in 2006 by the NASD (now FINRA, the Financial Industry Regulatory Authority). According to the study, certain people are more open to sales pitches and sharing information about themselves. Not surprisingly, they are also the ones most likely to be victims of high-pressure sales or fraud.

This chapter explores the lessons of the fraud study in order to raise your awareness of persuasion techniques. We'll also review some cases that illustrate potential problems to avoid. Throughout the chapter you'll find "Don't-Be-Fooled Rules" to protect yourself in day-to-day dealings with financial advisers.

Profile of a Scam Victim

The following profile of a victim was provided by FINRA.

Henry was a successful businessman who was married for thirty years, raised a family, and lived a good life. He had accumulated a significant nest egg for his retirement. Shortly after his wife's death, he received an overnight package containing professional-looking materials detailing an

A Closer Look:

There's No Such Thing as a Free Lunch

Retirees increase their odds of being unduly persuaded by exposing themselves to sales pitches at "free lunch" seminars. Securities regulators examined firms that sponsor such seminars. In half the cases, they found claims in sales materials that appeared to be exaggerated, misleading, or unwarranted. "[R]egulators are concerned about the possibility of unscrupulous and abusive sales practices and investment frauds targeted towards senior investors."

Let's face it: seminars are designed to sell. If you are tempted to go to such a seminar, prepare to be sold—and decide whether you want to be. Better yet, don't go. After all, why subject yourself to influence? It's better to find an adviser who is right for you—a topic covered in the next chapter.

investment in oil and gas wells. The next day, a salesperson called him and persuaded him to invest $40,000.

In his conversation, the salesperson used the following phrases:

- "These gas wells are guaranteed to produce $6,800 a month in income."
- "Some of the most successful investors in the country are interested in these wells."
- "There are only two units left in this project."
- "We drilled a well in Texas that had these same early gas readings, and the investors all made millions."

When Henry invested the initial $40,000, his journey into the world of fraud began. Within six weeks of making the first investment, he was contacted again by the same company. The caller told him the well was being dug, but that in order to access the "vast gas fields" the company would need another $50,000 to drill deeper.

Over a three-year period, Henry was contacted twelve times and invested his life savings in four different wells. He ultimately lost more than $500,000 to this oil-and-gas scam, investing in wells that always seemed promising at first, but then ran into trouble and were all capped.

The startling question the FINRA study sought to answer was this: how could a successful, financially intelligent investor fall prey to such a scam and lose his life savings?

A Closer Look:
What Makes Someone Vulnerable?

If you are retired or near retirement, you are more likely to be pursued and you are more likely to be victimized. How so? People who are experiencing major life changes (retirement; the loss or illness of a spouse; a change in living arrangements; problems with children or grandchildren) are more likely to be persuaded to do something against their self-interest.

The FINRA study reported that people "may make themselves vulnerable by their willingness to listen to sales pitches," including a willingness to listen to pitches from unknown sources.

Details of fraud victims' demographic profile may surprise you. According to the FINRA research, men are more likely to be victimized by investment fraud than women. Victims are likelier to live with someone else than are members of the general public, likelier to be married, have higher education, and have higher income levels than those of the overall population.

Going Undercover   To learn how con artists persuade normally cautious people to fall for a con, researchers involved in the fraud study analyzed audiotapes of con artists pitching undercover law-enforcement agents posing as retirees. More than 1,000 influence tactics were coded in 128 transcripts, for an average of 8.6 tactics per transcript. (You can find the results by going to www.finrafoundation.org/resources/research/index.htm.)

The person making the pitch typically used multiple tactics and customized his approach depending on his assessment of the victim. Here are some frequently used techniques identified by the fraud study:

1. Phantom fixation: promising the victim riches. For example: "These gas wells are guaranteed to produce $6,800 a month in income."

2. Commitment: exacting a commitment from the victim and then using it against him. For example: "You can vote to stop drilling, but if you do, all the rest of what you have invested will be lost."

3. Authority: playing the role of an authority figure to gain the victim's trust. For example: "I have been in the oil business for over thirty years and I have seen it all."

4. Social consensus: making it seem that everyone is buying the product. For example: "I know it's a lot of additional money to spend, but I am in this thing just as deep as you are and I say it's worth every dime."

5. Scarcity: making it seem that the product is rare to increase its perceived value. For example: "There are only two units left in this well."

The fraud study noted that using multiple tactics puts the victim into "a kind of psychological haze." During the haze, the victim's otherwise robust ability to spot and resist persuasion is lost. As a result, it is "little wonder that victims often say to law enforcement people after the fact, 'I don't know what I was thinking' or 'It really caught me off guard.' The con criminal wants to extract as much money from the person as possible before that haze is lifted."

Here are some additional tactics to be aware of:
- Source credibility: claiming to represent a "known legitimate business."
- Comparison: offering a more expensive alternative to make the cheaper option seem more desirable.
- Friendship: pretending to be the victim's friend.

- Reciprocity: performing a small favor so the victim feels he needs to reciprocate by agreeing to the con artist's wishes.
- Landscaping: making the victim feel "that all roads lead to where the con artist wants them to go."
- Profiling: using extensive questioning to identify "psychological hot buttons."
- Fear: playing on fears and using intimidation.
- Dependency: pretending to be a "young, helpless dependent" so that the victim feels compelled to help the con artist.

Don't Be Open to Sales Pitches According to the Fraud Study:

> The extent to which con criminals bombard prospective victims with a barrage of complex and sophisticated persuasion tactics . . . together with the finding that victims tend to be more open to listen to such sales pitches, creates a kind of perfect storm in which the victim has little chance of surviving. . . . Investors should be warned that such openness to sales pitches, without some education and training about the effects it can have on decision-making, can leave them highly vulnerable.

Even the more astute investor is at risk, as pointed out by FINRA, because of three additional factors:

1. The "knowing-doing gap": Beware of what Stanford Business School professor Jeffrey Pfeffer calls the "knowing-doing gap," in which investors should know better, based on their education or experience, than to fall for a scam. However, when presented with a con, they fail to use their knowledge to protect themselves.
2. The "expert snare": In the expert snare, the con artist praises the victim for his expertise, putting him "in the position of not wanting to ask tough, probing questions..."
3. "Low persuasion literacy": Even though an investor may know enough about finance to make informed decisions with a legitimate adviser, he may not be sufficiently steeped in the persuasion techniques used by criminals, leaving him vulnerable to them.

Now let's turn to some examples of situations in which people lost money dealing with both fraudsters and legitimate financial advisers. We'll also look at some practical rules to live by to help prevent you from suffering a similar fate.

Training Salespeople to Use Multiple Persuasion Techniques

Some financial firms train their advisers to use legitimate sales techniques, and some go further than they should. Let me share with you a bizarre real-life situation that was short-circuited by Massachusetts regulators. As you read ahead, ask yourself how you would have responded to these sales tactics.

The firm in question recruited people to sell insurance to retirees through seminar presentations. The insurance agents attracted attendees to the seminars by using direct-mail pieces and newspaper inserts. The materials targeted retirees over age 55 who were "unsophisticated investors" and owned their own homes.

According to court documents:

> [I]n an effort to cloak their associates with legitimacy as financial advis[e]rs… [the firm] used such specious titles as "Certified Elder Planning Specialists" ("CEPS") to mislead the elderly and disguise the fact that the associates were insurance salesmen… [The firm] plaster[ed] the title "Certified Elder Planning Specialist" on everything that [was] presented to the public—business cards, newsletter publications, seminar presentations and ghostwritten books.

The problem is, "the associates [were] not 'certified' by any state agency or educational board. CEPS [was] a self-certification title developed entirely by the [firm] to appeal to the senior market and obtain credibility as financial advis[e]rs."

All an agent had to do to get this special certification was pass a test after completing a course. According to regulators, one agent remarked, "[A] moron could pass it okay. . . it took me about 20 seconds."

To mislead the elderly, the firm fraudulently touted the investment knowledge and expertise of its agents. In the firm's publications, agents were presented to the public as investment advisers specializing in financial planning for retirees. And in order to bolster the credibility and image of its agents, the firm published purported client testimonials in its marketing materials.

Marketing materials prepared by an affiliate of the firm contained disclosures regarding the financial background and experience of the individual agents. Marketing brochures stated that each agent was "the perfect advis[e]r for those seeking solid counseling and total financial planning" and utilized "the latest estate planning and investment techniques to design and implement personalized plans that will reduce financial risk, lower taxes, avoid probate and protect assets from nursing home care costs." As a result, regulators said that the firm misled the elderly by presenting its agents as total financial planners, when in fact the firm trained its agents to sell annuities because those were the only products from which the firm profited.

The firm also used a ghostwritten book, *Alligator Proofing Your Estate*, designed to look like it had been written by the agent, whose picture appeared on the cover. Each agent had an identical book, personalized to suggest that he was the author. Agents handed out the book to create the impression that they were "investment advis[e]r[s] with expertise in senior financial planning."

After reviewing the training program, the regulators concluded that trainees had been taught to trigger disturbing emotions—using fear-inducing statements such as "[M]any senior citizens in America today will end up penniless"—and then to present the firm's insurance products as solutions, without mentioning any of the products' negatives. They were taught to talk to seniors as if they were "blind yet smart" twelve-year-old children, incapable of making decisions on their own.

The purpose of the seminar system was to sell annuities, regardless of suitability, age, financial status, time horizon, or investment returns. Trainees were instructed to persuade attendees not to disclose their decision to purchase an annuity, preventing others from interfering with the sale: "While we are waiting for the monies in your CD to be transferred to the Insurance Company . . . I would like to ask that you not mention a word about this to your kids."

If an attendee hesitated, trainees were taught to "[M]ake the decision for them. So when you close, you don't ask, you automatically enroll them. . . . You're like a Kamikaze Pilot. Focus, when you find your target then zoom in. . . Strike, Hit or Close!"

Julie's Don't-Be-Fooled Rules

• Don't underestimate the power of persuasion in a group setting where multiple tactics will be used to get the audience to buy something.

• If you feel pressured to sign something, to reveal information about yourself, or to buy something, it's likely that others are struggling with the same problem. Don't go along. Take a stand. Report your experience to your local state securities administrator, whose telephone and address you can find online at www.nasaa.org (the North American Securities Administrators Association).

Regulators

Take Action The Massachusetts case is an extreme but real example. Let me share a few more situations that attracted the scrutiny of regulators. Only the first involved outright fraud; the rest were legitimate advisers who caused retirees to lose substantial amounts of money—in some cases, all of their money. By reading the tips after each scenario and going through the process outlined in Chapter 20, you'll be able to raise your awareness, know where to voice your concerns, and avoid dangerous situations such as those below.

Ponzi Scheme   An unlicensed individual posing as a financial adviser offered retirees a "safe" way to invest their retirement savings. He succeeded in soliciting retirees in Colorado and New Mexico with free lunch seminars and presentations at retirement and senior centers.

Instead of investing the retirees' money as promised, however, he used the money to pay for his personal living expenses. To keep money coming in from new "investors," he created a Ponzi-like scheme in which he paid his first batch of clients "dividends" with money he got from new investors. This made his earlier investors think their money had been invested legitimately.

The bogus adviser defrauded twenty-five people, mostly retirees, robbing them of about $600,000 in all. When caught, he pleaded guilty to securities fraud. In 2006 the state of Colorado sentenced him to twenty years in jail.

Though pleased with the strong sentence, former District Attorney Scott Storey warned investors, "Seniors need to be very cautious and seek second or third opinions before moving their retirement savings and consult with friends or family about these decisions [emphasis added]."

How can you make sure this doesn't happen to you? Do your homework before investing.

Julie's Don't-Be-Fooled Rules

• Don't assume that the person soliciting your business is properly licensed and regulated. Resist the temptation to buy something before you check him out. Before writing a check to anyone, thoroughly—and independently—vet that person's credentials (see Chapter 7).
• Better yet, don't buy anything from an adviser who finds you. It's much smarter to do your own search for an adviser who suits your needs (see Chapter 20).

Bad Advice on the Job   A financial adviser targeted a company that was undergoing a reorganization. He received permission from the company to give seminars to employees, who were offered lump-sum retirement payments in lieu of pensions.

A number of pre-retirees became his clients—and lost a significant amount of money because of his bad advice. Here is what happened to some of these individuals, as reported by the New York Stock Exchange's Division of Enforcement:

A 50-year-old female refinery technician with a disabled husband and two dependent daughters had no experience in stock investing. She lost

$160,000 of her $220,000 retirement fund. (The adviser had promised that her account would be worth $800,000.)

A 53-year-old divorced technician with no previous investment experience lost $112,000 of his $135,479 retirement account.

A 61-year-old instrument technician lost $523,000 of his $1,129,978 retirement account.

Julie's Don't-Be-Fooled Rules

• If an adviser makes a presentation at your place of work, don't assume your employer checked him out beforehand.

• Even if you investigate the adviser's background and find he has a clean record, he still may not know what he's doing. Check the adviser's references and be sure to ask the interview questions listed in Chapter 20.

The Self-Serving

Broker   A registered representative who worked in the White Plains, New York, office of a nationally known brokerage firm for four years mismanaged her customer accounts by engaging in excessive, unauthorized, and unsuitable trading, which generated large commissions for her—at her clients' expense. According to the New York State attorney general's office, "Many of the defrauded customers were senior citizens or people with little knowledge of the stock market."

In one case, the representative failed to inform a retiree of the risk of investing "on margin" and lost the retiree's entire savings. ("Margin" means a loan, so when you "buy on margin" you are borrowing money to make a purchase.) In another, she made more than $1 million in trades in an account worth only $60,000; the client lost "almost everything in less than a year." In yet another case, the adviser signed her client's name on wire-transfer documents and wired $20,000 out of her client's account into an escrow account so she could close on the purchase of a home for herself.

During her employment, two clients filed arbitration claims against the adviser. These were settled for $1.9 million and $300,000, respectively.

The New York State attorney general's office went after the adviser's firm. After an investigation, the attorney general's office found that the firm had failed to supervise the adviser properly, had failed to notify her clients of her wrongdoing, and had failed to conduct an internal review of her accounts. FINRA barred the adviser from associating with any FINRA member firm (a "bar" means the adviser cannot sell securities through a brokerage firm).

The firm agreed to settle the matter by paying restitution to the adviser's clients in the amount of $741,000, plus costs and penalties totaling $300,000.

Julie's Don't-Be-Fooled Rules

• Don't assume that if your financial adviser works for a nationally known financial firm he is honest and skilled.

• Don't assume that the firm he works for is properly supervising his activities. Be alert and monitor your own investments on a regular basis.

• If you sense that something is wrong, pursue the issue with the adviser's supervisor. Write a letter stating your concerns.

Bait and Switch   In this case, hundreds of retirees responded to advertising in local Arizona newspapers for high interest rate CDs. When people arrived at the advertiser's office, they met with "a salesperson who would offer them additional investment opportunities in insurance products" as part of a "bait and switch" operation, according to court records.

Investors thought they were buying CDs. Instead, they had been sold high-risk financial products. The firm took in more than $8 million, which the court ordered returned to the investors.

Julie's Don't-Be-Fooled Rules

• If you respond to an advertisement for a financial product, you're asking to be persuaded to buy something.

• Be particularly wary of advertisements for familiar products, such as CDs—your guard will be lowered because you will think you know what you're getting. Read Chapter 13 on the different types of CDs. Watch out for a bait and switch.

401(k) Rollover

"Expertise"   After an increase in complaints from retirees, the New York Stock Exchange (NYSE) warned its members to be certain they supervised 401(k) rollover sales activity. The NYSE regulates the activities of member firms, which represent "the world's largest, most complex financial services firms"—in a nutshell, financial services firms whose names you would instantly recognize.

The NYSE recognized that financial advisers "make targeted marketing presentations or sales pitches concerning rollover IRAs to individuals with assets in 401(k) plans," and that occasionally the presentations are directed to employees of a particular company and occur on company premises.

The NYSE reminded the firms to check that a financial adviser's representations about his experience with retirement assets are "factual, not misleading," and urged firms to "impose enhanced supervision on certain marketing presentations or sales pitches relating to rollover IRAs."

Julie's Don't-Be-Fooled Rules

• Be aware that pre-retirees with 401(k)s are rollover candidates representing "money in motion." As such, they are attractive to financial advisers who are building their books of business.

• Make sure you thoroughly interview any adviser you plan on working with, no matter what company he works for.

• Don't be in a big hurry to do the type of 401(k) rollover your presenter suggests. Consider other options—including whether you are better off keeping your 401(k).

Hint: Be sure to check out the SEC website devoted to seniors at www.sec.gov/investor/seniors.shtml.

Put Yourself
in the Driver's Seat

If you need financial advice, take the controls and find someone to work with who fits your needs. Doing that puts you in charge. Doing anything else puts you in a situation where promoters (both legitimate and illegitimate) will be trying to fulfill their own objectives—which is money in their pockets, not yours. The next chapter explores how to turn the tables by finding an adviser who meets your needs.

20

Do You Need a Retirement-Income Adviser?

In this Chapter, let's discuss whether you need help with creating retirement income, and if so, how to find the right adviser. Keep in mind that when we're talking about retirement income, we're addressing something much broader: Achieving retirement security by successfully supporting yourself and your family in the style you want for the rest of your life—and leaving a legacy if you so desire.

Defined this way, a goal can be set for your personal situation and a plan to reach that goal can evolve—irrespective of your age or personal financial circumstances, whether you are a retiree or a "future retiree" who just started earning a living.

The path to achieving retirement security needs to be well laid out. The first question to ask is whether you can do the planning and execution on your own. That's quite possible if: 1) you are a successful investor in your own right; 2) you know how to create retirement income from your savings; and 3) if you are married, your spouse shares those skills—if he or she doesn't, what happens if you become incapacitated or predecease him or her?

Let's start with a self-assessment that can help guide you. Then, if you decide you would like to find an appropriate retirement income adviser, we'll discuss how to do that. I'll also provide you a list of interview questions for potential advisers and for references.

Alert: Keep in mind that the law is in flux about requiring all financial advisers to be fiduciaries. That is, regulators have been, and still are, addressing whether the financial advisers who are not fiduciaries should be. In addition, the DOL is focusing on its own fiduciary rules for 401(k)s and IRAs.

Is an Adviser for You?

Chapter 7 discussed the different types of advisers—how they are regulated and compensated, and the degree to which they are accountable to you. Now let's see if you should do your own investing or work with an adviser who can help you create retirement income.

Self-Assessment

Take the test on page 275 to see if you want to "do it yourself"—or whether you'd prefer to work with a registered representative, an insurance agent, or an investment adviser.

Finding a Retirement-Income Adviser

To find an effective retirement income adviser requires initiative on your part: You will need to conduct a search.

The goal of your search is to find a professional who has the skill, experience, and resources to help you embark on a new type of investment program, one that needs to be planned appropriately and executed correctly.

continued on page 276

Test Yourself

		Yes	No
1.	I do my own research.	☐	☐
2.	I want to decide what to buy or sell.	☐	☐
3.	I want to be responsible for my investments.	☐	☐
4.	I feel comfortable that I know how to create retirement income.	☐	☐
5.	I do my own taxes.	☐	☐
6.	I subscribe to and read financial newspapers.	☐	☐
7.	I read my confirmations and brokerage statements when I receive them.	☐	☐
8.	I'm not looking for guarantees.	☐	☐
9.	I am experienced in handling losses.	☐	☐
10.	I keep track of how my investments are doing.	☐	☐
11.	I know I will not outlive my money.	☐	☐
12.	I have less than $1 million in savings.	☐	☐

What's Your Score? Count Your "Yes" Answers.

Nine or more "Yes" answers

You are a do-it-yourselfer. Consider a discount broker or a no-load mutual-fund family. If a spouse or family member depends on you, be sure to read "Married or Not, It's a Family Affair" in Chapter 21.

Five to eight "Yes" answers

You need some guidance with your investments. Consider a brokerage firm where a registered representative can offer recommendations. If you answered "no" to question 3, 7, 8, 10, or 12, consider a registered investment adviser.

Four or fewer "Yes" answers

You need more than recommendations. Consider a registered investment adviser. If you answered "no" to question 12, consider an investment counsel who structures customized portfolios (see Chapter 7).

Alert: An investor with an inheritance received recommendations from friends and was ready to make a decision to go with a seasoned adviser. I recommended that she check his Form U-4 before going forward. She did, finding that he had a number of customer complaints filed against him.

According to a Finra survey, fewer than one out of four people check an adviser's background with a regulator.

If you like your current adviser—and if he meets your needs based on the self-assessment exercise above—ask him if he creates retirement income for any of his clients (not all advisers do). If the answer is yes, include your current adviser in the list of prospective advisers you plan to interview for that role.

What's the Best Way to Conduct Your Search?

Finding a retirement income adviser is a lot like finding a doctor, lawyer, or accountant. Most people start by calling a few trusted advisers or colleagues. If you need heart surgery, for example, you would very likely gather several names, then narrow down the list and make a decision after consulting with a few doctors and asking a lot of questions. You probably wouldn't go to the doctor with the biggest ad in the phone book.

Discount referrals from people whose goals differ from your own. If a friend raves about his adviser because he made a 25 percent return for him, he is investing for growth, not creating retirement income. That's not what you need. If a colleague loves his adviser because he's a good stock picker, that adviser is not the one for you either.

Alert: Be leery of recommendations from people who have a financial interest in making a referral. Your attorney, accountant, banker, insurance agent, and others may receive referral fees from (or share revenues with) the adviser to whom they refer you. (Be sure to ask.) I'm not a fan of referral fees or revenue sharing because they muddy the waters—who is the adviser really representing?

A Closer Look:
Does a Referral Fee Pose a Conflict?

One of my students had just lost her seemingly healthy 55-year-old husband to a heart attack. With no experience in making financial decisions—and uncertain what to do with the multimillion-dollar investment account her husband had managed—the widow asked her accountant to recommend an adviser she could trust.

The accountant introduced the widow to a young adviser at a big brokerage firm, who was paying the accountant an ongoing referral fee of 1 percent of her account balance per year—an arrangement that netted the accountant tens of thousands of dollars per year.

The accountant didn't believe that accepting the referral fee posed any problems in his relationship with the widow—until, that is, he was asked to testify on the widow's behalf about her lack of financial acumen in a case against the adviser. He couldn't testify, he told the widow, because he had a conflict of interest. Interpretation: his loyalty was to the financial adviser paying him the referral fee, not to the widow.

WARNING!

One of the biggest risks that retirees face is making the wrong choice of a financial adviser.

Questions to Ask

After you have interviewed a select few advisers whom you found through your research and you are satisfied that they understand your objectives and the risks you are comfortable with, conduct a job interview. Your goal is to confirm two things: aptitude and attitude. Aptitude: Is the adviser skilled at creating retirement income, based on experience with clients in circumstances similar to yours? Attitude: Is the adviser someone you want to work with?

The following list of questions includes some drawn from "Cutting through the Confusion: Where to Turn for Help with Your Investments," published by the North American Securities Administrators Association; the Investment Adviser Association; The Financial Planning Coalition; and the CFA Institute. (For your convenience, a list of these questions also appears in Appendix A; take it with you when you visit an adviser.)

Caution: you may encounter an adviser who resists answering questions. Proceed warily, if at all, for this type of adviser wants you to put your trust in him before he has earned it.

Here are some interview questions you should be sure to ask:

1. Tell me about your background and education.

Listen for signs of skill and experience, particularly with creating retirement income. Interview the adviser as if you were hiring an employee, a sitter for your newborn grandchild, or a contractor to undertake a major home renovation. Watch out for inexperience, such as someone who is new to the financial-advisory business, someone who was recruited for sales experience, or someone who was not successful in previous jobs.

2. Tell me about your licenses and registration; what products/services are you licensed to offer?

You'll want to know what the adviser is licensed to sell you: stocks, bonds, and mutual funds (Series 7)? Mutual funds only (Series 6)? Insurance products only (life insurance license)? Variable annuities (life insurance and Series 6 or 7)? Is he a fiduciary who manages portfolios (registered investment adviser /series 65)? Or is he perhaps not regulated at all?

Regulation determines the type of product or service you will be offered and the standard to which the adviser is held when he deals with you. Be sure to review Chapter 7 before conducting the interview.

Don't confuse licenses with designations such as a CFP. FINRA, the self-regulatory body that governs brokerage firms, does not approve or endorse any designations, nor does any designation carry legal weight. For more information, go to apps.finra.org/datadirectory/1/prodesignations.aspx.

3. What qualifications and experience do you have to offer the products and services described in 2?

You'll need to listen carefully to the response as you are trying to judge skill.

4. Will you provide me with regulatory disclosure documents that describe your services and disciplinary history or paperwork that you will want me to sign?

You can look up an individual adviser's background, including any disciplinary history, by going to FINRA's BrokerCheck (www. finra.org/brokercheck). To look up an SEC-registered investment adviser, go to www.adviserinfo.sec.gov. For state-registered investment advisers, go to your state regulator (a list is available at www.nasaa. org). For information on insurance agents, go to your state's insurance department.

5. How would you describe your ideal client?

You want the adviser to describe you. You don't want to be the lone wolf in the adviser's customer base in any respect, whether in terms of experience, finances, risk level, or goals. You also don't want to be the smallest client, financially speaking, unless you can confirm that you will get the attention you need.

6. Tell me what you see as my objectives, experience, risk tolerance, and financial circumstances.

You would expect the prospective adviser to have asked you about these factors. Now it is time to turn the tables and see whether he was listening. You want to establish that the adviser interviewed you carefully and that he heard what you had to say about yourself.

7. Tell me about your experience with clients in circumstances similar to mine.

You need to know that the adviser has a lot of experience with clients who need to create retirement income, and that he is experienced in working with people like you. You do not want to train an adviser with your portfolio. You also want to know how, specifically, he is achieving retirement income for these clients. For example, is he selling living benefits such as those discussed in Part II?

8. How do you assess your performance for these clients?

You don't want to hear, "I made X percent a year for my clients." That suggests the adviser can repeat past performance. Likewise be leery of anyone who claims his clients lost no money during the global financial crisis of 2008; though possible (by keeping money in CDs or going short, for example), that is also unlikely. Rather, you want to hear how the adviser succeeded in meeting the retirement income objectives of clients like you.

9. How would you propose to meet my objectives?

You want to hear a reasoned explanation of what the adviser intends to do or recommend. If he recommends a specific product, you want to hear the pros and cons of the product, and you want him to offer you sales literature and legal-disclosure documents before he asks you to buy anything. You want an adviser who gives you enough time and opportunity to read about the recommendation to fully understand what you are buying.

10. What should I expect of you if I become a client?

This question will help you identify the level of service you will receive. You'll also want to confirm this with client references (more on references later). At one extreme, expect that a transaction-based adviser will see clients only occasionally, when there is additional money to invest. At the other extreme, expect a registered investment adviser who supervises a customized portfolio to meet with you each quarter to review not only your portfolio, but also whether anything has changed in your life that would trigger a change in investment objectives or the composition of your portfolio. You also need to know whether the adviser handles all your requests and calls personally or whether he has a "sales assistant" or staff take calls.

11. How do you monitor investments to make sure you are meeting my income objectives?

If you are talking to a product salesman, expect little or no monitoring. If you are talking to a discretionary money manager, expect a description of reasoned procedures that are followed regularly to review positions in the portfolio and the portfolio as a whole, with a view to ensuring that your objectives are being met.

12. What type of reports can I expect to receive from you? I'd like to see some samples.

Reports also help distinguish the type of adviser you are working with. If you are buying an insurance product, you will receive a confirmation of the purchase and an annual statement. If you are buying a mutual fund, you will get a confirmation of your purchase, plus either a monthly or a quarterly statement. If you are working with a registered investment adviser, you will get the same confirmations and brokerage statements; in addition, you will normally get a more detailed report that shows you how you are doing compared with appropriate benchmarks and if you are meeting your objectives.

13. What happens when there is a problem?

Expect the adviser to go through the various types of problems that might arise, such as lost mail or a delayed check, a missing or incorrect IRS Form 1099 (which is issued at tax time), or even an incorrect required minimum distribution from a tax-deferred account (see Chapter 18). These are the types of administrative issues that can go awry with any type of firm. What you want to hear is how problems are addressed. What resolution mechanisms are in place? Does the adviser make it his business to correct the problem, or is it up to the client to initiate a fix?

14. How do you get paid?

You want to know whether the adviser is paid when you buy an investment, or whether the payment is ongoing based on the value of your account (or some other calculation, such as an hourly fee). For more information on how advisers are paid, see Chapter 7.

15. Do you pay a referral fee to anyone—in particular, the person who told me about you?

Referral fees present potential conflicts of interest. You want to know if your adviser is beholden to anyone. (See the story of the widowed student under "A Closer Look: Does a Referral Fee Pose a Conflict?" on page 277.)

16. What type of person would be better off with another adviser?

Listen for clues to see whether you do not fit the profile of the clients the adviser typically serves. For example, if you are a retiree, you don't want to choose an adviser whose expertise is working with young executives.

Ask for References

After you're finished with your interviews, pick one or two candidates you feel are suitable for you, and ask for the names of a few clients who are in a similar situation to yours in terms of age, financial circumstances, and retirement-income needs.

Client References

You will want to call a few of the adviser's clients to ask them about their experiences with the adviser. Your purpose is to determine if the client's story is consistent with what the adviser told you. Tell these people that you are looking for an adviser who creates retirement income for someone in your circumstances.

There is a fundamental reason to be thorough: the adviser you choose will be vital to helping you meet your retirement-income objectives. You want to identify the best adviser you can find for your particular situation. Here are some questions you might ask:

- Does this adviser create retirement income for you? How does he do that?
- Have you had any misunderstandings or disappointments with this adviser? If there have been problems, how have they been resolved?
- What is the client experience like? How often does the adviser meet with you? What happens at the meetings? Who schedules the meetings? What if you need something between meetings? Who answers the phone when you call? How soon can you expect a return call?
- How do you know if the adviser is doing a good job for you? Does the adviser provide you with any reports that measure how you are doing and whether you are meeting your objectives?
- How long have you worked with the adviser? How did you find him?
- Please compare and contrast this adviser with any others you've worked with in the past.
- Do you know how the adviser gets paid for his services? (That is, does he disclose his compensation, or is it packaged into products he sells?)
- How would you rate this adviser on a scale of 1 to 10, with 10 being the highest?
- Would you hesitate to refer your closest friend to this adviser, assuming he had the same investment objectives? Why or why not?
- Is there any reason you would not recommend this adviser to someone?
- If you had it to do all over again, would you choose this adviser?

In Appendix B, you'll find a list of these questions in a notepad format; use the notepad when you interview the adviser's clients.

Go Back to the Adviser

These interviews will prepare you to go back to the adviser to see how he will handle your account. This is the time to clarify exactly how the adviser intends to meet your retirement needs: Will he sell you a product? Will he structure and manage a portfolio? Will he make recommendations for individual investments? Will he suggest an SMA?

The time you invest in the process described in this chapter will repay you many times over. Turning over your life savings to someone whom you haven't checked out is as big a risk as betting the ranch on a twenty-to-one shot at the race track.

Married? Don't Go It Alone

Here is one last thought on choosing an adviser. If you are married, consider making your search a joint project. After all, you and your spouse are partners in retirement. Should one of you become ill or disabled or die, the other can carry on secure in the knowledge that the family finances are in good hands.

The Finish Line

You've come to the finish line: you're ready to create a retirement-income plan.

At this point, you have the basics you need to do a self assessment and distinguish retirement-income products, services, and service providers. Still, when it comes to creating a plan of action, you might be wondering, "Where do I begin?"

In this chapter, I'll put you on the right track in just a few steps.

First, I'll share some thoughts on how to involve your family in the process. If you have no immediate family, I urge you to review this section on your own or with a friend. Why?

Setting expectations in advance, both for yourself and for your loved ones, creates a mindset that will help keep you on the path to a safe and secure retirement.

Next, I'll take you through a Retirement-Readiness Test to help you understand your individual circumstances. Your test results will help you identify your financial goals and needs for retirement—which, in turn, will determine the actions you take. I'll give you some thoughts on handling those next actions and suggest some guidelines for the months to come.

Finally, I'll provide you with a Retirement Risk Assessment—a valuable set of questions that you'll want to revisit throughout your retirement. By understanding how to keep your risk level under control, you'll be able to protect your retirement assets in all types of markets.

Now let's get started.

Married or Not, It's a Family Affair
If you are married, engage your spouse in a retirement dialogue. How do you do that? Arrange a date and time in the near future to discuss your more distant future. Ask your spouse to voice his expectations. Are they in sync with yours? If not, now is the time to talk things through so that the two of you can reach common ground.

If you are widowed, divorced, or single, do these exercises on your own, recording your thoughts in a notebook. Better yet, enlist a relative or friend in similar circumstances to compare notes.

Considerations
Set aside some time to really think about your fears, hopes, and dreams for the future. Consider, for example, your use of credit. Ideally, you will have paid off your mortgage and credit-card debt well before you retire.

Do you want to leave an inheritance for your children? Some financial decisions result in zero or minimal "terminal value," meaning nothing is left for heirs. If you have no heirs, preserving principal beyond your lifetime may not be a priority; in that case, you may want to provide for charitable bequests.

A Closer Look:

Setting Expectations

In the case of a couple I spoke with recently, the breadwinner was distressed. He had always provided his wife with every indulgence—a practice he knew could not continue after he retired. There would simply not be enough money coming in from his pension and Social Security. When he raised these concerns with his wife, however, she could not "hear" him. Asked how she felt about retirement, the wife replied that she had one life to live. She wanted a happy retirement, she stated, and she was certain her husband would find a way to make that happen.

Having pinpointed their differing views, the husband realized he had a choice: continue working, or address realistic expectations.

Talk about risk. What will you do if you lose a substantial amount of money early in your retirement? Will you invest too conservatively and run out of money later because your investments are not outperforming inflation and taxes?

Review your tax return. If married, discuss your income-tax situation, your taxable and tax-deferred assets, and consider how you intend to withdraw money to pay for expenses.

Review Chapter 5: How do you feel about withdrawal rates? What do you consider safe in your situation? Keep in mind that how you invest will determine what is "safe." Generally, it is safer to withdraw a lower amount (4 or even 3 percent) if you retire early, have a family history of longevity, or want to leave an inheritance. Perhaps you can justify a higher percentage if you are an effective investor, monitor your performance regularly, and reduce or suspend your withdrawals in bad market periods. A higher withdrawal rate may likewise be acceptable if your likely payout period is short and you have no interest in leaving a legacy.

Confer on whether or not you need a financial adviser as you move into retirement. If you do, review Chapter 7, which covers different types of advisers, and Chapter 20, which explains how to interview and select the best adviser for you.

If you are married, think about retirement as a joint venture. Both partners need to understand what's happening financially in order to feel secure—especially because one spouse will almost certainly outlive the other. If the survivor must face the trauma of losing a life partner at the same time he is struggling to figure out his finances, he may not be able to make rational decisions. The solution is to choose and meet with your adviser together now, not later, and jointly decide on a retirement-income program that feels right for both of you.

Your Step-by-Step Retirement-Readiness Test

Now it's time to do some figuring. Steps 1 through 4 will help you determine your cash flows and whether you need to turn to savings for retirement income. Step 5 will help you determine how much you need in savings in order to be able to retire, assuming a thirty-year retirement. If you are already retired and have a shorter time horizon, you should be aware that this Quick Test will result in too high a savings requirement.

step 1: Estimate your expenses in your first year of retirement (or this year, if you are already retired) and categorize them as Essential or Lifestyle. (See Chapter 2.)

step 2: Calculate how much income above and beyond your pension and Social Security you will need to create in your first year of retirement (your "Income Gap"). For example, if your pension and Social Security bring in $30,000 and your total expenses are $40,000 ($20,000 Essential Expenses and $20,000 Lifestyle Expenses), you will need to create $10,000 of retirement income from your assets. (Make a note of your Income Gap; you'll need it for Step 5. See also Chapter 3.)

Ideally, as in this example, your Essential Expenses are covered by pensions and Social Security. If not, consider purchasing an immediate annuity (Chapter 9) to cover your Essentials, or working longer, or cutting back your Lifestyle Expenses by $10,000 per year, if you can manage such a reduction.

step 3: Factor in inflation. Your goal is to be able to cover these rising costs as time goes on. That means your investment choices must return more than inflation takes away. (The Quick Test uses a 3 percent inflation rate.)

If you're purchasing an immediate annuity and you want to protect yourself against rising inflation, your cost to buy the annuity will be higher. For example, a couple both age 65 can purchase a lifelong income stream of $1,000 a month for about $224,000 (in 2017). If the income stream is designed to increase by 2 percent per year, the purchase price jumps to about $285,000. These figures are quotations for a joint life immediate annuity with a ten-year-certain period, which means that the payments continue until both spouses die: if they both die before the tenth anniversary of the purchase, their beneficiary receives the payments they would have received until that date.

step 4: Determine your "Current Savings." How much have you saved now that you are ready to retire? You will need this number shortly.

step 5: Take a Retirement Quick Test. The test uses a future-value factor to give you a quick estimate of whether retiring now is an option, based on your current savings and income needs, and assuming your retirement will last thirty years.

You'll need two pieces of information: your Income Gap, from Step 2, and your Current Savings, from Step 4. It's an easy calculation: you simply divide your Income Gap by the factor in Table 21-1.

Let's try an example together. Assume your Income Gap is $10,000 and your Current Savings equals $160,000. Let's use the Quick Test Factor (see Table 21-1) for a 6 percent annual after-tax return on savings, which is at the bottom of the table. (The factor is 5 percent.) Divide $10,000 by 0.05 and you get $200,000. That's your Quick Test Result.

If your Current Savings is less than $200,000, as in this illustration ($160,000), consider postponing retirement. Why? Because you won't be able to generate enough income to cover inflation for the thirty-year period you should plan on living, even if you achieve 6 percent after-tax returns year in and year out. (Note that this illustration uses a thirty-year payout period, a 6 percent rate of return on your investment, and a 3 percent inflation factor. For more tables, see Appendix C.)

This result tells you that you have two choices: lower your retirement-income needs by cutting back on Lifestyle Expenses, or wait to retire until you have more savings. Although you might be thinking in terms of increasing your returns, it's safer not to plan on that possibility.

THIRTY-YEAR PAYOUT PERIOD	QUICK TEST FACTOR
Factor at 3% Annual After-Tax Return on Savings	3.30%
Factor at 4% Annual After-Tax Return on Savings	3.85%
Factor at 5% Annual After-Tax Return on Savings	4.40%
Factor at 6% Annual After-Tax Return on Savings	5.00%

Table 21-1: Quick test factors for thirty-year payout period

Remember that the Quick Test calculates the minimum amount you'll need to have in savings when you retire, assuming a thirty-year retirement. It assumes that you will spend all your money over a set period of years. It also assumes that you achieve the rate of return you choose to use in the Quick Test. (See Chapter 16 for a discussion of realistic rates of return. It's always safer to use a lower rate.)

Next Steps

Based on this review, you should have a good idea of your goals, how much income you need to produce from savings, the risk level you wish to assume, and whether you can retire soon as opposed to some day in the future.

Now, consider your options. Create a chart showing the pros and cons of each possibility. In each case, focus on the drawbacks to make sure you're willing to live with them—it's too easy to believe the promises of a financial product or strategy and gloss over the negatives.

Keep in mind that this is not an all-or-nothing situation. Each product and service can represent another piece of the retirement puzzle.

Before committing to a financial service, product, or investment program or strategy, recruit a friend to listen to your reasons for wanting to go forward. His job is to listen for signs that you should not go ahead. There are always factors that militate against buying something; now is the time to pinpoint what they are.

Go ahead only after you are convinced that you're on the right track. Before you sign anything, read all the important documentation. Be sure you understand what you are signing and what you are buying. If anything is unclear, ask questions—and confirm the answers.

Create a file for each product you purchase. Keep copies of all the paperwork you signed, as well as the disclosure documents (prospectuses, contracts, illustrations) and your notes.

Alert: Be especially alert at the beginning of your relationship with a new adviser; this is the best time for you to direct the course of action and set a tone for your relationship. Open and read every piece of mail you receive from your financial institution. Keep good records.

Set a specific time each calendar quarter to review your holdings and assess your progress toward meeting your objectives. Review your statements regularly to make sure everything is in order. If you see a problem or have a question, call your adviser and take notes during the call—and mention to the adviser that you are doing so. You want to make sure that there are no surprises, and that everything is going as expected.

Each January, review your prior year progress. Raise questions. Revisit your plan. Consider whether your objectives should be changed in any way. Monitor your performance religiously; if you spot anything you did not expect, be prepared to correct your course.

Bad Markets

At some point in your retirement journey, you will find yourself in a bad market. At these times, expect your income advisor to help you manage your portfolio's risk level, adjust your withdrawals downward (unless they are "covered" by interest or dividends), and remain flexible about your needs.

To help you, let me take you through a risk self-assessment. You'll want to revisit this test at least once a year—or more frequently, in down markets.

Retirement
Risk Assessment

1. If you own the stock of the company you worked for, is it worth more than 10 percent of your portfolio? (When you do the calculation, include all stock and retirement plans, as well as your individual holdings.)

2. Do you have more than 10 percent in any one stock?

3. Do you have more than 20 percent in any one sector?

4. Does your portfolio consist of more than 60 percent stocks or stock mutual funds?

5. Have you borrowed money to buy stocks (margin) or other investments?

6. Do you own any investments that are leveraged, such as closed-end funds?

7. Are you uncertain about how your investments are performing?

8. If retired (or about to be retired), are you unsure of where your retirement income is coming from?

9. Are you unclear on how much you are spending on Essential Expenditures every month?

10. Are you spending more than you earn from all income sources?

11. If you are retired, do you still have a mortgage? If you are still working, is your mortgage more than the value of your house?

12. If you are retired, do you have any consumer debt? If you are still working, is your "personal debt-to-equity ratio" more than 1:2? (Add all of your debt, including your mortgage. Then total all of your assets. Compare the two numbers. Is your debt higher than your assets?)

13. Do you have less than six months of living expenses set aside in an FDIC-insured bank account or money-market mutual fund?

14. Are you uncomfortable with your financial adviser's skill in creating retirement income? (Or, if you lack an adviser, are you insecure in your own ability to do so?)

If you answered "No" to all of these questions, you are less likely to be at risk than others, even in difficult financial markets. On the other hand, if you have any "Yes" answers, reassess your situation right away. Go through your answers to those questions and explore the underlying facts.

If your house is worth less than your mortgage, for example, you need to be especially vigilant about other risk factors. While you can't control the value of your house, you can control what you spend and how you invest. If you find that you have more debt than you would like, or are spending more than you know is reasonable, do something about that now.

As for your investments, watch out for company stock in particular. Behavioral economists tell us that people hold onto their company stock out of familiarity. For example, General Electric employees and alumni I've come across seem to want to hold onto that stock even if it represents a substantial part of their net worth. When you retire, it doesn't pay to hold employer stock in higher esteem than any other stock.

Likewise, you must reassess your strategy if you have been betting on a particular sector of the financial markets, or buying on margin. Concentration and leverage can improve returns in booming markets; these speculative techniques expose to you to higher risk in sideways or down markets.

Always make sure you don't act or react based on emotion. In early 2000, for instance, greed could have moved you to speculate in technology stocks. In 2008, fear could have driven you to put your money under the mattress. Neither state is a good way to make retirement-income decisions.

Get together with your retirement-income adviser on a regular basis. As markets change, review all income-producing investments, checking to see whether your retirement income expectations will continue to be realized. Also review your tax situation and your estate plan.

Don't Stop Thinking
about Tomorrow
As you move forward to the many tomorrows of retirement, your job will be to study your own situation as it evolves over time. At its heart, creating retirement income is all about you: no one else has your particular profile, so the more you know about managing your personal cash flow (and the tools available to do that), the better equipped you will be to build your own retirement security.

Take small steps. Don't rush. After all, you're getting ready for a vacation of a lifetime.

PART V

More Retirement Resources

Prospective Adviser Notepad

Name of Prospective Adviser: _____

Date of Interview: _____

1. Tell me about your background and education.

2. Tell me about your licenses and registrations; what products and services are you licensed to offer? Are these limited in any way (proprietary products or certain types of products)?

3. Will you provide me with regulatory disclosure documents that describe your services (including disciplinary history for you and your firm) and paperwork that you will want me to sign?

4. How would you describe your ideal client?

5. How do you find new clients?

6. Tell me what you see as my objectives, experience, risk tolerance,

and financial circumstances.

7. Tell me about your experience with clients who are in circumstances similar to mine.

8. How do you assess your performance for these clients?

9. How would you propose to meet my objectives?

10. What should I expect if I become a client?

11. How do you monitor investments to make sure you are meeting the client's

income objectives?

12. What types of reports can I expect to receive from you? I'd like to see some samples.

13. What happens when there is a problem?

14. How do you get paid?

15. Do you pay a referral fee to anyone—in particular, the person who told me about you?

16. What type of person would be better off with another adviser?

Client Reference Notepad (Chapter 20)

Name of Prospective Adviser: _____

Name of Client: _____

Date of Interview: _____

Does this adviser create retirement income for you? How does he do that?

Have you had any misunderstandings or disappointments with this adviser?
If there have been problems, how have they been resolved?

What is the client experience like? How often does the adviser meet with you? What happens at the meetings? Who schedules the meetings? What if you need something between meetings? Who answers the phone when you call? How soon can you expect a return call? Does the adviser get back to you right away?

Does the adviser provide you with any reports that measure how you are doing and whether you are meeting your objectives?

How long have you worked with the adviser? How did you find him?

Please compare and contrast this adviser with any others you've worked with in the past.

How does the adviser get paid for his services? Is compensation fully disclosed?

Would you hesitate to refer your closest friend to this adviser, assuming he had the same investment objectives? Why or why not?

Is there any reason you would not recommend this adviser to someone?

If you had it to do all over again, would you choose this adviser?

Quick-Test Factors for Different Retirement Periods and Rates of Return

Quick Test Factor for Thirty-Year Retirement

At 3% annual after-tax return on savings   3.30%

At 4% annual after-tax return on savings   3.85%

At 5% annual after-tax return on savings   4.40%

At 6% annual after-tax return on savings   5.01%

Quick Test Factor for Twenty-Year Retirement

At 3% annual after-tax return on savings   5.00%

At 4% annual after-tax return on savings   5.45%

At 5% annual after-tax return on savings   6.00%

At 6% annual after-tax return on savings   6.50%

Quick Test Factor for Ten-Year Retirement

At 3% annual after-tax return on savings   9.78%

At 4% annual after-tax return on savings   10.50%

At 5% annual after-tax return on savings   11.00%

At 6% annual after-tax return on savings   11.50%

Case Study

The following case study is provided courtesy of InFRE, the International Foundation for Retirement Education (www.infre.org) and is reprinted here by permission.

InFRE is a non-profit education foundation founded in 1997 in response to America"s impending "retirement crisis." The Texas Tech University Center for Financial Responsibility, recognized as a national leader in financial planning curricula, the National Association of Government Defined Contribution Administrators (NAGDCA), and the National Pension Education Association (NPEA) are behind InFRE.

To build a foundation for a lifetime of income needs, InFRE teaches advisers to cover Essential Expenses through lifetime income sources such as Social Security and pension and immediate annuities. Lifestyle Expenses (called "Discretionary" in the case study) should be covered through other assets that can create retirement income, such as taxable assets, retirement accounts, employment income, and variable sources.

Retirement Income Management

Goldin Case Study Planning Worksheets

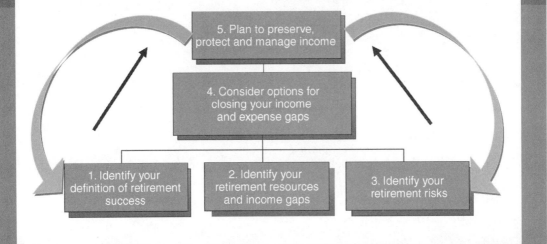

Five steps to preserve, protect and manage your retirement income

Case Study: Meet the Goldins!

Assume it is June, 2017 and Jim and Linda Goldin contact you because Mr. Goldin is seeking someone to help manage their money. He wants to be sure that Mrs. Goldin has the help she needs if he dies before she does.

During your initial meeting, the Goldins tell you that they want to maintain the lifestyle to which they are accustomed during the remaining years of their retirement. To do this, they expect they will need $85,500 in real income per year for at least the next ten years, which includes $54,300 in essential expenses. They have a moderate investing risk tolerance for their managed assets. Due to the market events throughout the 2000s, they want to keep 20% of their assets in cash and short-term securities. When possible, they do not want to give up entire control of their assets.

The other data you have collected is given below.

Mr. Goldin is 72 and Mrs. Goldin is 69. She will turn 70½ in 2018.

RMD
Mr. Goldin's RBD was April 1, 2016, and Mrs. Goldin's RBD is April 1, 2019.

Social Security benefits
They receive a total of $28,000 per year in combined Social Security benefits.
- His benefit is $21,000 per year.
- Hers is $7,000.

Home Equity
They live in a $500,000 home with no mortgage. They do not want to consider their home as a retirement resource at this time.

Working
Neither is currently working nor expects to in the future.

Insurance
They do not have any long-term care or employer-provided retiree medical insurance. Their only health insurance coverage is Medicare and a Medigap F policy.

Pension
Mr. Goldin also has a pension:
- It is from a struggling steel manufacturing company.
- It pays him $10,000 per year.
- The pension ceases when he dies.
- There are no survivor benefits.

Case Study Continued: Meet the Goldins!

IRAs
- Mr. Goldin has a traditional IRA (no basis) worth $400,000 (RMD of $15,625 in this year based on a RMD factor of 25.6).
- Mrs. Goldin has a traditional IRA (no basis) worth $300,000, but she is not required to take an annual distribution since she is not yet 70½.
- On a combined basis, the IRAs are split 30/70 between stocks and bonds.
- Each IRA lists the spouse as the only beneficiary; there are no contingent beneficiaries.

Other assets and information
- $35,000 in a checking account (earmarked for emergencies and is not intended to be used for retirement), earning 1% a year.
- $300,000 in a taxable stock portfolio (growth) earning 0.9% per year in dividends, and in which there are $125,000 in unrealized long-term capital gains.
- $100,000 in tax-exempt bonds (AA), earning 3% per year.
- $65,000 in a defined contribution plan from a long-ago private employer for Mr. Goldin, all in cash (RMD of $2,539 in this year based on a RMD factor of 25.6).
- They are in the 15% marginal tax bracket.
- Assume the Goldins pay all their taxes out of their $85,500 annual income.
- Mr. Goldin's father and two older brothers all passed away before age 78 due to heart trouble. Mrs. Goldin is in relatively good health.
- They have two adult children (ages 38 and 35) and four grandchildren (ages 13, 12, 10 and 9).

Managing Retirement Income Planning Worksheets

Step 1: Estimate Duration of Retirement Assets Worksheets

A) Personal data:

	Self	Spouse
Name:	Jim Goldin	Linda Goldin
Address:	123 Orange Blossom Rd.	123 Orange Blossom Rd.
	Clearwater, FL	Clearwater, FL
Phone #s: (w)		
(h)	727-555-1234	727-555-1234
(c)		
Email:		
D/O/B:	5/15/45	2/22/48
Profession:	retired	retired

B) Please identify the following longevity and health risks that are of concern:

	Major	Minor	Not a Concern
☒ Prescription drug costs		X	
☒ Health costs beyond insurance coverage	X		
☐ Providing for long-term care costs		X	
☒ Providing for a spouse if you die first	X		
☐ Providing for you if spouse dies first			X
☐ Possibility that you or spouse will outlive assets		X	
☐ Healthcare needs of parents/in-laws			X

C) Why did you retire? Please rate in order of priority played.

_____	Social Security	
X	Had enough money	
_____	Certain age	
_____	Job situation changed	
_____	Declining health of self or spouse	
_____	Started receiving pension	

_____ Switched to another career
_____ Got tired of working/had enough
_____ Met age/years of service requirement
_____ Spouse stopped working
_____ Switched to part-time work
_____ Other

D) Please rate your top retirement goals in order of importance.

Self	Rank	Spouse	Rank
Play golf	1	Move closer to grandchildren	1
Travel	2	Volunteer work	2
Have a 2nd home	3	Travel	3
Work in the yard	4	Take computer classes	4

2

E) Monthly Income Need:

Common Monthly Expenses	A) Current monthly Expenses	Stage 1 # of years _10_ age _72_ age _69_	Stage 2 # of years ____ age ____ age ____	Stage 3 # of years ____ age ____ age ____
Essential Expenses				
Housing (include property taxes)	$ 800	$ 800	$	$
Utilities	300	300		
Health care (including medical insurance)	150	300		
Household (furnishings, equipment and supplies)	200	200		
Transportation	400	300		
Food at home	600	500		
Insurance (life and other personal)	350	350		
Debts				
Income taxes	1,550	675		
Other	1,000	1,100	= 64% of income needed	
Total Essential Monthly	$ 5,350	$ 4,525	$	$
Total Essential Annual	$ 64,200	$ 54,300	$	$
Discretionary Spending				
Meals out	$ 450	$ 650	$	$
Clothing	150	100		
Entertainment (recreation, books, etc.)	750	1,250		
Personal care (products and services)	167	150		
Professional services	75	75		
Charitable giving	100	100		
Gifts	275	275		
			= 36% of income	
Total Discretionary Monthly	$ 1,967	$ 2,600	$	$
Total Discretionary Annual	$ 23,604	$ 31,200	$	$
MONTHLY TOTALS	$ 7,317	$ 7,125	$	$
ANNUAL TOTALS	$ 87,804	$ 85,500	$	$

3

F) Income Resources and Gaps:

Name: __The Goldins__
Ages: M __72__   F __69__
Year No. __1__ Date: _____

Essential Expenses
$_____54,300_____

Discretionary Spending
$_____31,200_____

Income from Lifetime Resources:	Essential Expenses		Discretionary Spending	
Pension	($ 10,000	)	($	)
Social Security	(28,000	)	(	)
Veteran's Benefits	(	)	(	)
Fixed Annuities	(	)	(	)
Variable Annuities	(	)	(	)
	(	)	(	)
	(	)	(	)
	(	)	(	)
	(	)	(	)
	(	)	(	)
SUBTOTAL Less:	(38,000	)	Less: (	)

Income from Managed Resources:				
Employee Savings Plans	($	)	($	)
Traditional IRA	(	)	(	)
Roth IRA	(	)	(	)
Brokerage Account	(	)	(2,700	)
Other Savings	(	)	(	)
Home Equity	(	)	(	)
Employment Income	(	)	(	)
Municipal Bond	(	)	(3,000	)
	(	)	(	)
	(	)	(	)
SUBTOTAL Less:	(0	)	Less: (5,700	)
GAPS	A. $ 16,300		B. $ 25,500	

total income gap = $41,800

4

G) Retirement Savings Available to Fill Gaps

Bank Accounts	Current Value
Checking	
Savings	
CDs	
Other	
Taxable Brokerage Accounts	
Money Market	
Stocks	300,000
Bonds	100,000
Mutual Funds	
Other Investments	
IRA Accounts	
Money Market	
Stocks	210,000
Bonds	490,000
Mutual Funds	
Other Investments	
Employer savings accounts	65,000
Other savings available now or in the future	
TOTAL SAVINGS AVAILABLE TO FILL GAPS	1,165,000

H) Estimate Duration of Retirement Assets:

Assuming your investment returns were exactly offset by inflation and taxes throughout your retirement, how long might your savings last?

Total savings available to fill Gaps (from G above).	$ 1,165,000	(1)
Forecasted annual essential income Gap A plus annual discretionary Gap B (from F above).	$ 41,800	(2)
Divide Line 1 by Line 2 to determine how long savings might last.	$ 28	(3) years

Step 2: Identify and Manage Retirement Risks Worksheet

Which of the following risks are of special concern?

Risk	Client	Spouse	Indicate Action(s) to Take
1) Longevity Risk:			✓ More annuitized income
a. outliving resources		✓	___ Access home equity
b. death of spouse		✓	
2) Inflation Risk:			___ Control expenses over time
a. healthcare	✓	✓	✓ Secure income streams that are/can be protected from inflation
b. food	✓	✓	
c. home value	✓	✓	
d. college	✓	✓	
e. other	✓	✓	
3) Health and Long-Term Care Risks:			___ Review Medicare and other health insurance coverage
a. expected and unexpected health and long-term care expenses	✓	✓	✓ Identify long-term care options
b. loss of ability to live independently			___ Obtain long-term care insurance
c. changing housing needs			___ Identify housing options
d. lack of available facilities or caregivers			___ Identify potential care givers and facilities
4) Investing Risks:			___ Ladder fixed investments
a. stock market reluctance	✓	✓	___ Ladder fixed annuity purchases
b. declining interest income	✓	✓	___ Better diversity assets
c. negative point-in-time	✓	✓	✓ Rebalance assets
			✓ Identify if objecive is to "die broke" or "leave legacy"
			___ Do Monte Carlo analysis/projection

6

Step 2: Identify and Manage Retirement Risks Worksheet (continued)

Which of the following risks are of special concern?

Risk	Client	Spouse	Indicate Action(s) to Take
5) Family Issues:			_____ Enter marital/family counseling
a. divorce of retiree or adult child			
b. disability or health issues of retiree or adult child			_____ Review disability/health policies
c. unexpected death of retiree or adult child with dependents			_____ Review/update will and beneficiary designations
d. job loss of retiree or adult child			_____ Identify adult/child care facilities
e. care of grandchildren or other dependents			
f. elder care for retiree parents			_____ Obtain long-term care insurance for parents
g. paying for college while in retirement			_____ File for financial aid
6) Business and Public Policy Risks:			_____ Build an emergency fund of one year's worth (or more) of health insurance premiums
a. employer bankruptcy			
b. employee benefits reduced or eliminated	✓		
c. insurer solvency			_____ Closely follow employer's financial status while in retirement
d. employment risk: physical			
e. employment risk: job availability			_____ Have routine physical examinations; exercise regularly
f. lack of diversification: employer stock			_____ Take job skill training classes regularly, such as computer skills
g. lack of diversification: annuity insurer			
h. changes in Social Security or Medicare			_____ Diversity employer stock holdings into other stocks
i. income tax rate change			
j. tax bracket change after death of spouse			_____ Use 1035 exchanges to diversify annuity holdings
k. estate tax rate change			
			_____ Conduct annual tax review
			_____ Conduct annual estate plan review

Step 3: Identify Distribution, Tax and Estate Issues and Opportunities

A) Capital Gains Planning and Opportunities:

Assets with Current Capital Gains	Purch. Date	Current Value	Cost Basis	Est. Gain
Stock Portfolio	12/31/97	300,000	175,000	125,000

Circle Marginal Tax Rate:

2017 Ordinary Income Tax Rate	Single Taxable Income	Joint Taxable Income	Long-Term Capital Gain Rate[1]
10%	Up to $9,325	Up to $18,650	0%
15%	$37,950	$75,900	0%
25%	$91,900	$153,100	15%
28%	$191,650	$233,350	15%
33%	$416,700	$416,700	15%
35%	$418,400	$470,700	15%
39.6%	$418,401+	$470,701	+20%

[1] Long-term = more than one year.

B) RMD Information:	Client	RMD Information	Spouse
a. Required beginning date (RBD).	April 1, 2016	a. Required beginning date (RBD).	April 1, 2019
b. Retirement accounts that require mimimum distributions:	12/31/08 balances	b. Retirement accounts that require mimimum distributions:	12/31/ balances
1. IRA	$400,000	1.	$
2. DC Plan	$ 65,000	2.	$
3.	$	3.	$
4.	$	4.	$
5.	$	5.	$
TOTAL	$ 465,000	TOTAL	$
c. RMD factor for current year:	25.6	c. RMD factor for current year:	
d. Require minimum distribution for this year (total dollars in (b) divided by RMD factor (c))	18,164	d. Require minimum distribution for this year (total dollars in (b) divided by RMD factor (c))	

8

C) Estate Planning:

Estate Planning Status:	Client	Estate Planning Status:	Client
Estate current estate value:	$ 932,500	Estate current estate value:	$ 767,500

Client	Spouse	
Yes (Yes) No	Yes (Yes) No	1. Have all of your (and spouse) beneficiary designations been reviewd and update recently? Date most recently updated. _last year_
Yes (Yes) No	Yes (Yes) No	2. Do you (and spouse) have a will? Is it current? Does your executor know where to find it and other estate planning documents? Date most recently updated: _3 years ago_
Yes (Yes) No	Yes (Yes) No	3. Do you (and spouse) have powers of attorney for healthcare and finances?
Yes (No) Yes	(No)	4. Do you (and spouse) have a plan to fund potential long-term care costs? If yes, what is the plan?
Yes (No) Yes	(No)	5. Have you (and spouse) considered a revocable living trust to reduce probate costs?
Yes (No) Yes	(No)	6. If married, have you and your spouse considered a Credit Shelter Trust (also known as a by-pass or AB trust) to reduce estate taxes?
Yes (No) Yes	(No)	7. Are you making gifts to family members that take advantage of the annual gift tax exclusion (currently $13,000)?
Yes (No) Yes	(No)	8. Have you considered charitable and other irrevocable trusts that could provide lifetime income, estate tax and income tax benefits?

Estate Planning Wishes	Client	Estate Planning Wishes	Spouse

Designated beneficiaries: Name	Age	Amount	Designated beneficiaries: Name	Age	Amount
1. Mary (daughter)	38	40%	1. Mary (daughter)	38	40%
2. Thomas (son)	35	40%	2. Thomas (son)	35	40%
3. Paul	13	5%	3. Paul	13	5%
4. Sarah	12	5%	4. Sarah	12	5%
5. Jessica	10	5%	5. Jessica	10	5%
6. James	9	5%	6. James	9	5%

9

D) Taxation Estimate of Social Security Benefits:

1. Add your AGI and tax-exempt interest income.

   1. 55,000

2. Enter half your annual Social Security benefits (if married filing jointly, enter half of your combined benefits).

   2. 14,000

3. Enter total of lines 1 & 2.

   3. 69,000

   If the total of line 3 is less than $25,000 and you are unmarried**, or less than $32,000 and you are married filing jointly, none of your Social Security benefits are taxable. If you are married, filing separately and live with your spouse, go to line 8.

4. If the total of line 3 is greater than the figures above, subtract $25,000 if you are unmarried** and $32,000 if you are married filing jointly and enter amount.

   4. 37,000

5. Divide line 4 by one-half and enter amount.

   5. 18,500

6. Enter the smaller of line 2 or line 5.

   6. 14,000

   If the figure on line 3 is less than $34,000 and you are unmarried** or less than $44,000 and you are married filing jointly, the figure on line 6 is the Social Security benefits subject to taxation and stop here. Otherwise, go on to line 7.

7. Compare the figure on line 6 with $4,500 if you if you are unmarried** or $6,000 if you are married filing jointly and enter the smaller amount.

   7. 6,000

8. Take the figure on line 3 and subtract $34,000 if you are unmarried**, $44,000 if married filing jointly and nothing if you are married, filing separately and live with your spouse. Enter this amount.

   8. 25,000

9. Multiply line 8 by 0.85 and enter amount.

   9. 21,250

10. Enter the sum of figures on lines 7 and 9.

    10. (27,250)

11. Multiply your annual Social Security Benefits (combined benefits if married filing jointly) by 0.85 and enter amount.

    11. 23,800

The smaller of the figures on lines 10 and 11 is the amount of your Social Security benefits subject to taxation.

*   *The worksheet is for estimate purposes only. Consult a tax advisor for actual determination of Social Security benefits taxation.*
** *Also includes head of household filing separately and living apart from spouse.*

10

Step 4: Identify Options for Addressing Gaps Worksheet

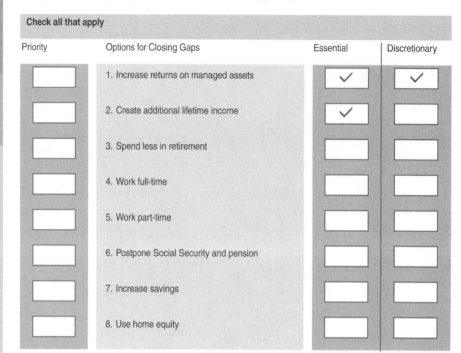

Check all that apply

Priority	Options for Closing Gaps	Essential	Discretionary
	1. Increase returns on managed assets	✓	✓
	2. Create additional lifetime income	✓	
	3. Spend less in retirement		
	4. Work full-time		
	5. Work part-time		
	6. Postpone Social Security and pension		
	7. Increase savings		
	8. Use home equity		

Notes:

_____

_____

_____

_____

_____

_____

_____

_____

_____

_____

_____

_____

11

Step 5: Convert Resources into Income Worksheets

A) Income Conversion Trade-off Evaluation:

Read the statements and check the box next to the response that is most appropriate for you.

A. I plan to use the money invested in my retirement accounts (401(k), 457, 403 (b)) . . .

☐ 1. *Here and there, whenever I wish,* I want the freedom to change my income from year to year, depending on my needs and plans.

☐ 2. *To pay some of my daily living expenses but save some for extras.* I need a certain amount of regular income from invested assets, but I want the freedom to splurge when I want to.

☒ 3. *To pay the bulk of my daily living expenses regularly.* This will be a primary source of ongoing income for me.

B. With my wealth, I plan to . . .

☐ 1. *Pass on as much as I can.* I want to leave as much money and property as I can for my beneficiaries and/or charities.

☒ 2. *Spend what I want and pass on the remainder.* I want a certain level of guaranteed income but the flexibility to spend or pass on the rest.

☐ 3. *Spend it all during my lifetime.* I want to use my money for my needs and wants in my golden years. My family and friends are OK financially.

C. When it comes to managing my investments, I want . . .

☐ 1. *To have total control of my money.* I'll be responsible for managing it throughout all of my retirement.

☒ 2. *Someone to provide me with some help.* I still want some say in how my money is invested, but also want to have help in managing my money.

☐ 3. *A financial company to guarantee me income for life.* The company can worry about how to invest my money and make it last.

D. Having a guaranteed lifetime income is . . .

☐ 1. *Not a high priority.* I have more than enough resources for my needs. I'm more interested in growing my wealth for beneficiaries

☒ 2. *Somewhat important, along with creating a legacy.* I want a certain level of regular income. But I want to leave something for family members and charities as well.

☐ 3. *Essential.* I want to know I have a regular "paycheck" no matter how long I live in retirement.

Now add up your numbers!

Uses the space provided to write down the number next to the statements you selected.

Add up your	A. _____3_____
numbers to	B. _____2_____
get your total	C. _____2_____
score.	D. _____2_____
TOTAL ⇨	_____9_____

Now that you know your score, look below to find out which income distribution option on the following page might meet your needs.

If your score is 4-6 You may have a greater desire to use a **Systematic Withdrawal Plan/ Periodic Distribution** option when converting resources into income.

If your score is 7-9 You may have a greater desire to combine a **Systematic Withdrawal Plan/Periodic Distribution** and **Lifetime Income/Annuitization** options when converting resources into income.

If your score is 10-12 You may have a greater desire to use **Lifetime Income/Annuitization** options when converting resources into income.

Note: A more detailed analysis might suggest different strategies

B) Retirement Income Distribution Options:

Option	Score	How it Works	Impact on Beneficiaries	Pros and Cons
Systematic Withdrawal Plan/Periodic Distribution	4-6	Leave your retirement accounts invested and withdraw a dollar amount adjusted for inflation on regular basis (monthly, quarterly, semi-annually or annually). In addition to regular withdrawals, you can also withdraw any dollar amount whenever you wish.	Your beneficiary may choose to withdraw the remaining balance all at once or continue to receive payments until the account balance is depleted.	You can change how much you withdraw each year, and you have the flexibility to make "big" withdrawals for special needs. But since your income isn't guaranteed for life, you could run out of money before you die. If you're a "spender," stay away from this option.
Combining Systematic Withdrawal Plan/ Periodic Distribution and Lifetime Income/ Annuitization	7-9	Convert a portion of your retirement accounts to an immediate annuity, to provide the desired amount of lifetime/ longterm income (such as to cover your essential living expenses). Leave the remaining retirement assets invested and withdraw any additional amounts when needed or on a regular schedule.	Your beneficiary may choose to withdraw the remaining balance from the systematic/partial withdrawal accounts or continue to receive payments until the account balance is depleted. Depending on the Payout Option chosen (see next page), your beneficiary may receive some income from your annuity.	A certain amount of your income is guaranteed for life, while you retain control over the rest of your retirement account assets. You are choosing less certainty/ more opportunity than total lifetime/longterm income but more certainty/less opportunity than systematic/partial withdrawal.
Lifetime Income/ Annuitization	10-12	Convert a portion of your retirement accounts to an immediate annuity. The amount of your income is determined by the Payout Option you choose (described on the next page), your age, your beneficiary's age, and current interest rates or expected market returns.	You can guarantee your beneficiary(s) a certain amount of income for a certain time period or even for their lifetime. Alternatively, you can totally eliminate your beneficiaries from receiving any income at all, if you so choose.	Your income is guaranteed for life. If you are a "spender," this option will help keep you from overspending. You give up control over how much and when you can take withdrawals. You also limit or eliminate the amount of money you can pass on to your beneficiaries. With "fixed" lifetime/long-term income, you'll get a set dollar amount regularly; but inflation will make this money worth less and less in the future. With "variable" lifetime/longterm income your initial income may be lower and will go up and down over time, but you have a better chance of fighting inflation during retirement.

Identify Your Appropriate Annuity Payout Option(s)

To determine which annuity payout option might best meet your needs, read the descriptions below and check the box next to the one that is most appropriate for you.

I want the most income I can get for as long as I live.

No one else depends on me financially. When I die, whether it's in 20 days or 20 years, nothing will be left for any beneficiaries.

→ You've chosen a **Single LIfe** option.

I also want to take Systematic/Partial Withdrawal payments.
　Yes　　No

I want income for life with at least a certain number of payments.

I know I'll have income for as long as I live. If I die before receiving all of my payments, my beneficiaries are guaranteed to receive the rest.

→ You've chosen a **Life Annuity with Guaranteed Payments** option.

I also want to take Systematic/Partial Withdrawal payments.
　Yes　　No

I want income for a certain number of years.

Instead of lifetime/long-term income, I know I'll only receive payments for a set number of years. But if I die before I've received all my payments, my beneficiaries are guaranteed to receive the rest.

→ You've chosen a **Period Certain** option.

I also want to take Systematic/Partial Withdrawal payments.
　Yes　　No

I want to receive income for _____ number of years.

I want income for as long as my beneficiary and I live.

I know we will have guaranteed income as long as we live, even if one of us dies. But once we pass away, there will be nothing left for any other beneficiaries.

→ You've chosen a **Joint and Survivor** option.

I also want to take Systematic/Partial Withdrawal payments.
　Yes　　No

14

5th step: Specify the new target asset allocation

C) Asset Allocation

Asset Class	Asset	Current Dollar Amount	% of Portfolio	Amount to Reposition	Desired Dollar Amount	% of Portfolio
Cash	401(k)/457/403(b)	$ 65,000	%	$	$ 65,000	%
	IRAs	$	%	$ 165,594	$ 165,594	%
	Brokerage Account	$	%	$ 100,000	$ 100,000	%
		$	%	$	$	%
	Subtotal Cash	$ 65,000	4 %	$ 265,594	$ 330,594	20 %
Fixed Income	Pension	$ 121,581	%	$	$ 121,581	%
	Social Security	$ 366,389	%	$	$ 366,389	%
	401(k)/457/403(b)	$	%	$	$	%
	IRAs	$ 490,000	%	$ (416,782)	$ 73,218	%
	Brokerage Account	$	%	$	$	%
	Muni Bonds	$ 100,000	%	$	$ 100,000	%
	Subtotal Fixed Income	$ 1,077,970	65 %	$ (416,782)	$ 661,188	40 %
Domestic Equities	401(k)/457/403(b)	$	%	$	$	%
	IRAs	$ 210,000	%	$ 251,188	$ 461,188	%
	Brokerage Account	$ 300,000	%	$ (100,000)	$ 200,000	%
		$	%	$	$	%
International Equities	401(k)/457/403(b)	$	%	$	$	%
	IRAs	$	%	$	$	%
	Taxable investments	$	%	$	$	%
		$	%	$	$	%
	Subtotal Equities	$ 510,000	31 %	151,188	661,188	40 %
Real Estate*		$	%	$	$	%
		$	%	$	$	%
	Subtotal Real Estate	$	%	$	$	%
	TOTALS	$ 1,652,970	100%	$ 0	$ 1,652,970	100 %

Do not include home if you do not want to consider it as a potential source of retirement income.

Identify Client Risk Tolerance

Current Allocation (Stocks/Bonds/Cash)*

- [X] Conservative (20/50/30)
- [ ] Balanced (40/40/20)
- [ ] Growth (60/30/10)
- [ ] Aggressive (85/15/0)

Desired Allocation (Stocks/Bonds/Cash)*

- [ ] Conservative (20/50/30)
- [X] Balanced (40/40/20)
- [ ] Growth (60/30/10)
- [ ] Aggressive (85/15/0)

* Asset allocation percentages are for illustrative purposes only, and are not held out or intended to be recommendations for actual retiree or other client portfolios. Please refer to your broker/dealer compliance department's guidelines and other internal resources for retiree asset allocation targets to use.

15

D) Income Allocation:

7th step: Calculate withdrawal rate

	Taxes O/C B/N	Current Asset Value	Amount Converted	Post Conversion Asset Value	Essential Income $ 16,300 Gap A	Discretionary Income $ 25,500 Gap B
Lifetime Sources:						
Pension	0	$ 121,581	$ 0	$ 121,581	$ 10,000	$
Social Security	0	366,389		366,389	28,000	
Veteran's Benefits						
Fixed Annuities						
Variable Annuities Linda's IRA	0		100,000	100,000	7,217	
			fixed income to equity			
SUBTOTALS		$ 487,970	$ 100,000	$ 587,970	$ 45,217	$ 0
Managed Sources:					*1/2 RMD*	*1/2 RMD*
Employee Savings Plan	0	$ 65,000	$ 0	$ 65,000	$ 1,270	$ 1,270
Traditional IRA	0	700,000	(100,000)	600,000	7,813	7,813
Roth IRA						
Brokerage Account	C	300,000	0	300,000		19,117
Other Savings						
Home Equity					2,700	
Employment Income					+ 16,417 19,117	
Muni Bond	N	100,000	0	100,000		3,000
SUBTOTALS		$ 1,165,000	$ (100,000)	$ 1,065,000	$ 9,083	$ 31,200
TOTALS		$ 1,652,970	$ 0	$ 1,652,970	$ 54,300	$ 31,200

Text Key:
O = Ordinary Income
C = Capital Gains
B = Both
N = Non-taxable

Managed sources total income: $ 31,200 [1] + $ 9,083 [2] = 40,283

$$\frac{\text{Managed Income}}{\text{Managed Assets}} = \frac{\$\ 40,283}{\$\ 1,065,000} = 3.78 \%$$

16

Step 6: Maintain and Update the Plan Worksheet

Annual Review Step	Date Last Performed/ Checked for Client	Date Last Performed/ Checked for Spouse

1. Are Income Goals Being Met?
 	
Reminders:
  a. avoid converting capital gain assets into ordinary income
  b. use annuitized money to meet living expense needs; use non-annuitized money to meet living expense wants
  c. review the timing of investment, annuity and reverse mortgage cash flows		

2. Are Assets Optimized?
 	
Reminders:
  a. Check how long retiree/spouse hope to work
  b. Check portfolio asset allocation; include "bond" assets like Social Security or pensions
  c. Liquidate taxable assets first
  d. Check SWP percentage
  e. Check required minimum distributions		

3. Is There a Need for Additional Lifetime Income?
 	
Reminders:
  a. convert tax-sheltered assets into annuities
  b. use variable annuities or fixed annuities with a COLA feature
  c. consider delayed annuitization when actual spending is unknown and investment control is important
  d. SWP up to 4-5% of the non-annuitized portfolio
  e. avoid changing the overall portfolio asset allocation when you annuitize		

4. Did or Might the Tax Situation Change?
 	
Reminders:
  a. capital gain income is more income tax-efficient than ordinary income, but capital gain assets carry estate tax advantages
  b. if retiree doesn't need the income now, delay Social Security until age 70
  c. spend taxable or tax-sheltered money depending on the current year's income tax situation
  d. forecast RMDs out several years, especially if there are large retirement balances in order to minimize potential taxability of Social Security		

Bibliography

Altman, Nancy J., and Eric R. Kingson. *Social Security Works! Why Social Security Isn't Going Broke and How Expanding It Will Help Us All.* New York: The New Press, 2015.

Bartiromo, Maria. *The Weekend That Changed Wall Street.* New York: Penguin Group, 2010.

Carlson, Charles B. *The Little Book of Big Dividends.* Hoboken, NJ: Wiley, 2010.

Cloonan, James B. *Investing At Level 3.* Chicago, IL: American Association of Inividual Investors, 2016.

Cramer, James J. *Get Rich Carefully.* New York: Plume, 2014.

Gerstein, Marc H. *Screening the Market.* Hoboken, NJ: Wiley, 2002.

Greenblatt, Joel. *The Big Secret for the Small Investor.* New York: Crown Business (Random House), 2011.

Greenblatt, Joel. *The Little Book that Still Beats the Market.* Hoboken, NJ: Wiley, 2010.

Heiserman, Hewitt Jr. *It's Earnings That Count.* New York: McGraw-Hill, 2005.

Hinden, Stan. *How to Retire Happy.* 4th ed. New York: McGraw-Hill, 2013.

Kobliner, Beth. *Get A Financial Life Personal Finance In Your Twenties And Thirties.* New York, NY: Touchstone, 2016

Lefevre, Edwin. *Reminiscences of a Stock Operator Annotated Edition by Jon D. Markman.* Hoboken, NJ: Wiley, 2010.

Lange, James. *Retire Secure!* Pittsburgh, Pennsylvania, James Lange, 2015.

Larimore, Taylor, Mel Lindauer, Richard A. Ferri, and Laura F. Dogu. *The Bogleheads' Guide to Retirement Planning.* Hoboken, NJ: Wiley, 2011.

Lindauer, Mel, Taylor Larimore, and Michael LeBoeuf. *The Bogleheads' Guide to Investing.* 2nd ed. Hoboken, NJ: Wiley, 2014.

MarksJarvis, Gail. *Saving for Retirement (Without Living Like a Pauper or Winning the Lottery).* Upper Saddle River, NJ: Pearson Education, Inc., 2012.

Milevsky, Moshe E. *The Calculus of Retirement Income.* New York: Cambridge University Press, 2006.

Miller, Jeremy C. *Warren Buffett's Ground Rules: Words of Wisdom from the Partnership Letters of the World's Greatest Investor.* New York: HarperBusiness (HarperCollins), 2016.

Moeller, Philip. *Get What's Yours for Medicare.* New York: Simon & Schuster, 2016.

Peters, Josh. *The Ultimate Dividend Playbook.* Hoboken, NJ: Wiley, 2008.

Quinn, Jane Bryant. *How to Make Your Money Last.* New York: Simon & Schuster, 2017.

Rittenhouse, L. J. *Buffett's Bites: The Essential Investor's Guide to Warren Buffett's Shareholder Letters.* New York: McGraw-Hill, 2013.

Ross, Nikki. *Lessons from the Legends of Wall Street.* Chicago: Dearborn, 2000.

Slott, Ed. *The Retirement Savings Time Bomb and How to Diffuse It.* New York: Penguin Books, 2012.

Slott, Ed. *Your Complete Retirement Planning Road Map.* New York: Ballantine Books (Random House), 2006.

Smith, Gary. *Money Machine: The Surprisingly Simple Power of Value Investing.* New York: American Management Association, 2017.

Zwecher, Michael J. *Retirement Portfolios: Theory, Construction, and Management.* Hoboken, NJ: Wiley, 2010.

Acknowledgments

This book is the result of a collaboration of experts and supporters who saw the need for an educational consumer-protection guide for soon-retiring baby boomers.

The original edition came to life in 2006, when my agent, Marilyn Allen of Allen and O'Shea, took the idea to Sterling Publishing, Inc., who saw a fit with the mission of AARP Books: to publish books that enrich the lives of older Americans.

The AARP posed a question: you serve a select clientele—can you write this book for a broader audience? If it weren't for that challenge, the message of this book may not have reached those who need it most: people who have not saved enough to retire, as well as those who do not consider themselves astute investors. But for that nudge, I would not have delved into the world of guaranteed products nor developed the self-assessments, checklists, and tools (such as the rating system and the "Don't Be Fooled Rules") that are designed to help even the neophyte ask informed questions.

This new edition, under the editorial guidance of Kate Zimmerman of Sterling, updates and enhances the message to be even more demographically inclusive.

The first edition and this edition are the product of many resources and subject matter experts, notably: the US Social Security Administration and US Department of Housing and Urban Development (HUD); Thomson

Reuters; Brentmark Software, Inc.; K&L Gates LLP; Morningstar, Inc.; the Vanguard Group; T. Rowe Price; Ed Slott & Company; Behavioral Research Associates, LLC; NOLHGA, the National Organization of Life and Health Insurance Guaranty Associations; III, the Insurance Information Institute; FINRA, the Financial Industry Regulatory Authority; and InFRE, the International Foundation for Retirement Education (InFRE provided the case study they developed to train financial advisers, which is reprinted with their permission as Appendix D).

Then there are the many individuals who offered a reader's perspective on the first edition, among them, Manny Bernardo, Ed Cashin, Jason Cavallo, Scott Chevrier, Richard Delaney, Ellie DeRidder, Jeanne Fraioli, Ed Hynes, Grace Luz, Joe Maffei, Durrie Monsma, Mike Novosel, Frank O'Connor, Tom Raabe, Marlon Richards, Jim Riordan, Peter Spielman, John Swensson, and Chris Vaccaro.

Last but not least, are the Jackson, Grant employees who helped behind the scenes, namely Peter DeWitt, Bob Carroll, David Hennessey, Janella Joyner, and Michael Tenreiro.

My heartfelt thanks to you all for your contributions.

About the Author

The trusted voice of retirement investing, Julie Jason, JD, LLM, developed her perspective on financial services over a 30+ year career in law and money management.

Through her award-winning weekly investor education column (syndicated by King Features) and books, Ms. Jason troubleshoots financial problems for a broad audience of readers of every age and financial means. Through her Investment Counsel firm (Jackson, Grant Investment Advisers, Inc. of Stamford, CT), she and her team manage retirement-income portfolios for wealthy families who want a fiduciary experience removed from the sales culture of Wall Street.

Ms. Jason's website is juliejason.com. She welcomes comments and questions from her readers (julie@juliejason.com).

Index

A

A.M. Best financial-product ratings, 95
Accumulation of 401 (k), 211, 212
Adjusted gross income, 243
"Amortization schedule," 194
Annuities
    deferred versus payout annuities, 99
    fixed, 121–136
    immediate, 98, 103–120
"Asset class," 218

B

Baby boomers, and budgeting, 14, 15
Balanced index returns, 55
"Balanced" mutual funds, 232, 233
Bank employees and trust companies, 88, 89
Barring advisers, 270
Base amount, 243
Basics
    achieving a secure retirement, 3–12
    financial advisers, 73–90
    improving your situation, 59–72
    money, how long will it last, 47–58
    personal cash flow, 13–22
    retirement income, sources of, 22–32
    social security, income from, 33–47
Bonds
    and commissions, 87
    credit risks, 222, 223
    investing for income, 219, 220
    maturity date, 219, 222
    municipal, tax-free, 240, 241
Broker, self-serving, 269
Brokered CDs, 180, 181
"Brokers." See Registered
    representatives.
Business, income from a, 28
"Buyer's Guide to Fixed Deferred Annuities
    with Appendix for Equity-Indexed
    Annuities," 134
"Buy on margin," 269

C

Callable CDs, 179
Capital gains, long term, 239, 240
Cash equivalents, 220
Cash flow, personal
    boomers, and budgeting, 14, 15
    debt, 14
    determining where the money goes, 18,
      19, 20
    exercise, 13, 14
    and expenses, 15, 16
    and inflation, 21
    and importance of expenses, 23
    and "Lifestyle Balance Register," 17,
      18, 19
    and longevity, 21, 22

Certificates of Deposit
    brokered, 180, 181
    callable, 179
    checklist, 182, 183, 184–185
    equity-linked, 181, 182
    how they work, 177
    interest, 178
    look-alikes, 177, 179
    recommendations, 177
    and retirement, 175, 176
    "step-up" or "step-down," 179, 180
Compounding
    and age, 60, 61, 62
    "negative," 62, 63
    and retirement income, 59, 60
    and target decades, 66, 67–69, 70
    using, 64, 65, 66
Consumer price index, 219
"Credit risk," 222, 223

D

Deferred annuities, 99
"Defined-contribution plan," 204, 205
"Demands-based" formula for stock, 230, 231
Diversification of stocks, 220, 221
"Dividend," 219
Divorce, "benefits of," 41

E

"Effective income-tax rate," 238
Employer stock, 251
"Equity-Indexed Annuities: Fundamental Concepts and Issues," 133
Equity-indexed annuity. *Also see* Fixed Annuities
    costs and taxes, 131, 132
    description of, 123, 124
    fixed, 125
    guarantee, 130, 131
    how it is sold, 127, 128
    how it works, 125, 126
    important considerations, 132, 133, 134
    and interest to retirees, 124–125
    questions to ask, 134, 135
    riskiness of, 130
    and salesperson commission, 129, 130
    understanding the, 128, 129
    when do you get the money?, 127
    who should consider?, 135, 136
Equity-linked CDs, 181, 182
Estate planning, 246
"Excess of cap amount," 99
"Expert snare," 264

F

Federal Deposit Insurance Corporation, and CD insurance, 176
Federal Truth in Savings Act, and CDs, 178
Financial advisors
    commissions and fees, 86, 87–88, 89
    and compensation, 85, 86
    description of, 81
    determining need for, 8, 10
    four categories of, 75, 76–82
    and Investment Adviser Association, 73
    and legal violations, 84, 85
    and licenses, 83
    and regulation, 74, 75
    and standards of conduct, 84
Financial Industry Regulatory Authority (FINRA)
    and best interest standard on broker-dealers, 89
    and equity-indexed annuities, 129
    and registered representatives, 76
Financial planners, 81, 82, 85
Fitch Ratings, and financial-product ratings, 95
Fixed immediate annuity. *See* Immediate annuity
Fixed income annuities.
    anecdote about, 121–123, 124
    equity-indexed, 124, 125–136
"Forward mortgage," 188

401 (k) plan
    advantages of, 204
    amount to contribute, 205, 208, 209
    company match, 206, 207, 208
    investment selections, 214, 215–216
    life cycle of, 211
    pretax advantage,
    phases, 210
    and retirement, 24, 204, 213, 214
    rollover expertise, 271
"Free-look period," 106, 107

G
Glass-Steagall Act, 88
Gramma-Leach-Bliley Act, 88
Guaranteed minimum income benefit
    advantage of, 137, 138
    case study, 142, 143–145, 146
    conditions, 141
    costs and taxes, 150, 151, 152
    description of, 138
    how they are sold, 146, 147, 148
    how they work 139, 140
    important considerations, 152, 153–157
    promises of, 141, 142
    and prospectus, 138
    riskiness of 149, 150
    and taxes, 242
    terms you should know, 140 141
    understanding, 148, 149
    when you get your money, 142
Guaranteed minimum withdrawal benefit
    case studies of, 162–165
    complexity of, 167,168
    costs and taxes, 169, 170
    how it is sold, 166
    how it works, 160, 161
    interest to retirees, 160
    nuts and bolts of, 160
    overall recommendation, 172, 173
    people who should consider buying, 172
    questions to ask before buying, 171

    and problem with managing retirement
        savings, 159–160
    rating, 166,167
    rating for safety, 169
    rating for value 170
    riskiness of product, 168, 169
    trustworthiness of guarantee, 169
    understanding the product, 167
    what can go wrong, 170
    what happens when you did, 170
    what it promises, 161
    what the salesperson makes, 166
    what you should read, 171
    when do you get your money, 161
    "withdrawal limit," 161

H
Holding period of stocks, 226–229, 230
Home
    equity conversion mortgages, 189, 190–199
    reverse mortgages, 187–199
    as personable asset, 26
    sale exclusion, 244, 245

I
"Immediate annuity"
    advantages of, 105, 106
    costs and taxes, 111, 112
    and death of owner, 113, 114
    determining whether you need, 118, 119
    getting into trouble with, 115
    how they work, 107
    importance of, 106
    important considerations, 112, 113
    innovations, 115, 116
    options, 114, 115
    as a personal pension, 103
    pensions, problems with, 104, 105
    present value of, 98
    promise of, 107
    questions you should ask, 117
    reading before buying, 116, 117

risk of, 111
sales of, 108, 109, 110
tax advantages of, 113, 241, 242
tips when buying, 117, 118
understanding, 110, 111
when you get your money, 107
woman's experience with, 108
Income annuity. *See* Immediate annuity
Individual Retirement Accounts *See also* 401
    (k) and Tax-deferred accounts
taking money out of, 249–258
tax advantages of, 249, 250
Inflation
protection with annuities, 116
and retirement income, 21, 63
and stock market, 219
"In-kind transfer," 251
Insurance agents, 78, 79, 82, 85
Insurance companies
regulation of, 97
solvency of, 97
Insurance producers. *See* Insurance agents.
Insurance products, pricing of, 87
Interest rate risk, 223, 224
Investment Adviser Association, and financial
    advisers, 73, 74
Investment advisory services, and
    commissions, 87, 88
Investment counsel, 80
"Investment objective," 219
"Investment pyramid," 123

J
"Joint life" annuity, 114

K
"Knowing-doing" gap, 264

L
"Life only" annuity 114
Life with period certain annuity, 115
Life-insurance industry, and solvency of

companies, 97
Lifelong income, guaranteeing, 93–102
"Lifestyle Balance Register," 17, 18, 19
"Load." *See* Mutual funds and commissions
Long-term capital gains, 239, 240
"Low persuasion literacy," 264
"Lump-stock distribution" of employer stock
    251

M
Markdown, 87
Market risk, 223, 224
Markup, 87
"Maturity date," 219
Median life expectancy, for men who reach the
    age of 65, 21, 22
Modified adjusted gross income, 243
"Money manager," 80
Money-market mutual fund
definition of, 51
investing in T-bills, 224, 225
"Monte Carlo simulators," 56, 56
Moody's Investors Service, and financial-
    product ratings, 95, 96
Mutual funds
and commissions, 87
money-market, 51
selecting, 222
Thomson fund for "balanced," 232, 233

N
NASAA's Investment Adviser Guide, and
    licenses for financial advisers, 83
National Center for Health Statistics, and
    median life expectancy, 21, 22
National Organization of Life and Health
    Insurance Guaranty Associations
    and state's insurance guaranty association,
    99
    and list of failing insurance companies, 97
"Negative compounding," 62, 63
"Net unrealized appreciation," 251

"Networking," 88
New York Stock Exchange, and 401 (k) rollover
    "expertise," 271
"Nonrecourse" loan, 190

O
"On margin," investing, 269
Optimal withdrawal rate, 48, 4–54, 55

P
"Participation rate," 125, 126
Payout annuities, 99
"Payout period," 49
Period certain annuity, 115
Personal assets
    leaving to your spouse, 246, 247
    and retirement, 24, 25,26–27
    taxable, 26
"Portfolio," 221
"Portfolio manager," 80
Probate, 247
"Proprietary" reverse mortgages, 191
Provisional income, 243

Q
"Qualified dividends," 26

R
Rebalancing of 401 (k), 212
Registered investment advisers, 79, 80, 81,
    82, 85
Registered representatives, 75, 76–77, 78, 82,
    85
"Required beginning date," 255
"Required minimum distribution" rules, 252,
    253–258
Retirees and scams, 259–272
Retirement, taxes in
    adviser, 248, 297, 298
    assets, leaving to your spouse, 246, 247,
        248
    estate planning, 246

    and home-sale exclusion, 244, 245, 246
    immediate annuities, 241, 242
    IRA, 237, 238
    social security, 242, 243, 244
    tax-free sources of income, 240, 241
Retirement income, determining how long it
    will last
    inflow and inflation, 47–47
    "Monte Carlo Simulators," 56, 57
    withdrawal rate, optimal, 48, 49–54, 55, 57,
        58
Retirement income, sources of
    determining how much needed, 24
    improving, 59–72
    and inflow, 31
    lifelong, 93–102
    personal assets, 24, 25, 26-27
Retirement income advisers
    determining whether you need one, 271,
        272
    finding a, 274, 275, 276, 277–284
    notepad, 297, 298
    risk assessment, 292–294
Retirement income plan
    case study, 301–320
    considering your options, 291, 292
    and the markets, 202–292
    involving your family in, 285, 287, 288
    step-by-step readiness test, 288, 289, 290
Retirement sources
    bibliography, 321
    case study, 300–320
    client reference notepad, 298
    prospective adviser notepad, 297
    Quick-Test factors, 299
Reverse mortgages
    borrowing through, 191, 192
    complication of, 196, 197
    cost of loan, 193
    and default, 194, 195, 196, 197
    and your heirs, 195, 196
    home equity, 189, 190–199

overall recommendation, 199, 200
popularity of, 187, 188
things to know before buying, 198–199
what they offer, 188, 189
"Right of survivorship," 247
Roth IRAs
    "qualified" withdrawals from, 240
    and RMDS, 252, 253
    as tax-free asset, 27

S
"Salary deferrals," 205
S&P 500 Index Fund, returns, 54
Scam victim, profile of a, 260, 261, 262
Secure retirement, securing a
    experience in, 7, 8–9, 10
    and financial advisors, 8
    retirement income, amount needed, 3, 4–5
    retirement plan, need for, 7
    thirty year, test for, 299
    for you and your spouse, 10–12
Separately Managed Accounts (SMAs), and
    commissions, 87, 88
Sequencing, 27, 28
Single premium immediate annuity. *See*
    Immediate annuity
Social Security
    applying early, 36
    applying later, 38
    benefits, taxation of, 43, 44
    breaking even with, 37, 38
    and divorce, 41
    and divorce before retirement, 41, 42
    eligibility for, 34
    how to apply, 44, 45
    how much will you receive?, 34, 35
    importance of, 33, 34
    and retirement, 29–31
    and sickness, 36, 37
    spousal benefits, 38, 39, 40
    and supplemental security program, 45,46

survivor benefits, 40
and taxes, 242, 243, 244
working while retired, 42, 43
Spouse, leaving assets to your, 246, 247
"Stability of principal," 219
"Standard deviation," 53
Standard & Poor, and financial-product
    ratings, 95
"Step-up or step-down" CDs, 179, 180
Stock brokers. *See* Registered representatives.
Stock market
    asset classes, 218
    cash equivalents, 220
    creating retirement income, 230,
        231–232
    deflation, 219
    diversification, 220, 221
    bonds, 218, 219
    holding period 226–229, 230
    inflation, 219
    investing as you approach retirement, 225,
        226
    making it work for you, 217, 218
    market risk, 223, 224
    treasury bills, 224, 225
Stocks, and commissions, 87
Suitability standard, and registered
    representative, 77, 78
Supplemental security program, 45, 46

T
Target decades, 66, 67–69, 70
Tax-deferred accounts
    401 (k), 204–216
    and retirement, 26
    retirement plan landscape, 204
    taking money out of, 249–258
Taxes in retirement, 237–248
Tax-free assets, and retirement, 27
Tax-free sources of retirement income, 240,
    241

T-bills
    description of, 51
    interest on, 50
"Ten years certain option," 114
"Terminal value," 49
Thomson index for "balanced" mutual funds, 232, 233
"Total annual loan cost," 194
Treasury bills, 224, 225
Trust companies, definition of, 88, 89

U

Uninsured private reverse mortgages, 191
"Unlimited marital deduction," 247

V

Variable annuities. *See* Guaranteed minimum income benefit
"Volatility," 53

W

Wealth creation, and retirement, 25
Withdrawal of 401 (k), 212
Withdrawal rate, optimal, 48, 49–54, 55
Work, income from 28, 29

Y

"Yield spread," 131